Do you want to know what the "Age of Aquarius", the "New Age" is really about? Then you must read **The Shiny Herd**. Mr. Houck describes over 8,000 years of astrology, astronomy, history and religion for examination. He has apparently spent years researching ancient books and scripts, symbology, history, and religious documents. Clearly and powerfully, he shows how our "modern" religious-philosophic concepts are a distortion of much older concepts of reality. These ancient truths come from teachings brought to human-kind by the "Watchers" millennia ago. The "Watchers" taught the human race principles of creation and evolution using images that could be readily understood: the stars!

Mr. Houck shows how modern astrology is only a partial use of this ancient holistic knowledge. He then goes on to give us that lost, forgotten cosmic astrological knowledge anew! And, in doing that, he brilliantly returns astrology to its original place in history. **The Shiny Herd** reviews each of the astrological constellations and "with each sign we find the material out of which organized religions have built their self-serving myths." For many, this book will be highly controversial and disturbing, perhaps even sacrilegious; for new age thinkers, it will be a breakthrough in personal responsibility, soul consciousness and human evolution.

The Shiny Herd is a must read for all who believe in self-creation and the goodness of evolution. It answers profound questions and clarifies old ambiguities. Mr. Houck is to be congratulated for this ambitious and courageous book.

Linda and Michael Brady
Astrologers for Creative Choices, Inc.
Holistic Educational Center
Baltimore, Maryland

The Shiny Herd

Ancient Secrets Hidden in the Sky

Charles M. Houck

Noble House

Baltimore, Maryland

The Shiny Herd

Copyright © 1994 Charles M. Houck

Library of Congress
Cataloging in Publication Data
ISBN 1-56167-164-9

Cover design by Chuck Shauck
Book layout and design by Patricia Mitchell

Published by

Noble House

8019 Belair Road, Suite 10
Baltimore, Maryland 21236

Manufactured in the United States of America

To Nick,
whose three magic words
brought this book into matter-form:
"Go for it."

Table of Contents

Preface

In this book there will be found numerous references to prehistoric geniuses who presented the Earth with the celestial hieroglyphs known to us today as the Zodiac. These beings were known to our ancient ancestors as the "Watchers." There is reference of the "Watchers," for example, in an old work called **The Book of Jubilees**. This work is also known as the "Apocalypes of Moses" because it was said to have been written down by Moses as dictated to him by an angel and the work claims to relate the history of earlier times. The work is reliably dated, however, as from the second century before the present calendar.

When this work was written need not concern us. Pertinent to our consideration is this reference: "For in his days (of Jared) the angels of the Lord descended upon the Earth -- those who are named "the Watchers" ---that they should instruct the children of men."

Throughout the ancient world there was common acknowledgment of these "Watchers," generally in regards to the wise minds that set down the foundations upon which world traditions have sprung. Most notably these are in regards to cosmological understandings and the origins of the celestial picturings known to us today as the Zodiac. These geniuses were the Earth's residents in that long-ago prehistory time, and are only vaguely known to us today through mythopoetic legends and tales.

Because this planet was rocked more than once in ancient times by interstellar catastrophies, most direct evidence of the sojourn here of these ancient Watchers has been lost. For a few persons whose eyes are not blinded by emotional pride and/or spiritual prejudice, however, evidence confirming their existence here can still be found. They are spoken of in legends passed down in oral accounts, and alluded to in mythological and scriptural writings. More convincing are the unexplainable architectural master-works such as the predeluvian Baalbeck Terrace in present day Lebanon, the Great Pyramid in Egypt, and others. The precision and technology needed to accomplish similar architectural feats cannot be matched by technology available to us even today, so it is unlikely that our primitive ancestors were capable of such wonders.

These prehistory "Watchers" possessed a remarkable understanding of what we refer to as cosmology-comogony. Using this understanding and their knowledge of the celestial realm, of planets, stars and the Earth's place in space, they fashioned a kind of textbook upon the observable heavens so this understanding could be passed on to succeeding inhabitants of our planet. This knowledge was presented to the world as an astonishingly detailed picture mapping of the heavens. The remnant of their celestial mapping, taken from their secondary use of these picturings, is known today as the Zodiac. Their celestial picture book was fashioned for instructional purposes in two interrelated zodiacal, text-like presentations, which we will translate as the greater Zodiac of Constellations and the lesser Zodiac of Signs.

After the Watchers had departed and Earth suffered through a number of cataclysmic events, this knowledge become scattered and confused. Old lessons only half remembered served as the cornerstones for belief systems which contributed to the elevation of the priest-class. The result is that the world's religions have their roots in celestial chartings used by the Watchers to present cosmological understanding.

Most western religions of today vehemently deny any astrological-zodiacal association. The intent of this book is to touch upon what is regrettably only a few of the deciphered Zodiac lessons which have served as the cornerstones for the Judeo-Christian-Islamic articles of faith.

In the Old Testament book of Job, the ever-verbalizing
god is quoted as asking this question of Job:

Do you know the ordinances of the heavens;
Can you put into effect their plans on Earth?"

*   *   *

"The mysteries of the Incarnation, from Conception
to the Ascension into heaven, are shown to us on the face
of the sky and are signified by the stars."

-- Albertus Manus

(a Dominican scholastic philosopher who did much to introduce
Aristotle's scientific methods into Christian thought -- for which he
was awarded the title of "saint.")

In the Beginning

No one knows the origin of the Zodiac. It has been in existence from at least 6000 B.C.E. (before common era). Because it was in its complete form even at that time, the Zodiac has to be considerably older than that. Without exception, all ancient astronomer-priests attributed their knowledge of the heavens to older celestial beings whom they referred to as "the Watchers." In this book the unknown geniuses who presented the world with the Zodiac will also be referred to as the Watchers.

What we know today as the Zodiac is but a remnant of a secondary celestial text concerning life lessons and the individual's interrelation with the universal energies. This instructional course was regarded as the Lesser Zodiac, or more properly, the Zodiac of Signs. It is from this secondary use that we received our familiar Zodiac which begins with the sign of Aries.

The subject of this book will focus primarily on the Greater Zodiac, which in prehistory times was known as the Zodiac of Constellations, and which began the lessons of Creation with the sign of Aquarius.

Evidence is presented with pieces of broken tablets and cylinder seals which seem to show that the two Zodiac presentations were salvaged for the world by those ancient peoples of the land of Shumer -- which is today commonly spelled Sumer. There are Sumerian astronomical tables, tablets of planetary information, descriptions and lists of constellations, lists of stars, and studies of our solar system.

These predate the better known Egyptian civilization.

Sumer (Shumer) is the land which is presented in the Old Testament references as "the land of Shin'ar," and was located in what is today designated as southern Mesopotamia. The name Shumer comes from the ancient Akkadians and identified with reverence their wise predecessors. The word Shumer translates as "Land of the Watchers."

This same land was referred to in the nation of ancient Egypt as *Ta Neter*, meaning "Land of the Watchers." Ancient Egyptian writings freely presented the idea that their concepts and model of civilization, as well as their spiritual understandings, began and issued out of the Land of the Watchers.

The Akkadians, close ancestors of the Sumerians, called the governing beings -- and probable founders -- of Sumer the *Ilu*, meaning the "Lofty Ones." This word became the root-source of the Hebrew words Elohim and El used in the early pages of the Old Testament. The Canaanites and the Phoenicians also received their word Ba'al from the same source, and it translates loosely as "Lord."

The Sumerians themselves, in the earliest references found on tablets, called their governing beings DIN.GIR. There is some question of the precise meaning, but it is generally accepted as meaning "the Righteous ones."

Whoever these "Righteous Ones" or "Lofty Ones" were -- wherever they came from -- they seem to be the prime candidates as the ones who presented the two Zodiacs and their lessons to the world.

There was, from the *very first appearance* of the Zodiac figures in Sumerian tablets, an astonishing familiarity with the universe so awesomely spread with myriad stars. The mechanics of the Zodiac presented an astounding knowledge of the true workings of our own solar system. To this day, all the constellations of the northern skies and the majority of the constellations of the southern skies are known by the names given them in Sumerian astrological tablets. Even more astonishing is the fact that the constellations were all listed from the very start in their correct order.

Of all the various constellations, the most important for teaching purposes were the twelve that appeared to form a primary band about this solar system as seen from Earth. These twelve major constellations were called UL.HE by the Sumerians which translates as "The Shiny Herd."

Where the Watchers who compiled the lessons of the Zodiac came from may never be explained. All we have is the certainty that all the trappings of high civilization sprang forth suddenly and seemingly out of nowhere in the Mesopotamia region. This instant civilization unaccountably had all the trappings and refinements we commonly think of as rather recent acquisitions. They possessed planned cities with carefully surveyed networks of streets. There were multistoried buildings of brick, marketplaces, schools, places of worship, medical centers, law and courts of law, record keeping and libraries, granaries, systems of weights and measures, textile mills, wharves, international trade, and even zoos. They made use of irrigation, domestic animals, carts -- with wheels, and metal making. Their amusements included music and musical instruments, dance, acrobatics, theater productions, races, and prostitution.

With this highly refined civilization that appeared so complete all at once over eight thousand years ago there was an intimate familiarity with things celestial.

We have only a few clues on some incomplete tablets that present a tale of where the Righteous Ones -- or the Watchers -- may have come from. The modern world, unfortunately, finds the suggestions too far-fetched -- a flight of fancy. These people with their unaccountable knowledge of the celestial realms have been regarded as without credibility because of one startling assertion. Among the incomplete tablets is found reference to an unknown planet of this solar system, the orbit of which took it far beyond Pluto's orbit and which then passed back between the orbits of Mars and Jupiter.

This planet's orbital pattern is supposed to take about 3600 Earth years to complete. Since no modern astronomer has ever confirmed such a planet it must be regarded skeptically. The Sumerians, however, took it seriously, and they knew this planet by the name of Nibiru, which means "Planet of Crossing."

The later civilization of Babylonia revered this same planet as a "Celestial Lord," which did not then carry the meaning of a god. They knew this planet as Marduk. Over a considerable time the Babylonian priesthoods came to personify the planet and cast it in the role of a "god."

In about this same period of time, Egypt, another offspring of the Sumer civilization, also knew and referred to this same Celestial Lord by the name of Ra. Here is where much error and confusion has issued, for Ra was not originally a sun god nor even a personification of the Sun. Ra originally signified the "Planet of Crossing," and its most ancient symbol is a *winged* disk or orb. The Babylonians, too, used the winged disk symbol for this unverified planet. The Egyptian symbol often included serpent-like wing struts and double serpent heads, which do not inspire a concept of the Sun. The inclusion of serpent images with the symbol is a powerful clue. In nearly all the world's ancient civilizations serpents commonly served as symbols for knowledge and wisdom which were never regarded as being gifts of the Sun. Ra was linked in some manner to wisdom, and in this regard it eventually was understood as a great god of heaven and Earth.

The winged disk was used to symbolize the Celestial Abode of Ra, and it was understood by the ancients to be a *large distant planet*, not the Sun. This claim is proved by numerous depictions in which both the orb emitting rays representing the Sun and the winged orb representing the mysterious planet are present. A good example of this, where both symbols are present in the same depiction, is the coffin top from a tomb in Thebes which also shows the hieroglyphs of the twelve constellations. Since the Earth has never had twin suns, the one with wings has to represent something else. For our purpose now it is of little consequence if the planet Nibiru exists or not. Still, we do have much to learn of our own solar system, and our space probes have only scratched the surface.

*   *   *

Upon that circled celestial blackboard we know as the Zodiac, the Watchers inscribed the twelve major constellations with the symbols for the twelve Patriarchal Principles which animate all life. It is from the Watchers' teachings of Patriarchal Principles that so much emphasis was placed upon the so-called Patriarchs in biblical myths. For this reason, what the Patriarchal Principles stood for should be made clear. There was no disguised ancestral worship in the teachings of the Watchers.

In the ancient lessons on Creation and cosmology given with the celestial codex called the Zodiac of Constellations each sign presented a *principle of Creation*. These taught the successive planes of development and growth -- from Involutionary through Evolutionary stages. At each stage a power and virtue is developed by means of which matter-form and individual conscience is gradually built up. These are the Patriarchal Principles, or which religious jargon might call the spiritual causes of all reality.

Although much of the Watchers' cosmological knowledge has been lost, the constellational symbols they used for instructional purpose have remained remarkably similar for countless millennium. The symbols survive today in the Zodiac most commonly recognized through newspaper astrological gibberish.

The signs of the Zodiac were common to all peoples of the very ancient prehistory world, and have remained to this day a part of the common interpretive understanding of astronomical science and astrological analysis.

The Watchers, as mentioned before, employed the Zodiac in two forms for instructional purpose. Both of these used the same constellational groupings and picturings which, because of their familiarity, made the lessons given with them easier to comprehend. Each Zodiac served as a kind of textbook. The Zodiac of Constellations concerned itself in the main with teaching of Creation -- or more precisely, cosmology, the process of Creation. The Zodiac of Signs, with which most people are more familiar, concerned itself with spiritual and life lessons. It is from this use that it came to be superstitiously associated with predictive quality.

The difference in the Zodiac presentations which used the same constellational groupings as their basis was subtle. The Greater Zodiac of Constellations began its lessons with the constellation of Aquarius and ended with Capricornus. The Lesser Zodiac of Signs began with the constellational sign of Aries and ended with Pisces; figuratively from head to foot. These differences and their interplay will be touched upon in more depth in later chapters.

The important thing to remember is that it was never the intent of the geniuses who gave us the Zodiac that it be used as a forecast tool for personal day-to-day directioning. The twelve major constellations were presented only to serve as symbols of the twelve Patriarchal Principles upon which and out of which all Creation is structured.

The twelve Zodiac signs served to illustrate the steps of progression and the apparent conflicting elements to be overcome at each step in order to reach higher -- or Evolutionary -- fulfillment. Science today is aware that what we know as material-matter is but congealed energy. Albert Einstein formulated this fact as $E=MC^2$. Elements differ from one another in the structure of their atoms upon which depend their physical and chemical properties. This is what the Zodiac of Constellations taught -- as *involved in the process of becoming* -- without getting mired down in heavy technical explanations.

Only here will we momentarily detail scientific understanding of the conflicting elements of Creation. Elements differ in electronic configuration (valence), boiling point, melting point, density and specific gravity, hardness, specific heat, spectrum, and radioactivity. The elements also differ in malleability, ductility, compressibility, elasticity, thermal expansion, electrical conductivity, and magnetic properties. How these attract or repel to consequently develop and build accounts for all things in Creation. This was what the lessons given with the Zodiac of Constellations sought to bring into understanding.

Each constellation in what was regarded as the Lesser Zodiac (with which we are most familiar) was presented as symbolically representing some portion of human anatomy. Together they composed what was known as the "Cosmic Being," or "Celestial Man," or "Divine Man." This figure served much the same function as a classroom illustration. From the anatomical divisions was traced the intent, aim, development and Evolutionary purpose of personal awareness which we each perceive as *self.*

Using these ancient cosmological, spiritual and life-lesson illustrations as tools for prediction of daily confrontations is like using a photograph of some waves of an ocean as general navigational tool. If the stars truly did indicate some written program for each individual to follow, other things should be taken into consideration. Paramount among them is the fact that if we consider the entire width of the Zodiac and not simply the ecliptic, the Sun passes through or touches upon not just twelve constellations but forty-eight predominate ones.

Another consideration is the fact that the accepted stars in the constellations have changed through the ages. The constellational reference point used by conventional astrologers of today was determined for the year 221 C.E. (our Common Era). The true constellation positions of the planets in today's sky are nearly twenty-five days different from that reference point. During the intervening centuries, due to the Earth's shifting axis, the Zodiac had moved forward at the rate of one day in seventy-two years. This makes the practice of astromancy suspect at least, but it does not alter the lessons given by the Watchers.

Astrologer-forecasters argue that these variations from the original charting are of little importance; that only the signs of "houses" of the Zodiac have meaning, not the location of the constellations. Ignoring the polar wanderings, which in some cases have thrown the constellations into a different "house," seems a precarious way to chart one's destiny.

For astromancy purposes these changes have been allowed for by only a small percentage of astrologers, and this is called sidereal astrology. Even with this allowance, however, the fact remains that the Zodiac was not conceived and presented to humanity as a device for determining any individual's assigned worldly fate.

The Zodiac's hieroglyphic figures hold little value except in the larger understanding of Creation processes and the human purpose presented with the Cosmic Being lessons. The lessons presented the process of Creation and our role within it. The lessons taught of matter formation and explained the manner by which each of us is to take up our Divine nature through the process of Involution and Evolution.

It is in this larger regard that we will soon look at each of the twelve Zodiac signs. With each sign we will find the material out of which organized religions have built their self-serving myths.

When Venus Wore Horns

To understand and express the interactions of Nature, time and natural occurrences, the prehistory Watchers drafted into the Lesser Zodiac -- upon the blackboard of the heavens -- the symbolic representation of the Celestial Man. This representative figure is recognized to this day in association with the Zodiac where each sign is given a different portion of human physical anatomy. For example we accept the premise from common astromancy practice that Aries "rules" the head, that Virgo governs the breast, Sagittarius influences the hips and thighs, and so on.

The so-called "ruling planets" of each Zodiac sign that are played up in astrology-horoscope practice today were not a factor in the Watchers' lessons on Creation actions and cosmology. Nor were they a factor in the life lessons given with the Lesser Zodiac of Signs. The notion of planetary "rulerships" arose much later. The idea of planetary "rulership" was probably inspired when careful watch was kept on Mars and Venus after the latter's entry into the solar family line-up some time around 3000 B.C.E. Both of these planets made an obvious impact on life on Earth from that time on.

There is a curious fact about our solar system's planetary line-up that seems to have been swept under the rug. In spite of the proof that careful records were kept of celestial observances in the ancient past, and these included notations on stars outside our own galaxy, there were then only four planets recorded as being in our solar system. Prior to the third-second millennium B.C.E the planets observed and listed were Mercury, Mars, Jupiter and Saturn. Astronomy records from all over the world in that ancient period recorded only these four planets as members of our solar family. For some reason it seems that all the planets which are presently regarded as house "rulers" were not then present.

This brings us to an idea that is hotly denied in scientific circles. In spite of scientific scoffing, evidence suggests that the planet we know as Venus entered our solar family as a comet some time between 4000 and 3000 B.C.E. If such was the case, the event exerted undeniable influence upon Earth in that era. Knowing this as a possibility it is easy to see how the superstition could arise that planets could be used as a means of prediction.

The practice of attempting to project the times for the more severe upheavals on Earth due to the interactions of Venus and Mars seem to have begun in the last-gasp period of Sumerian times and extended into the early Babylonian times. The troublesome celestial events which brought calamities to Earth in that epoch time would naturally become the foundation of using planetary positions in an attempt to predict future conditions.

There was a distinct recorded change in the role played by the astrologer-priests during this cataclysmic era. The astronomer's study of the heavens became focused more and more upon trying to determine how and when celestial bodies influenced the cataclysmic events experienced on Earth. Well into Babylonian and Egyptian times the position of the planets, particularly of Venus and Mars, and their interactions were meticulously recorded. The studies of the disturbed planets Venus and Mars and their influence became buried and lost beneath legends and myths.

The time frame during which the celestial terrors were played out lasted over many generations. Over this extended time there were two extremely close encounters to Earth and Mars by the invading comet. The disturbances on Earth were catastrophic. For Mars it was even more disastrous. After the comet's second close pass to Mars, the electromagnetic exchanges between the two celestial bodies probably drained off what atmosphere Mars might have possessed.

The second major encounter threw Mars from its long peaceful orbit to rebound across the heavens, and in the process earn for itself the reputation as the planet of destruction. Even after Venus had stabilized in its present orbit around the Sun, Mars continued to rampage through the heavens. This continued for several more generations before taking up its present orbit between Earth and Mercury.

Only after these occurrences did the astrological records from different areas around the world suddenly begin a new method of time calculation and calendar observances -- and included in the solar family a new planet, Venus.

During the "war in heaven," when Venus and Mars were engaged in genuine deadly battle, Venus appeared to display horns and was trailed by a long luminous tail as it rushed across the heavens. For this reason Venus was likened to a bull figure in many of the world's astrological records. This image in the Age of Taurus was not regarded as being auspicious. The bull-like figure presented by the comet was never confused as being the celestial Bull of Taurus. It is likely that it is from the charging bull appearance that Venus came to be regarded as the "ruler" of Taurus in astromancy practice.

This charging bull image across the skies was presented in numerous myths. Probably the most telling account of where Venus originated is in the Greek myth of Athena springing "fully armed" from the "head" of Zeus (Jupiter). Generations of Greeks and Romans likened Zeus-Jupiter with a bull, depicting the thunderbolt god standing upon the back of a charging bull. It was always made clear, however, that the bull charging across the heavens was not associated in any way with the celestial Bull, Taurus.

If Venus existed as a planet of our solar system prior to around 3000 B.C.E., why is it that around that general time the peoples of the world suddenly became so awed and terrified of it? In Asia Minor in that time period the dominant gods and goddesses that arose in public veneration were looked upon as being intimately linked to the sphere we now know as the planet Venus.

All Venus-as-goddess characterizations such as Nana the Babylonian goddess, Astarte of the Phoenicians, Ishtar of the Assyrians, and Aphrodite of the Greeks entered the family of deities only after the general time mentioned. When Venus was personified as a goddess she was characterized as the ultimate practitioner of the art of attraction-repulsion. In consequence of this the raw natural principle which the comet-planet came to represent was commonly depicted as a naked girl. From this association Venus came to be viewed as presiding not over love *per se*, but over attraction which was epitomized as sensuality and pleasure. In Greek myth, for example, it was Venus-Aphrodite's need for sensuality and pleasure which more often than not brought trouble to those about her.

In Babylonia, the planet Venus was distinguished from the other planets and was worshiped as a member of a trinity consisting of Venus, Moon and Sun. This triad eventually developed into the Babylonian holy trinity around 1400 B.C.E. Ishtar, the Assyrian Venus, was regarded as the "star of lamentation." In Babylonian psalms, Ishtar is recorded *as making the Earth to quake, making blazing fire rain upon the land, making mountains to fall down*, and similar terrors.

In Assyrian presentations from that time, Ishtar was said to have "slain her thousands and her tens of thousands." Fire was said to be her raiment -- and with her flames she allegedly consumed the enemies of king Assurbanipal (d.626? B.C.E.) Assurbanipal is probably the Asnappar or Osnapper mentioned in Ezra 4:10. Assurbanipal himself wrote, "Ishtar, the fearful dragon," and that Ishtar was "...clothed with fire and bears aloft a crown of awful splendor." He added also that she "raineth fire over Arabia."

Out of the pestilence, plagues and assorted ills which spread upon the Earth due to the celestial upheavals, there arose strong fears which fed superstition. In this broiling atmosphere a belief in demonology spread like a plague of spirit. Genii, it was believed, swarmed everywhere. They crept in under doors and through cracks to hide in every nook and cranny; they lurked behind walls and hedges, in hollows and depressions. These superstitions were fanned by the priest-class who said such genii demanded magical incantations and/or prayers and religious veneration for their appeasement.

The planet Venus continued to hold such terror for the world that in Babylonia a yearly sacrifice of a boy-surrogate for the king was made to the goddess Ishtar. In the course of these yearly observances the boy to be sacrificed was hurtled through the city streets aboard a chariot in symbolic reenactment of the comet-planet's wild celestial course. The culmination of the rampaging ride was the actual sacrifice of the boy victim.

To the Phoenicians and Philistines among others, the comet-planet Venus was regarded as the Queen of Heaven. The Jewish women of this general time were of the custom of offering cakes to her, and incense was burnt upon the roofs to her. This is recorded in the biblical book of Jeremiah 7:18 and elsewhere.

When we read in Jeremiah 44:17-18, for example, of Jeremiah's flight with other refugees to the nation of Egypt, there is much concern expressed about honors to the Queen of Heaven, meaning the comet-planet Venus. Even after many years the planet Venus still evoked dread and profound fears. This was so deep-felt that the fleeing refugees believed that the fall of their nation to Babylon was the result of Josiah (c640-c608 B.C.E.) not honoring the planetary entity. The verses make it clear that the people did not think their plight and the horrendous upheavals and catastrophes were due to Josiah turning away from god but from his failure to honor the goddess (Venus).

The close passage of Venus to the orbit of Mars which occurred a generation earlier, on March 23rd, 687 B.C.E. to be exact, marked the last major worldwide cataclysm to be triggered by Venus. This brought about the established orbit

of Venus as we know it today. Prior to that date there was
a long period of time in which the length of the year and the
months had to be repeatedly recalculated.

The necessity for repeated recalculating of monthly
and yearly lengths is attested to on an ancient clay tablet
which says that "eight years under Sennacherib (705 to 681
B.C.E.) and twelve years under Esarhaddon (681 to 668
B.C.E.) ...the New Year's festival was omitted." That was a
twenty year period. Esarhaddon was succeeded by
Assurbanipal mentioned earlier, and it was he who had to
recalculate the planetary movements, the precession of
equinoxes, and the periodic return of eclipses.

The length of the terrestrial year prior to this general
period was of 360 days. Ancient Babylonian tablets declare
that the walls of Babylon were 360 furlongs in compass "...as
many as there had been days in a year." It is from this ancient
360 day yearly cycle that circles came to be measured in an
area made up of 360 degrees. Further evidence that celestial
interference occurred in this time period is the fact that
Babylon, before the heavenly disturbances, had been situated from two to two and a half degrees further north than
the region is today. That means the region prior to the Venus-
Mars encounters had not been as hot or desert-like as it is
now.

Marduk, Bel, Ba'al, Ashur, Astarte, Ishtar and others
are some examples of personifications linked with Venus.
The wild entry of Venus through the solar inner circle
eventually dislocated Mars from its long peaceful orbital
path. This is accounted for in the Hindu myth of Siva's (Mars)
passionate lovemaking with Parvati (Venus) *which caused
the whole world to shake and move.* Because of the encounters of the planet with the planet-to-be Venus, Siva-Mars
then brought about such destruction on Earth that it came
to represent the principle of destruction. In the Vedic hymns
prior to this time in question, Siva-Mars was never even
addressed as a deity! Only in the later Brahmanic epic
poems and literature did placid Mars become the destroyer.

Venus is often referred to by astronomers today as a
"sister" planet of Earth due to its proximity and its being

similar in size. Close sisterly resemblance seems to end there, for Venus exhibits gaseous traits and a heated atmosphere that has more in common with the huge outer planets of Jupiter and Saturn. The planet Venus also has a slow rotation period, turning on its axis only once in every 247 Earth days. Another clue that Venus is an inner solar family member only by adoption is the fact that it is the only planet in our system to revolve backwards from all the rest.

Science and popular concept continue to regard Venus as the "sister" of planet Earth laboring under the belief that both planets formed during the same era of condensation. Science backs up this belief by counting craters on our "sister's" face, and by this method reckons the planet to be between four hundred million to eight hundred million years old. Everything fits neatly as they have set up their theory. The possible flaw in their carefully constructed supposition is that they assume that if the planet is there now, then it has always been there.

It is rather self-serving of science to ignore the fact that what we know as the planet Venus was never mentioned or known before c 3000 B.C.E.

By the time these terrifying events occurred due to the entry of Venus into the solar system, the Zodiac and its constellational symbols were hoary with age.

By then the Watchers had been gone so long from Earth that they were remembered only in legend. For those who lived through these ages of terror and who were not versed in the true meanings of events seen in the sky it was easy to slip into fear and superstition. Their descendants would certainly have continued to search the skies for any portent of disaster.

Through those terrifying times the lessons of Truth which the Watchers had fashioned with the Zodiac and its associate hieroglyphs remained boldly proclaimed in the heavens. Memories of the old lessons became as torn and tangled as the masses of wanderers and refugees who carried them. These in turn became the splinters upon which the new breed of astrologer-priests fashioned superstitions that developed into manipulative dogmas of tribal faiths.

Much of that understanding which developed into dogma then still serves as religious articles of faith even in today's technological age.

There is a curious footnote of Venus influence even well into our common era. The symbol used for the planet Venus is of the Ansate Cross. This is a cross having a handle or resembling a looped handle, which probably recalls the tail that tagged behind the invading comet. The Crux Ansata, most familiar in Egyptian symbolism as the *ankh* is regarded a symbol of life. The cross, as usual, represents matter. Perhaps the strangest connection to this Venus symbol is that it is this form, the Ansate Cross, which most cathedrals used as their pattern for the nave, transept, chancel and apse.

*   *   *

Astrology -- what we now term astronomy -- is the world's oldest science. It served as the keystone of all the astonishing knowledge possessed by the Sumerians, Babylonians, Assyrians, Egyptians, the Indus Valley civilization, China, and high cultures of South America. Their superior skills in natural sciences, medicine, and philosophy issued out of their observance of the celestial lessons once given with the Zodiac.

The ancient Sumerians had celestial observation down so precisely that they recognized a cycle of 3600 years in the unfoldment of world and human events. These cycles were known to them as *Saros*. The recognized cycle of 3600 years is the length of time it takes a "fixed" star to move from one degree of a 360 degree circle. This Sumerian wisdom is offered as testimony in their tablets that their ancestors had witnesses many Saros cycles.

A further example of their astonishing knowledge of things celestial is their understanding of the Precession of the Equinoxes. The Precession of the Equinoxes refers to retardation due to the Earth's axis being inclined relative to its plane of orbit around the Sun. This is incredible knowledge when you consider that in terms of human life spans the shift in the Zodiacal backdrop is a mere one degree of the three-hundred-sixty degree Celestial Circle. To place this in more comprehensible terms, it takes seventy-two years just to shift that one degree against the Zodiacal backdrop. As another means of comparison, it takes two thousand one hundred and sixty years to pass through a single Zodiac sign.

The Sumerian's own astronomical accounts began with the age of Taurus, which began around 6400 years ago. This period, too, was a torturous era that followed closely upon celestial movements that had brought about other worldwide cataclysms. People all around the world began in this period to adore the Bull with religious devotion. This is generally regarded as the time-setting for the story of Moses, and the references to golden calf adoration is based upon the Age in which the story is placed. Not only did the Hebrews, and later Jewish myths, give recognition to this period, but so did the peoples of the entire world. In Catal Huyuk in Anatolia (Turkey), for example, there is an unearthed Bull shrine which dates from this same general period.

The Sumerian descendents were fully aware of the shift into the Age of Aries (the Ram) which occurred around 2200 years prior to our calendar reckoning, or 4200 years ago. They kept careful accounts of Earth's entry into that Age. It was in this period of time that the sacrificial animal of the world's religions shifted from bull to ram (sheep, goats).

More astonishing than these recorded precessional shifts is the fact that the Sumerians possessed records of previous precessional shifts: of Gemini, about 8500 years ago; Cancer, about 10,700 years ago; and of Leo, about 12,900 years ago. The Sumerians believed that it had been in the Age of Leo that the Earth had come into its visible-matter form. In other words, the period when Earth entered its visible stage of matter, condensing and beginning to solidify from its gaseous elements. This understanding echoed the lessons of the stages in which energy develops toward its destined matter form, and it was with the lessons given with Leo that the Watchers taught how energy becomes visible as matter.

It should be noted that the ancient Sumerians, Assyrians, Babylonians, Egyptians, and later the Greeks, all recognized that the Earth was a planet, that it orbited the Sun, and that Earth was a "celestial wanderer." Much of this ancient wisdom became lost during the various cataclysmic events endured by Earth. There were, due to heavenly disturbances, mass migrations taking place all around the world. The last major mass movements occurred from about the year 700 to around 287 B.C.E. In this period of time Egypt and Babylon were the main western deposits of Zodiacal wisdom, with even Babylon eventually crumbling beneath the pressures of circumstance. In the east, astrologers of China and in the Indus Valley also kept safe their deposits of astrological knowledge.

The rescuers could be said to be the wanderers and seekers from Greece who visited both Babylonia and Egypt. Among the migrants who eagerly sought some understanding of the celestial influences that were causing world disturbances was Pythagoras (582?-500 B.C.E.). Pythagoras, known to us as a renowned Greek philosopher and mathematician, studied in both Chaldea and Egypt. It was through him, as well as Thales, Democrates, Democritus, Plato, and Eudoxus, that most of the information taught at the Alexandrian Library and School of Mathematics and Astronomy was gathered. That the ancient Watchers' lessons were not even then completely lost is shown in the teachings presented by these men. Democritus, for example, is credited with formulating the atomic theory and conceiving the idea of atomic energy. All of this, it is sometimes hard to remember, was advanced in classical antiquity.

During the Sumerian-Chaldean epoch astrology was not used as a means of discerning any individual person's lot in life. Birth dates were of no particular concern, and the only client the astronomer was likely to have was the king or perhaps certain important leaders. It was mainly the political and/or climatic events which were of most concern to the persons who sought out the astrologers. It was through such attempts to find an edge against the frightening forces affecting Earth that initiated the attempt to use astrology for predictive use. The astronomer-priests based their studies and calculations upon the appearance and disappearance of the troubling planets, particularly Venus and Mars, at the line of the horizon. From this came the practice used in astromancy of casting a person's horoscope using the planets that appeared upon the horizon at the time of the consultant's birth.

With the conquest of Chaldea by Alexander the Great in 331 B.C.E. the stage was set for the Greeks to take over the interpretive meanings of the Zodiac. It was the Greeks who codified the Zodiac in the pattern that is still in use today. Their understanding, translation and transfer was not always perfect.

After the Sumerian-Chaldean epoch, astrology seems to have developed along two different lines. One branch adhered more closely to the original intent of the Zodiac hieroglyphic figures. This branch spread by way of Egypt, India, and eventually reached as far as the South American cultures. In this branch the astrological speculations exercised heavy and undisguised influence upon religion and philosophy. This promoted a strong holistic interpretation with the universe viewed as being fundamentally alive and purposeful. The drawback to this understanding was that the priest-class, who had lost sight of what this means to the individual, tended to regard the individual as being of little importance to the overall scheme of things. This in turn generated a fatalistic view of life.

The other branch of astrological consideration was shaped and developed largely through the culture of Greece, and then in turn by Rome. This branch developed along rather refined lines, being gradually diminished in its obvious influence upon philosophy and religion. The Greeks were always more interested in astrology as a means of forecast. The Romans, however, whose state and religious leaders had for generations been counseled by soothsayers, at first resisted the use of astrology as a means of prediction.

With the passage of time the astrologers eventually

gained favor over the soothsayers to become sought after by the leaders for prediction and direction. In the economical crisis that developed in Rome as the Empire entered its decline, Christianity gained its foothold by promising the masses the "bread of life." Once Christian devotees managed to gain influence upon state power they actively opposed astrology and forced it into a channel of charlatanism. A multidimensional-polytheistic understanding of things was not something they could structure into an enslaving corporate business.

The young religious cult grew, nourishing itself by absorbing various tenets and rites and personages from the same "Pagan" cults they sought to destroy. More and more disguised astrological symbols were absorbed into the young religion's articles of faith. The founding church fathers busied themselves with formulating new myths to disguise the astrological symbolism upon which they were built. A number of these will be touched upon in the discussion of each Zodiac-constellational group.

Resuming the Star Search

In the sixth century before our present era the Greek philosopher Pythogoras was already thoroughly convinced of the "melodic" influence of the stars. To each of the seven then known celestial family members (Sun, Moon, Mercury, Mars, Jupiter, Venus and Saturn) he allotted a note of the musical scale depending upon its distance from Earth.

Hippocrates (c460-370 B.C.E.), regarded as the "father of modern medicine," about whom the Hippocratic or Coan school formed at the island of Kos (Cos), is credited with attempting to separate superstition from medicine. His attempt was noble if not entirely successful. Hippocrates followed the then current belief that disease resulted from an imbalance of the "four bodily humors." "Humors" was the designation given to glandular secretions and which were thought to influence other forces. His contribution was the concept that the "humors" were themselves influenced by outside forces. Hippocrates taught that there was a correspondence between every human rhythm, periodicity or cycle and planetary motions. He believed that there were astrological influences upon the body and that they could be used as indicators of health problems.

Plato (429-347 B.C.E.), in his writing of **Timaeus**, the same book that presented the Atlantis legend, developed a theory of planet-gods. Plato's notion of heaven was of a place where models of everything in existence were copies from divine ideas. This notion was like a slightly distorted echo of the ancient lessons of Creation-formation presented by the Watchers who used the Zodiac of Constellations as their instruction tool. Heaven was interpreted by Plato as a wheel, the axis of which rested upon the knees of Necessity. The "souls" of all living things were imagined to be sorted and sifted through this wheel, from whence they then fell to Earth to take up their form. All souls were, as a result, then thought to hold vibratory harmony with the orbs of heavenly influence (planets). It was but a short hop from this notion to the idea that planetary influences determined events in an individual's life.

Aristotle (382-322 B.C.E.), student of Plato (and tutor of Alexander the Great), carried this notion further and pitched the idea of astrological influence by connecting the power in our world to the movements of the upper celestial bodies.

Then around 280 B.C.E. a priest by the name of Berosus, from the temple of Marduk in Babylon, set about writing a three volume book called the **Babylonica**. Much of the information in this work came from the archives in the temple of Bel at Babylon and therefore held a great deal of history. More important for present consideration, this work devoted considerable space to astrology.

The Greeks were immediately fascinated with the book, leading Berosus to set up an astrology course at the Greek island city of Kos (Cos). The famed medical school established by Hippocrates was still in full operation there. It was not long before Berosus was instructing medical students, and his influence at the school became substantial.

The next influential personage in regards to astrological information was the Greek astronomer Hipparchus (190-120 B.C.E.). He was the first systematic astronomer of whom there are some remaining records -- thanks to the later writings of Ptolemy. Hipparchus made most of his observations at the island of Rhodes. It is Hipparchus who is credited with the discovery of the Precession of the Equinoxes. The fact that he *re*-discovered the points at which the Sun crosses the celestial equator does not lessen his achievement. He also made a comprehensive chart of the heavens, giving the positions of more than eight hundred and fifty stars. (Ptolemy was later to expand upon these.) In addition Hipparchus relayed a method of determining longitude by observing the parallax of the moon in eclipse. He is considered to be the first person to make systematic chords roughly equivalent to trigonometrical sines.

Claudius Ptolemaeus, commonly referred to as Ptolemy and who flourished from 127 of our present era to around 151, is our bridge into knowledge of the earlier times. He was an astronomer, mathematician, and geographer. His book known as **Tetrabiblos** was written at Alexandria where he made his observations. This work was destined to become the bible of astronomers until it was abandoned in the sixteenth century for the Copernican system.

In his astronomical and mathematical works, Ptolemy was indebted to Hipparchus. It was in his writing called **Syntasis** that Ptolemy gave some remaining records of Hipparchus, thus preserving them for posterity. From the works of Hipparchus, Ptolemy based his geocentric theory of the universe. He proceeded, unfortunately, to misinterpret Hipparchus' records and worked from the idea that Earth was the stationary central point of the planetary system. In this scheme of things the Sun, Moon and the planets were thought to revolve around Earth. Radiating outward, Ptolemy believed, were the elements of earth, water, air, fire, and ether. Beyond these, he suggested, lay other zones as immense spheres, each being a heaven. This notion was most probably encouraged by Gnostic and Mithran influences in Alexandria during the time Ptolemy was working there. It was from such fabric that the medieval Roman Catholic Church drew its erroneous conclusion of a cosmogony where Earth, instead of the Sun, was the stationary central point of the system.

*   *   *

Only after the Hellenization of Chaldean astrology did the notion arise that everyone had a right to know their personal destiny. The Greeks, by introducing the concept that at birth a newborn was influenced by the planets that were rising on the horizon at the time, ushered in an astrological doctrine that was more extensive than in use previously. It was this use of astrological pursuit that set the stage for astrology to be disowned -- but not abandoned -- by western religions. By the time Rome was in decline, astrological lore was shuttled from open study to the dungeon of forbidden "Pagan" knowledge. Exiled in the depths of churchy vaults, astrology became the secret basis for many of the Judeo-Christian-Islamic myths -- just as it had more openly done for countless other, more straight forward "Pagan" religions.

The Roman world, with a long tradition of fortune tellers, augurers and soothsayers, did not eagerly embrace astrology forecasting from the Greeks as it had accepted almost everything else from Greek culture. To the Romans religion and fortune prediction were intimately intertwined. The priestly class of augurers, who were quite often of the aristocracy, had for centuries participated in decisions of state. For this reason astrology was long held in contempt by the Romans.

After the death of Julius Caesar in 44 B.C.E., however, which coincided with the appearance of a comet, astrological prediction gradually gained favor over that of the soothsayers. Astrology continued to grow in favor in spite of the repeated attacks upon it by men in power. It is this Roman priestly class of augurers which influenced later Christian condemnation of astrology.

When the early Christian faith moved in to usurp the polytheistical faith of the Romans, the church fathers sought destruction of all possible rival influences. Astrology was denounced as a matter of course, being labeled fatalism, and the Zodiac was dismissed as a "Pagan" device. We will see in later pages concerning each Zodiacal division that most all of the Christian religion's claimed "holy" events such as virgin birth, the manger, events of their "savior's" life, calvary, and such are all taken from the lessons of the ancient Zodiac of Constellations which were reworked and presented as "historical" events.   In fairness it must be admitted that the Christian religion was not the only one to do this. The ancient Zodiac lessons served as the basis for Mithric, Orphic, Jewish and countless other religious inter-pretations.

*   *   *

        The twelve major constellations, so well known from newspaper and magazine horoscopes, were originally in-tended by the prehistoric Watchers to serve as symbols of the twelve Patriarchal Principles which underlie and activate all of Creation. Knowing their true purpose it becomes obvious that the twelve signs of the Zodiac were never intended to be used to discern personal destinies. Rather they were used as a means of teaching the processes by which creative action creates. Each of the Zodiac signs, in their original presentation, served to reveal the principle purpose at work *in various prephysical planes of development.*

        Out of this ancient wisdom once taught with the twelve major Zodiac lessons there arose the mythical and religio-superstitious importance attached to the number twelve.   Worldwide religious significance of the number twelve rests squarely upon these Zodiacal presentations of the Patriarchal Principles. It is the personification of these creative principles which have come to be called the Patri-archs in the Old Testament -- all of them presented as being before the appearance of the mythical Moses.

        The movements of the Earth and the Moon served as strong visual emphasis to support the suggestion that the number twelve was possessed of mystical or magical impor-tance. Anyone who watched the sky could see that the Earth completes its passage around the Sun in twelve months, passing through the influence of the twelve major divisions of the Zodiac. Furthermore, the Moon completed twelve passages around the Earth in approximately the same amount of time. These mysteries of movement seemed to prove the power of twelve and in religious myths everywhere the number is repeatedly emphasized.

The twelve Zodiac lessons which taught the Patriarchal Principles of Creation inspired the Greek tales of the twelve Titans and the twelve Olympian gods. Hercules, the Greek Celestial Man and savior figure had his twelve labors to perform, each linked to Zodiac figures such as the Nemean Lion which is Leo. There were twelve gods of the Brahamanical Zodiac. Even the legend of Atlantis and its legendary twelve great kings is linked with the Zodiac. In addition, Atlantis was described as circular in its layout, *ala* the Zodiac, and it was said to have bands of water defining its regions.

From the twelve divisions of the Zodiac also was drawn the averment that the Persian-Hindu god Mithra, the Egyptian god Osiris, the Aztec god Quetzalcoatl, the Gautama Buddah and all other "savior-gods" were attended by twelve disciples, just as is credited to Jesus. Evidence that the claim of Jesus being attended by a similar band of twelve is but another mythical tale is affirmed by the original Gnostic-based writings of "Paul." These writings were used to help shape Christian principles, but never once in the earliest writings was there ever any mention of the alleged twelve constant companions. The "disciples" are mentioned only once in writings attributed to Paul, and that is an obvious later insertion.

The number twelve is bantered about in numerous scriptural tales, playing important symbolic roles in both the Old and New Testaments. Jacob, for example, is deemed in Jewish myth to have had twelve sons who served as the founders of the mythical twelve tribes of the Hebrews. Solomon's temple, in which "there was neither hammer nor axe nor any tool of iron in the house while it was building," was also said to contain twelve divisions within it. Additional examples will be touched upon in later pages.

Of course the New Testament does not neglect the number twelve either. In the Book of Revelations, a jumble-mixture of misunderstood cosmology-astrology-numerology, the number twelve is again presented as pregnant with mystical meaning. In chapter 21, verse 13, for example, the number twelve is played up where we read, "On the East, three Gates; on the North, three Gates; on the South, three Gates; on the West, three Gates. And the wall of the city had twelve foundations and names of the twelve apostles of the Lamb."

The Zodiacal-astrological association is so obvious that it has been hidden from the masses by that familiarity. The three "gates" on each side of the new heavenly "city" refers to the quarterly division by threes of the Zodiac circle. Aquarius, Pisces and Aries comprise the "East gates." In occult usage east refers to the prephysical planes, or what religion often terms spiritual.

After the "East gate," the verse then speaks of the "North gate," moving the "revelation" in a counter clockwise listing of the "gates." The reason for this is because the listing of the Zodiac divisions follow the Earth's apparent movement through the twelve Zodiacal divisions of the sky. Because the Zodiac signs are always listed in a counter-clockwise listing, so too did the "gates" of the heavenly "city" have to follow form.

The north "gates" are therefore reference to Taurus, Gemini and Cancer, which in the Watchers' lessons concerned the process of *becoming* -- of energy substance -- the generating of prephysical substance toward visible form. That is why in occult "revelations" or "prophecies" of doom and gloom the destiny of the world is always said to come "out of the North."

The west "gates" refer to Leo, Virgo and Libra, the signs used in the Zodiac of Constellations lessons to teach of density, of matter formation, of temporary visible form. Because "spirit" is locked in matter-form at this point it was allegorically "dead" while experiencing matter form. For this reason west came to symbolize death in many cultures. Romans, for example, entered their camps by the East gates after achieving victory in battles. In contrast, funereal processions and people driven away to exile or in defeat or in shame were usually escorted away through the West gates of the city.

The south "gates" are Scorpio, Sagittarius and Capricornus which in the Zodiac lessons taught of ascension, or more correctly the evolution of quality.

Other examples of the importance of the number twelve can be seen in Shi'ite theology. Unlike the Summi Muslims, the Shi'ites hold a hardcore belief in the role of an intermediary between man and Allah. This belief allows for the seat of a strong religio-politico set up in the guise of god's mouthpiece. From the earliest days of Islam's spread, leaders of the Shi'ite faction encouraged the claim that there were Twelve Imams which served in the capacity of "mediator." These twelve, not surprisingly, were presented as the rightful successors to the Prophet Muhammad. The Twelve Imams were presented as having combined religious and secular authority.

Fundamentalist Shi'ites of today adhere to the belief that the twelfth Imam disappeared in the year 940 C.E. but will reappear to establish a cleansed Islamic state. This notion has much in common with some Christian factions looking forward to Jesus' "Second Coming."

Once again this myth of the Twelve Imam founder-authority beings is based upon ancient Zodiacal influence. Twelve, as usual, is drawn from the twelve major constellational lessons, and Muhammad (just as is Jesus) is posited in the Sun position as the representative of god. In this manner he is made the focal point about which all theological interpretations revolve.

By these few examples we can see that the number twelve plays an important role in every religion of the world although it is always disguised to suit their particular purpose. In the previous example from Revelations the astrological mechanisms are transposed as religious "revelation." The four triplicities of the Zodiac symbolized by the fire, earth, air and water signs are repeatedly played upon. Each one of these four symbolic divisions is further defined in astrology as the Cardinal, the Fixed, and the Mutable signs.

The "names" of the twelve "apostles" said to be in "the

wall of the city" are nothing other than the twelve constellations themselves which appear to revolve about the Sun. The ancient Zodiac of Signs figure, the Celestial Man, represented the Life Principle. This was taken as organized religion's "Lamb" who, as a solar god, was pictured as being accompanied by twelve loyal "apostles of the Lamb."

In the Book of Revelations, allegedly a saintly vision of a decreed horrific future, the River of Life is said to flow past the fabled "Tree of Life." The tree is described as miraculously bearing twelve different varieties of fruits -- a different fruit for each month of the year. This is such a transparent astrological reference that it seems incredible that billions of people have accepted it as some "holy" and mysterious revelation.

*   *   *

Bull, eagle, lion and man: these stand forth prominently in the Old Testament, especially with the so-called visionary "prophets" such as Ezekiel. In truth there is nothing prophetic or visionary about these "prophets" or in the symbols that they are said to have witnessed. The Bull, Eagle, Lion and Man are but Zodiacal hieroglyphs stolen for dramatic display. To understand the use of these symbols we must reconstruct the earlier time period and their view of the heavens.

During the past five thousand years the constellational divisions have moved eastward through sixty degrees. The earlier Zodiac lessons had established that the four Cardinal Points of the Zodiac were in the constellations of Taurus the Bull, Scorpio (which the Hebrews knew as the Eagle), Leo the Lion, and Aquarius the Man (Water Bearer).

It was during the time period of Ezekiel's influence that the Scriptures acquired their references to the "cherubim" mentioned in the book of Ezekiel and which were alleged to contain all those symbolic faces. The word cherub, incidentally, comes from the Assyrian word *kirub*, and its meaning is "Bull." (No further comment.) It was from these same Cardinal Points that the four "brigades" of Israel -- Judah, Ephraim, Rueben, and Dan -- received their emblems. A clue to the real Zodiacal meaning is that these "brigades" were said to be in "the four-square Wilderness Camp," a subtle reference to the prephysical planes, always allegorized as wilderness or desert in scriptural tales.

All of this only shows how intricately bound together were the tenets, dogmas and myths of Judaism with astrology and the Zodiac figures. Although the Old Testament denounces astrology, as in II Kings 23:4-5, the verses against it were later insertions. In this case the insertion was made by Jeremiah's scribe, Baruch ben Nerian, for Jeremiah himself was illiterate. The denouncing of astrology was included to counter popular acceptance of the more ancient teachings of cosmology that had been given through the Zodiac lessons. The Verse in II Kings 3 was inserted to give the Jewish priest-scribes the propaganda against the Zodiac teachings by claiming the constellational figures represented the "army of the heavens" false gods.

Judaism, as with all other religions of the Middle East region -- indeed the world -- clung instinctively to the elements of a more ancient and more comprehensive presentation' of cosmological understandings. Mosaics of the Zodiac were often prominent in numerous ancient synagogues. Among the more recently unearthed is the mosaic at Hammath Tiberias close to the edge of the Sea of Galilee. In this mosaic is shown the signs of the twelve Zodiac divisions surrounding the Greek sun-god Helios.

*   *   *

The arc of the night sky was the blackboard upon which the ancient Watchers fashioned their lessons of Creation-cosmology. From it the Watchers sought to explain both the actions of Creation and it purpose. The Zodiac symbolically presented the covenant of the Creator with

Creation. It was the great and original Arkite Mystery.

Long after the great meanings taught with the Zodiac had been lost or hidden the arc that taught the covenant of Creation was remembered in legend and was thought of as having been something tangible. Out of this there arose among most of the cultures of the Near East region a standard practice of priests to fashion a portable construction in which "god" was said to dwell. There was a strong parallel between the arkite ceremonies among many of those ancient peoples, and in the scriptures it is given prominence as the "Ark of the Covenant."

The Jewish priesthood, dedicated to promoting a political god who took to his bosom the Jews as his "chosen people," therefore fashioned a physical dwelling place to inspire the populace of his closeness. This was, as said before, standard religious practice among most of the cultures of the Near East region during this period. Even in this perverse misinterpretation of the ancient Watchers' teachings, however, the "mysteries" remained the same, for although the Ark remained fully visible to all the "Holy of Holies" -- priestly jargon for the ultimate action and purpose of Creation -- remained veiled from profane gaze.

To the prehistory Watchers the arkite mysteries were explained fully upon the Arc of the Sky. There they found set forth the Patriarchal Principles and the manner and purpose of the cosmological processes. With this the ancient Watchers set forth their great doctrine of the Renovation of Humankind.

From this most sacred arcana of the ancient world the Jewish priesthood plagiarized and structured their "holy scriptures." In doing so, even though they did not fully understand what they had borrowed, they provided the means of survival for those arcane teachings.

Academic Studies of the Zodiac

The ancients classified four of the signs of the Zodiac as "fixed" or "foundation" signs. These served to divide the academic studies of the Zodiac into four *Logia.* We receive this word Logia from the Latin, through the Greek word *logo* which means "ratio, proportion," and which is now generally accepted to mean word or speech.

The word *logi* is an extremely ancient Zodiacal-astrological term and was used in the instructions of the twelve Zodiac divisions which contain the questions of Creation and life. These chapter-like divisions -- or *logi* -- corresponded to the twelve major constellational divisions of the visible heavens, with Logos being used to designate the "cosmic source."

Out of this arose a body of occult cosmology and life lessons commonly known in prehistory times simply as the Logia. Following the Earth's catastrophic upheavals brought about by the Venus-Mars encounters the teachings from the Zodiac lessons were salvaged in disordered form but still known as the Logia.

Some of these salvaged teachings underwent a number of translations and interpretations. In time some of the writings managed to find its way into the New Testament, a little reworked and mythologized but from the ancient Logia, nonetheless. For example, reworked for Christian religion's use was **Ur-Markus**, known to us today as the "gospel" of Mark. From the ancient **Logia of Matthew** came the carefully edited and reworked version which is today honored as the "gospel" book of Matthew. We are indebted to the follower of Manes -- known as Mani in western references -- by the name of Seleucus for the copy from which these "gospel" books were recopied into the canonical version used today.

Pagan understanding of the words Logi and Logia is echoed in the Greek language usage and which is credited with the origin of the word. It is from the same root source that the Greek word *legein* was derived and which means "to speak."

The early Pagans understood the word Logos to refer to planetary creativity as originally used with the cosmology lessons taught with the ancient Logia divisions of the Zodiac. Humankind still recognized through the earlier part of worldwide tribulations that planetary creativity arose out of energies in action. Obliqueness, however, was already creeping into popular understanding of this.

It became a practice in those uncertain times to personify the creative energies for elementary instructive use. Presenting the creative processes in this way served much the same purpose as fairytales serve to prepare children for understanding life's harshness and uncertainties. Adults, supposedly, learned the difference between tales of personified energy actions and the true higher functions that had been represented. Until ambiguity set in, that is. When all this became gradually reworked by priest-mythographers the elementary personifications of the creative energies became the "gods" in their religious interpretation.

Planetary creativity, even in the ages that followed closely upon the world disturbances, was still part of most "Pagan's" understanding of cosmology. The creative action which underscored all the universe was still understood as being a part of the Life Principle. In their understanding the Life Principle -- or Logos -- it was commonly recognized and comprehended as the light and life of all things. Out of this arose the Christian claim wherein the light and life was personified as Jesus the Christ.

The Greeks stand as the preservers as well the point of division for much ancient thought. Since we received this word Logos through the Greeks, we will follow in through the Greek usage which rather loosely represented it.

In Greek philosophy Logos came to be considered the "word" by which the inward thought is expressed -- or the thought itself. This pretty well balances in its meaning with the first lesson given with Aquarius in the Zodiac of Constellations on the creation process. The Greek philosophical exercise reflected the Zodiac lesson where Divine Consciousness is presented as the Creative thought, the source of all things.

The Christian fathers' concept of Jesus as being the "Word of God" is taken directly from this Greek philosophy. In this manner, through their constructed labyrinth of theology, they were led to the presentation of Jesus as Christ being the second person of their Trinity. In the ancient Zodiac of Constellations teachings the source contained within itself three equal and principle aspects of creative power. These triple aspects within the source were taught with the lessons of Aquarius, Pisces and Aries.

Jesus, then, is the personification of the second aspect of the creative source which had been taught with the Logia of Pisces in the Zodiac of Constellations. This personification has served the Christian religion well through the Age of Pisces. The religious claim of Jesus as the second person of their trinity became established and presented by the priest authors in the reworked Logia of Matthew by inserting the suggestion into the "gospel" of Matthew 28:19. This was then reinforced by repeating the suggestion that the Logos was personified as Jesus in the fourth "gospel" of I John.

Once this meaning of Logos was incorporated into Christian jargon it was further remodeled to disguise the original meaning. In the "mystery" put forth in the garbled book of Revelations, the Logos is then said to have "seven spirits" who come before "his" throne. These are none other than the seven Involutionary planes of energy through which matter comes into form as had been taught with the ancient

Zodiac of Constellations. These "seven spirits" were more correctly and honestly presented in ancient Pagan cosmology based upon the Zodiac teachings where they were understood as being the seven formation divisions of planetary matter.

The transformation of the Zodiac lesson divisions known as Logia into Logos as the "word of God made manifest," -- or the "Son of God" -- in no way advanced with their claim any higher understandings of cosmic truths. The sneered upon Pagans, on the other hand -- from whom the basic concept of their Logos was stolen -- at least presented a crude understanding of cosmology through their stories of the "gods" whose amoral actions symbolized the indiscriminate energies at Creation's source.

The Pagans never pretended that any morality attended the amoral creation functions which they personified as gods. The Pagans knew with correct and absolute certainty that morality and ethics are not found in the source energies but are qualities which evolve through a process of refinement. Raw forces at work in Nature, the Pagans understood, could only be controlled and shaped through the painful Evolutionary exercise of human intelligence and compassion. Only by honing these out of the energy-conscience we know as *self* can humankind pull itself up to the edge of its intended higher purpose.

The use of the Zodiac lesson divisions, the Logia, to the interpretation as the "Son of God" was a cunning move to present a secondary god into what was and is still professed to be a monotheistic faith. The "Son of God" claim is based entirely upon the Zodiac lessons of cosmology which taught how the primordial elements reached the SUN stage of development. From this lesson of cosmology religion contrived the theological claim of the "Son of God" made manifest. This opened the way so disguised polytheism could then be freely pursued by the installation of hierarchal bands of "archangels" and "saints." Most of the earliest of these claimed hierarchal beings were personifications of various constellational signs and the planets themselves.

From common usage at the time the word Logia

gradually came to serve as reference to the maxims attributed to any religious leader. In Christianity, therefore, the
word logia came to refer to the sayings attributed to Jesus,
but which were not recorded in the "Gospels."

*   *   *

The twelve major academic studies given with the
ancient Zodiac of Constellations were presented in four
divisions -- or Logia. These were marked by the four "fixed"
signs much as lesson headings. These four divisions were
marked by Aquarius, which concerned the sources; Taurus,
which concerned the substances; Leo, which concerned the
densities; and Scorpio, which explained ascension -- or
Evolutionary planes.
     The "fixed" signs were regarded as representing a
uniformed balance of the reservoirs of energy which appear
to human comprehension as conflicting forces -- chaos. Over
the passage of ages the logia divisions came to be used as
symbols for symbols. These came to be thought of as the four
"elements" presented symbolically as air (Aquarius), earth
(Taurus), fire (Leo), and water (Scorpio). That these "elements" were only symbolic representations in themselves is
seen in the inclusion of fire as a *physical* element.
     When the original intent of the Zodiac lessons became
confused and lost through planetary disasters and priestly
interpretation of Zodiac lessons, understanding slipped into
the whirlpool of superstition. With the world still trembling
from its brushes with celestial shifting it was easy for the
ancient "fixed" signs to become confused as "elements."
These "elements" were then accepted as being the "foundation" signs, and the original or true cosmic meaning was lost.
     The ancient teachings had been saved and were still
known in their correct form among two or three groups of
peoples. Some impressive attempts to preserve that knowledge in the face of rising ignorance and superstition could
account for some mysterious monuments. The great Sphinx

in Egypt is one such possible attempt to preserve ancient knowledge. It may indeed whisper secrets of the universe, but only to those who hold the key. The Great Sphinx at Gizeh was known to the Egyptians as *Hu*. The name holds great meaning which relays some extremely important information about the status of the species we know as Hu-man.

In the ancient teachings given with both of the ancient Zodiac texts all references to Man, with the upper case M, always signified Divine Consciousness which resides within the fountainhead of Creation energies. Any references to man, with the lower case m, always referred to the true race of man. When "man" was spoken of, however, it was not in reference to the human species! This makes for confusion if we do not have the key to this distinction.

The *true race of man* refers to the *evolved, refined intelligence of the Evolutionary being.* We as a matter-form species do not fall into that category. We possess only the potential for that advanced stage.

The potential for ascending into the Evolutionary planes exists within us because we are the result of higher intellect which has been infused to mutate a primitive life form with intellectual capability. What we think of as the *hu*-man species, therefore, indicates only our elevation out of beasthood. We, as hu-man, stand apart only as candidate material for evolvement into higher planes of wisdom. The prefix of *hu* refers to our beast-being, and *man* refers to the higher intellect which was coded into the species. This is what the mysterious figure of the Sphinx at Gizeh represents, a beast-bound being destined to evolve into the true race of man.

The Great Sphinx was not built to represent the god of the rising Sun, nor was it built to protect the neighboring tombs from evil spirits as often presented. There is great meaning in the fact that the Sphinx crouches -- almost as in expectation -- gazing *eastward* directly down the thirtieth parallel. Both the Sphinx and the Great Pyramid are intricately linked to Zodiacal symbolism and are probable repositories of cosmological and human-purpose information to which the key has been long lost.

To preserve information could also be the reason for

the construction of the Great Pyramid. That incredible monument never served as a tomb as popularly believed, and was never intended to be one. The four corners can be said to suggest the four "fixed" signs. There are four triangular walls which face in "cardinal" alignment. It is possible that the north inclined wall is representative of Cancer; the east is for Aries; the west wall is for Libra; and the south wall is for Capricornus.

The edges of the Great Pyramid diverge from the four cardinal points by only a few minutes, and this divergence is probably due to past planetary shifts. Measurements by the most precise means presently available have discovered that the center of the Great Pyramid was at northern latitude 29 degrees 58' 55", which places it a mere one sixtieth of a degree from exactly at the thirtieth parallel.

That the older pyramids, especially the Great Pyramid, served some kind of astronomical function is not widely accepted. One of the strongest clues that the Great Pyramid possibly served some astronomical function is presented by the two pairs of narrow shafts within the structure. When the northern conduit into the so-called "King's Chamber" was first cleared cool air rushed in to stabilize the interior temperature at 68 degrees F. Because of this, these conduits have been presented more as a miracle of air conditioning -- for corpses yet -- and are continued to be explained as being "air shafts." Maintaining a stabilized temperature was undoubtedly part of the function of the shafts. The overlooked and purposely ignored fact is that these shafts are inclined one degree toward the Circumpolar stars. None of these facts have any critical importance for some burial site.

The Sphinx and the Great Pyramid are mentioned here only as examples of how information *might* be hidden from us in plain view. The pyramid could have been constructed for the purpose of preserving the ancient Zodiacal lessons of the Watchers in a way that we are not privileged to understand. The emphasis is on how something *could* be.

The mythological sphinx of the Greeks, not to be confused with the Great Sphinx, also owed its body shape to the combination of the "fixed" sign hieroglyphs. Its human head is from Aquarius, its bull's body is from Taurus, its lion's paws are from Leo, and its eagle's wings are from Scorpio. This mythological sphinx, regarded as being female, is said to have set forth the riddle of the universe to the Thebans. That this mythological figure was regarded as female hints that it represents the aspects of prephysical substance, -- Creation's "elements." The riddle of the sphinx was: "What is it which has four feet in the morning, two at noon, and three at night?" The answer to her riddle was given by Oedipus. The answer is man, for the hu-man species is the bridge into the Evolutionary plane -- the higher planes of being. The sphinx in this myth represented the prephysical planes. Once the plane in which man's higher purpose is achieved the primal elements then return to the elemental planes. This is the reason that this myth says that the sphinx hurled herself from a cliff in self-destruction once the riddle was solved.

To the Chaldeans the four "fixed" signs were known as their "Formators," which is to say the *builders of the world.* The Hebrews, before the advent of Judaism among them, regarded the "fixed" signs as "Cherubim" which were considered to be the builders of the world.

To the Greeks who were more philosophically inclined, the fixed quadruplicity was accepted as representative in a more refined concept. The complete being, they believed, is composed out of the interweavings of four categories which they termed the Physical, the Intellect, the Moral, and the Aesthetic. This is a more advanced understanding, for these could be said to be the "formators" or builders of the *Evolutionary being,* not the world.

Christian mythographers carried the Zodiacal quadruplicity into an entirely different direction. Upon the "fixed" signs of the Zodiac the church fathers fashioned their four "gospels." Matthew is Aquarius, concerned with the source; Luke is Taurus, concerned with the substances; Mark is Leo, more intent on the densities; and John is Scorpio, who allegedly presents the Evolutionary aspects following the ascension out of matter.

*   *   *

With the examples presented thus far it has been shown how both the Old and New Testaments of the "Holy Bible" were in reality structured upon the ancient lessons on Creation and cosmology presented by the Watchers with the Zodiac of Constellations.

Unlike the Zodiac with which most of us are familiar and which begins with the sign of Aries, the greater Zodiac of Constellations, dealing with Creation-cosmology processes, opened with the sign of Aquarius. With the hieroglyph figure of Aquarius the ancient Watchers represented the pouring out of the "waters" of Creation. The subject matter of the hieroglyph was the water itself, *not* the figure holding the urn.

Through the long ages after the Watchers had departed, as we have seen, world conditions contributed heavily to dissimilation of the ancient cosmological knowledge. By the time the Jewish priesthood had fully installed itself -- ages later -- as the controlling faction among the Hebrew tribespeople, little of the cosmological instruction held any meaning. The Zodiac figures, however, were always remembered. They were to serve, in various personifications, as the "Patriarchs" and alleged historical ancestors claimed by the priest mythographers of Judaism.

The Judaic priesthood set about revising whatever ancient material they had to draw upon to fashion an account of Creation. Of course the followers of Judaism were to be portrayed as "chosen" above all else in Creation. To the priest-scribes who took on this monumental task the world seemed to be the center of the universe. The human species, which seemingly dominated the world, was obviously the Creator's favorite, perhaps even his sole concern. The Jewish priesthood set out to convince the world that the followers of Judaism were the most favored of all.

There arose among the Judaic writings two versions of how Creation began. Both were incorporated into the Genesis account, and their conflicting elements were difficult to bring together in a satisfying merger. These were made up from the Jhwhistic account, and the priest mythographer's account. The Jhwhist, who wrote centuries earlier than the priests, drew more accurately from ancient material and spoke of a Creator that created through *its* many aspects. This is why the plural Elohim is found in the earlier verses of Genesis. These are in reference to the primordial energies. It is these that are quoted as saying, "Let us make man in our image."

The political minded priests were not interested in teaching Creation processes but were intent upon creating a god for themselves to give themselves the aura of authority. They chose to build upon the existing material that had once taught of Creation but fashioned for themselves a personal, political god to account for everything that was created. The priestly account therefore opened not with any generating primordial energies but with a self-determined god *already* in full control. The priestly account then dealt with cosmological unfoldment by having their invented god begin Creation by *verbalizing* over the primordial waters. Since this was a plagiarized account it should not be surprising that this priestly version of Creation became, both figuratively and literally, a word-of-mouth happening.

The opening of the Bible, therefore, opens upon a false premise. Although it has its roots in the interpretive and illustrated presentation once given with lessons from the Zodiac of Constellations, the priestly tale of "beginning" fails to give any valid understanding of the primal powers at work at the source. From this false premise the errors of interpretation proliferate.

From the scriptural tales as they read today it is obvious that the writers of the stories never comprehended that there were other worlds, other galaxies, perhaps even other universes. The Watchers, however, had once taught that there were other worlds and other galaxies, and the prehistory cultures had understood it.

The Watchers had taught also that the purpose of humankind is to achieve the qualities of higher being and through that achievement enter into the true race of *man.* There were no self-serving reasons behind the lessons of the Watchers, so you would never have found any reference to "sin" in their teachings. They knew with sublime certainty that if man is to find that destined godhood, it must be saved not from "sin" but from *ignorance.*

Those ancient sages, in fashioning the pictorial textbook upon the heavens itself, presented with their Zodiac figures a system that could not be successfully obliterated. In the hieroglyphic figures, signs and symbols used by them to present the true message of Creation and life's purpose there can still be found, by those willing to search, the genuine process of Creation and our meaningful place within it.

The maligned ancient Pagans understood fully the true character of the Creator-Cosmocrator, which was *not* regarded as a "god." They understood, without feeling threatened, that there was nothing one could do to tempt that indifferent creative force to favor them over something else. They understood that life was best fulfilled by learning to make use of the natural energies and patterns and cycles around them. They understood from the Zodiac lessons that it was in learning to move *with* these actions that they could exercise some favorable directive control over their own lives. They did not deceive themselves in the name of some religion that they possessed rights of "dominion" over Nature's forces.

Creation's and Nature's forces are there to be tapped and used. It is not the responsibility of those forces to make themselves available to us. Instead, it is up to each one of us to tap and direct those forces, for we are, as mystical as it may sound, each a part of them. We can take our first step toward higher beings when we understand that all "gods" are but the inventions of priesthoods to use as an excuse for whatever they do not understand.

On the other side of the coin, "gods" are eagerly accepted by persons wanting someone or something other than themselves to stand responsible for anything that happens in their lives. Never mind that "miracles" are accounted for only by the setting aside of universal order -- and if that really happened the universe would destroy itself. Never mind that a "savior" paying for our wrong doings would keep us chained to the practice of doing wrong. Never mind that the priest-class admits these concepts are all a farce when they try to sound wise and profound with such axioms as "God helps those who help themselves."

Genuine "salvation" can be found only by recognizing that no one else can stand responsible for you except you. No one died so you could go on "sinning" but not stand responsible for your actions. No one else can intervene for your failure to evolve anymore than someone else can breathe for you. Each individual point of energy conscious-ness -- the *self* -- destines itself to repeat its pilgrimage through this plane of matter until that lesson is learned. After millenniums of being fed priestly lies this is a shocking truth.   Once you wake up to it, though, it is the most exhilarating revelation of personal worth.

With this in mind we will be reevaluating Creation and life's purpose from the perspective of the Zodiac lessons given us by the ancient Watchers. Before entering the chapters on the Zodiac lessons themselves there are also a couple of other things to keep in mind.

One is that in some places in the following studies there are references made to the Zodiac of Dendera.   The name comes from the village of Dendera located on the west bank of the Nile River in upper Egypt. In ancient times the village was known by the name Tentyrah. It is here that there stood a temple which was dedicated to the goddess Hathor (Aphrodite, *Venus*). This temple, admittedly, was erected long after the prehistoric times of the original Zodiac presentations. Even so the Egyptian Zodiac did not stray as far off course as it did in other parts of the world.   For this reason the hieroglyphs of the Zodiac presented there are used as a means of comparison.

The temple was completed in the reign of the Roman Emperor Augustus, so it is comparatively recent as a storehouse of Zodiacal lore. Nonetheless, there was in this temple a spectacular celestial Zodiac which formed the ceiling of one of the upper chambers, and it provides us the means by which we can compare Egyptian with Greek presentations for clues to the original Zodiac figures. On the ceiling the major constellational groups were symbolized by human, animal and mythological figures, all engraved on copper. The ceiling was removed about 1820 and transported to the Bibliotheque Nationale in Paris. When the Zodiac of Dendera is referred to, it is as it was represented in the Egyptian temple.

There remains now only a general summary of what each sign represented in the lessons given with the Zodiac of Constellations.

Aquarius	=	Divine Consciousness
Pisces	=	Creative Consciousness
Aries	=	Creative Ideation
Taurus	=	Creative Energy
Gemini	=	Mental Matter
Cancer	=	Astral Matter
Leo	=	Etheric Matter
Virgo	=	Dense Matter
Libra	=	Plant Kingdom
Scorpio	=	Animal Kingdom
Sagittarius	=	Human Kingdom (generic force)
Capricornus	=	Wisdom Consciousness

Aquarius
The Water Bearer

*the first major sign of the Zodiac of Constellations
representing the prephysical plane
of Divine Consciousness*

The sign of Aquarius is commonly referred to as the Water Bearer. This sign is also commonly -- and erroneously -- presented in astrological descriptions as the servant of humanity. In this erroneous interpretation the waters which Man is pouring out is said to be the waters of knowledge which quenches the thirst of the world.

This interpretation was advanced in spite of the fact that water has never served as an occult symbol for knowledge. Besides, according to the Zodiacal hieroglyphs, the water which Aquarius pours forth is depicted as flowing toward and around a single fish, not the world. The single fish is the first decanate of Aquarius, the constellation of Piscis Austrinus. This is an excellent example of how corrupted the ancient Zodiacal lessons have become.

We know this constellation today by the Latin name Aquarius, meaning "the pouring forth of water." The Latin name is in keeping with the original presentation, for the constellation represented the inexhaustible reservoir of the primordial energies, symbolized as water waves, from which and in which all Creation takes place.

The ancient symbolic representation used as the sign for Aquarius has always been of two jagged parallel lines representing waves. These "waters" are symbolic of the action of *primordial creative energies*. It is these primordial creative energies which are the subject of the first lesson given with Aquarius in the Zodiac of Constellations.

The wave symbol represents the parallel lines of force, the vibratory undulations of primordial energies which is the material out of which all in Creation is created. Here is represented the beginning of coordinated energies. It is from priestly interpretation of this ancient Zodiacal lesson of the Watchers that we are indebted for the opening three words in the Bible: "In the beginning..."

The ancient Watchers who compiled the lessons of the two Zodiacs always regarded Aquarius as Man, with a capital M; not a human man but the symbolic subject of all ancient spiritual teachers and of cosmologists. Aquarius was Cosmic Man, and the figure served to symbolize the evolving *Life Principle*. This bit of information alone should already open up a lot of understanding for some incomprehensible biblical verses. Jesus being referred to as the "Son of Man" is one example.

With the Zodiacal sign of Aquarius, the Water Bearer, the ancient Watchers began their lessons of Creation and its processes. Borrowing from this ancient presentation of cosmological-spiritual knowledge the Jewish priest-scribes of a much later age opened their "Scriptures" with the outpouring of primordial waters.

With this sign of Aquarius the ancient Watchers presented the lesson of Causation, that eruptive issuance within the primordial energies which indicated the awakening or activating of those energies. The Man of the Aquarius hieroglyph stood symbolic of this first cause and the Watchers addressed it as Divine Consciousness. It is through this Divine Consciousness that creative action is instigated -- or pours forth.

The Old Testament authors, not prone to abstract thought, interpreted this ancient Zodiac figure literally, accepting that the Creator Intelligence was a male personage. From this they established their one-hundred-percent male Scriptural god. The Celestial Man of Aquarius had been refashioned then to become the Scriptural god who is said to *move upon the face* of Creation's waters.

The second verse of the first chapter of Genesis is traditionally translated from the Hebrew as: "And the spirit of god moved upon the face of the waters." This translation is open to dispute, however. The Hebrew scholar J. M. Vaschalde asserts that a more accurate meaning would be: "And the breath of the divine beings (the Elohim or Patriarchal Principles) agitated the surface of the waters" (primordial energies).

The zodiac hieroglyph of the Cosmic Man shows him pouring forth the waters of Creation from an urn. From this example of outpouring waters came all the world's stories of the River of Life. It is from this primordial outpouring that all creative energies take their source and are spoken of in myths and scriptural writings as rivers. In Persian tradition, for example, this symbolic River of Life was known as Arvanda.

In the Bible, Genesis 2:10, the "River of Life" is presented as issuing "...out of Eden to water the garden, and from thence it began to be parted and became, as it were, four heads." The "Garden of Eden" is spoken of as being planted eastward of Eden, which is the occult way of allegorizing the forward movement in the creative process. The four rivers "parting" to become "as it were, four heads," is an allegorical account of the four material elements of planetary invisible emanation or vapor. This is therefore really a tale of cosmology. In other words, where the energy substantives of the four material elements flow into the planes of substance to became the planetary aura.

The names given to these four scriptural rivers bear further proof that this story is but cosmology in occult dress. The first river is said to be named Pison. The name translates as meaning a multitude, and the inference is atoms. The verse giving this name says the river "compasseth the whole land of Havilah, where there is gold." Why would anyone be interested in gold at that early point of the story? Only because it symbolized the *mineral monads*.

The second river in scriptural myth is given the name

Gihon, which means "to break forth." This symbolized the
current of life force on the lower planes, which occurs at the
plane of Creative Energy.

The third river's name is given as Hiddikel which
translates as meaning "rapid motion." Freedom of mobility
is suggested here, the quickening of life currents that
activates living matter.

The name given to the fourth river in this scriptural
myth is said to be Euphrates which means "fruitful." This
served to represent the evolutionary fruitfulness or purpose
of matter life that culminates in the human kingdom.

The mention of Assyria with these rivers is a blind and
is used in a symbolic sense only, not to any real geographic
location. Four rivers still exist in that region today, and
because they served as models for the biblical tale the
abstract cosmological meaning is lost to the masses. The
tales of the "rivers" parting out of Eden have nothing
whatever to do with geology or history.

In considering the tales told in the book of Genesis we
should keep in mind the meaning of the word. Genesis is a
Greek word, and it means birth or *origin*, which is why the
book mythologizing the beginning of Creation bears that
name. All stories in this "book" therefore were structured to
relay hidden cosmology information, with the energies and
actions of Creation being personified as the starring characters. The entire Bible, in fact, is structured upon this
occult literary form, including the New Testament.

                    *   *   *

The waters being poured forth from the urn held by the
Cosmic Man of Aquarius became the basis for the waters of
the "deep" over which the biblical "god" presided. The
knowledge and understanding of Creation and its processes
offered with the Zodiac lessons was far superior to anything
the priest-mythographers offered in its place. The extent of
the knowledge and wisdom that the Zodiac lessons con-

tained can be exemplified by the symbol used for the lesson heading of Aquarius, ♒ . Discoveries in considerably resent times confirm the extent of the Watchers' knowledge.

In the field of quantum mechanics it is understood today that duality extends into matter. It was discovered in 1924 that electrons should be regarded as not only individual particles but also as being associated with systems of waves. Electrons is the name science has given to the most elementary charge of negative electricity and constituents of all atoms. An integral part of modern quantum mechanics involves wave mechanics.

We are talking of the subatomic levels which gives rise to matter-form. In other words, the starting point -- the causation -- of all material-matter things. This was the subject matter of the opening lesson of Aquarius in the Zodiac of Constellations which sought to explain Creation and cosmology.

Albert Einstein's general theory of relativity also presented two propositions that are important to the opening lessons of Aquarius. 1) That mass and energy are equivalent and interchangeable, and this proposition was proved through atomic fission. 2) That mass increases with velocity. Science has also discovered that when particles are observed on a subatomic level, they disclose seemingly contradictory behavior patterns. At times these particles behave like fluids, while at other times they behave like solids. In theoretical physics this is called wave-particle duality.

With this we are back to the Aquarius symbol, ♒ .

The lessons given with the Zodiac were used to present the general understanding of this in a simplified, symbolic form for easier understanding by the masses.

The lesson on Creation's source continued with the hieroglyphic figure of a single fish, the constellation of Piscis Austrinus.

*   *   *

Piscis Austrinus
or the Southern Fish
first decanate of Aquarius

In the Egyptian temple at Dendera this constellation was known as Aar, which translates as "stream." Piscis Austrinus, first decanate of Aquarius, is commonly depicted as the stream of water which flows from the urn being held by Man (Divine Consciousness). These waters are shown to flow to and around a single large fish. The fish hieroglyph itself symbolizes the primary ideation of life.

The single fish hieroglyph of this decanate-constellation represented the Life Principle which is shown as within the activating streams of primordial energies. This single fish, therefore, represents the homogenous -- or singular first cause which is raised into action from non-manifesting space (void).

This is the source material for various occult statements such as is found in the **Qubbalah** that God had his dwelling in the Great Sea (primordial energies) and was a fish therein. This second decanate of Aquarius is also the inspiration for the reference by Augustine (354-430 C.E.) to the effect that Jesus was "...a fish that lives in the midst of waters." These and similar declarations allude to the Life Principle present within the primordial energies.

The "eye" of the single fish hieroglyph for this constellation is known by the name of Fomal-haut, an Arabic word meaning "mouth of a large fish." The lesson which was given with this constellational hieroglyph explained the primary ideation of life which receives the waters of Genetic Consciousness. This is the carrier of creative intelligence, the cause of all creative activity.

Causation and Genetic Consciousness combine, activating the Life Principle and the first flickering fission of Creation's beginning is accounted for. In the Bible this prephysical state of Genetic Consciousness is accounted for only after Creation is already accomplished, and is then presented in the personification of Adam.

In Christian scriptures, the New Testament, the same

story is told in tighter personification form. In this tale, Jesus, personification of the Life Principle, is also called "Man" or "Son of Man," a direct reference to Aquarius. The first "miracle" thus attributed to the Son of Man is the turning of water into wine, which is to say turning the primordial energies into the wine of life.

The Christian mythographers in fashioning the "life" of Jesus follow the Zodiac lessons of Creation and cosmology. His first "miracle" had to be the bringing forth of the wine of life out of the primordial water. Jesus, orbited by his twelve faithful disciples, ala the Sun and its planetary disciples, are depicted as attending a wedding. Whose wedding? No one knows because it doesn't matter. The wedding itself symbolizes the union of the Primary Ideation of Life with Genetic Consciousness.

In the book of John, verse one of Chapter Two it says, "And the third day there was a marriage in Cana of Galilee: and the mother of Jesus was there." Nowhere is it ever explained from what point this "third day" was reckoned. Jesus personifies the Life Principle therefore the "third day" is in occult reference to the third plane of Creation as presented in the Zodiac of Constellations. The "wedding" is the lesson of Piscis Austrinus, the unity of raw, primal energy and ideation.

The story progresses by having the celebration being threatened by the lack of wine. Jesus' mother, who personifies unformed elementary substance, then asks Jesus to do something about the lack of wine. To this Jesus callously replies, "Woman, what have I to do with thee? mine hour is not yet come."

This haughty and belittling little speech to one's mother is certainly not worthy of any savior. Even though the motives of priest mythographers are always best viewed with suspicion this was not penned as a religious example suggesting that we should adopt some surly manner toward our mother. There is something hidden in the quote that has a different meaning. Aside from the apparent scornful address to his own mother as simply "woman," there is more evidence that this is the Life Principle addressing prephysical substance which Mary symbolizes. The clue is in the line, "mine hour is not yet come."

Creation must continue, so Jesus, the Life Principle, commands that water be poured forth. In Christian mythology the water is said to have been poured into six waterpots of stone from which he then miraculously produces more than enough wine. This is but the Zodiacal Aquarian Man pouring forth the waters of Creation which become the wine of life. The six waterpots of stone are a literary disguise for the six Involutionary Planes through which energy is to move into its dense matter forms. The twelve faithful disciples would have to accompany him, for they are the twelve creative forces -- the twelve Patriarchal Principles. These are the same Principles referred to in the book of Genesis as the Elohim.

This is another tale where facts are kept from the faithful. Where the ancient town of Cana of Galilee supposedly existed has never been revealed. Cana was supposed to have been situated near Capernaum. Two present-day towns claim to be the Cana of the New Testament myth. One is Kefr-Kenna, four and a half miles northwest of Nazareth, and the other is Khirbet-Kana, nine miles north of Nazareth. Neither claim has merit since the story is a myth.

From the ancient Zodiac presentation of the Aquarian lessons there can also be found the reason why Jesus' twelve disciples were referred to by Jesus as "fishers of men." The twelve Patriarchal Principles, the animating elements of physical life, can thus be figuratively referred to. From this tale plagiarized from the lessons of Aquarius in the Zodiac of Constellations, the popes and bishops of the Roman Catholic Church derived their symbol of their hierarchical office -- the so-called Fisherman's Ring.

*   *   *

Pegasus
the Winged Horse
second decanate of Aquarius

The "waters" presented with the hieroglyph of Aquarius represented the ocean of primordial energies out of which Creation arises. The emphasis was placed upon the issuance of Creation's waters and not the Man. The waters flow forth from the urn, and within the outpouring stream is the single fish, Piscis Austrinus. This single fish symbolized the homogenous or singular first cause becoming activated within the non-manifesting void.

It is at this point that the flowing waters were depicted as being activated, *becoming turbulent elements.* This is the subject of the second decanate of Aquarius.

With this decanate the Watchers presented as the lesson's hieroglyph, the first of several figures not found in zoology, a horse with wings. In Greek mythology Pegasus is said to have sprung from the neck of the Gorgon named Medusa when she was beheaded by Perseus. This explanation jumps ahead a bit to the Aries lessons of Creative Ideation, but since Aquarius, Pisces and Aries comprise the three-in-one aspects of Causation it is acceptable -- if confusing. The Greeks referred to Pegasus as "the horse of the gushing fountain."

The constellation of Pegasus is commonly shown as it was presented in pre-Grecian times, as the fore-parts of a horse lunging forward with great wings spreading from its shoulders.

This hieroglyphic figure is, for a reason, of the fore-parts only. Whenever a hieroglyph of a partial figure is used, as with Pegasus and Taurus, it always serves to indicate a stage of *incomplete* formation. In this case the figure indicates that the generative idea within Causation is not yet fully formed. Pegasus symbolizes the turbulent, gushing elements which are to soar -- as with wings -- through the "fourth watch" of the Involutionary Night.

Ancient wisdom given with the Zodiac lessons said that these were turbulent powers which only the Creator

could control. This straightforward teaching of primordial
elements was reworked into Scriptural jargon where "the
spirit of god" moves "upon the face of the waters," Genesis
1:2. This is a priestly falsehood presented as a foundation
stone upon which all Scripture is built. "Spirit of God" is an
empty term, totally without meaning. Causation, which we
may call the Creator, is not a personal deity, not a spirit, nor
does it have a spirit. It is, at this point, the morally
unqualified first principle. It is this morally unqualified first
principle that religion addresses as "god."

The Christian counterpart of this movement *upon the
face of the waters* is found in their mythology where Jesus is
depicted as walking upon the waters. In other words, the
Life Principle in Involution moving upon the primordial
elements.

*   *   *

Cygnus
the Swan
third decanate of Aquarius

The hieroglyph for the third decanate of the Zodiacal
sign Aquarius is that of the cross-bearing Swan, known as
Cygnus. The name Cygnus is the Latin word for swan, from
the Greek word *kyknos*, also meaning swan.

The swan has always been commonly regarded as the
most lordly bird of the waters. In this constellation the
principle stars which suggest the wings and length of the
Swan's body form what is perhaps the most beautifully
prominent form of a cross to be seen in the heavens. It is
sometimes referred to as the Northern Cross. Because of this
the constellation was presented as the "cross-bearing swan"
in the older Zodiac picturings and the hieroglyph showed a
swan with a cross borne under one of its wings.

It must be stressed that for all peoples of the ancient
and prehistory world the symbol of the cross always repre-

sented *matter.* The lesson given with Cygnus concerned the taking on of cohesiveness. In other words, the first binding of energies which is the means by which all Creation unfolds and takes on matter-form.

The Swan of the Zodiac lesson served to symbolize the advance of ideation upon the turbulent primordial waters. Here Genetic Consciousness makes its first movement through the prephysical elements to "take up its cross" of eventual matter-form.   The germ of all Creation is at this point activated. This is the original and true "Immaculate Conception."

With the lesson given with Cygnus, therefore, was presented the initial means of cohesion -- or spiritual impregnation. This is the Immaculate Conception of Divine Purpose that brings forth all things in Creation. It is a point of beginning that can be accomplished only in the spirit.

The ancient hieroglyph for this constellation served as the basis for the Greek myth of Zeus taking on the guise of a swan to visit and impregnate the lovely mortal woman named Leda. Zeus, in this tale, personified Divine Consciousness. Leda was presented as being the wife of the Spartan king, Tyndareus. This was the mythologist's way of explaining the overshadowing of spirit which implants the beauty of higher truth within the soul.

The result of the Zeus-Leda union was the birth of the too-beautiful Helen who symbolizes the beauty which all humankind honors, reveres and aspires to attain. In this mythological example, Leda personifies the impregnated Life Principle which, through conjunction of the rational and spiritual, is to reach its attainment as an intended life form. Through this Zodiac hieroglyph of the cross-bearing Swan the ancient Watchers honored symbolically the "feminine" aspect of the creative energies which could receive and conceive the creative intention of Divine Consciousness.

This Zodiac feature was drawn upon by the fathers of the Roman Catholic Church when they structured their allegations of Mary's immaculate conception. In Catholic belief, based on Judaic interpretation of Causation, the Creator is regarded as being male and male only.   The

elevation of Mary offered the only possible means of presenting what could be termed the feminine aspect within the
godhead.   The Roman Catholic Church, and consequently
all Christian faiths, have thus been compelled to resort to
the feminine prototype that had long been rationally recognized and honored throughout all "Pagan" antiquity.

To summarize the Aquarian lessons: Divine Consciousness pours forth the stream of primordial waters
(energies).   These activate the Life Principle within them,
which in turn activates elementary substance toward cohesiveness.

*   *   *

Aquarian Curiosity

Near the southern edge of the constellation of Cygnus
there was discovered about 1976 a pulsating star with a
timing sequence that is not regarded as natural.   This star,
located about 1000 light years away from Earth, has been
designated as JP-1953.   The J stands for Jodrell Bank, the
discoverer of the star, and the P stands for Pulsar.   The
numbers indicate the star's coordinates in the heavens.

This star gives out a radio pulse once every four-
tenths of a second, and it has not deviated from that pulse
since its discovery.   There has been no spin-down detected.
The pulse and the lack of spin-down are not a natural
phenomenon.

The age of this star has been calculated by Dr. Frank
Drake of Cornell University.   Data indicates that the
youngest the pulsar could be is five billion years old.   The
upper limit has been projected as being forty-five billion
years old.   The upper range, considered from all calculations,
is regarded as being the more likely.

That would mean the star would be four times older
than the estimated age of the rest of the universe!

Rationality responds that cannot be.   We are left to

wonder if perhaps some intelligence has altered it for some purpose that we cannot imagine.

*   *   *

The Age of Aquarius

The much heralded "Age of Aquarius," which popular astrology tells us we are now on the threshold of entering, is commonly looked upon as the age which is going to bring peace and love to humankind. In ascribing to this belief, humankind again seeks to sidestep any personal responsibility for this desirable condition.

Expecting the Aquarian Age to simply pour out such gifts upon the world is wishful thinking. It is not the duty of the Aquarian Age to bring offerings of peace and love to humankind. The Age of Aquarius extends only a period of time wherein human intellect is presented with the opportunity to pursue these blessings for Aquarian unfoldment.

Contrary to popular astrological interpretation, the ancient Watchers regarded the sign of the Waterman as the most dispirited of all the twelve Principle positions. This was due to the Zodiacal position of Aquarius which is located at the cosmic midnight. In other words, this is when the world is most turned away from light.

Pisces
The Fishes

the second major sign of the Zodiac of Constellations
representing the prephysical plane
of Creative Consciousness

The second major division in the Zodiac of Constellations as presented by the ancient Watchers is the sign of
Pisces. The figures which symbolize this sign consists of two
fishes, one facing the North Pole Star, and the other in a
parallel path with the Sun. These celestial Fishes, although
some distance apart, are shown as bound together by their
tails with a narrow band. This band, sometimes called a
ribbon or cord, is also shown as being fastened to the neck
of Cetus, the celestial Whale, the hieroglyph of the neighboring constellation which is the second decanate of Aries.

The constellational sign of Pisces continued the
lessons of primordial powers from which Creation has been
achieved. The two Fishes of the Zodiac lessons are regarded
as dwelling in the innermost regions of the primordial
waters, and they serve as symbols for the multiplication
action brought into force by the Life Principle.

For a moment we should refresh our mind that the
earlier lesson presented with the first decanate of Aquarius
symbolized the Life Principle with the figure of a single fish.
With the lessons of Pisces the Life Principle is shown, still
within the primordial waters, as having divided. This can be
likened to the way a single cell is known to divide. The

energies have established their poles, represented by the Fishes swimming in different directions yet still linked in their movement. The Life Principle is symbolized as having divided its energies so that it may "go forth and multiply."

The two Fishes of Pisces therefore present the lesson of where the homo is divided into hetro that it may multiply by fusion (blending).

Pisces, in the ancient Zodiac of Constellations, presented the lesson of the Law of Increase in Nature, which is consistent in the Involutionary and Evolutionary planes. The lesson of Pisces taught the means whereby primordial substance is vastly increased by dividing so that it can multiply itself into the Monadic host. Simply put, this is the division of the prephysical substances.

Pisces served to represent the stage of creative action where one becomes two. In the Book of Genesis this division of elementary energies is presented by having god create Eve by bringing her forth out of Adam's side. Adam is the Life Principle, Eve is the elementary substance out of which Life is projected. God then tells them to "go forth and multiply." In the scriptures these events were said to have taken place "eastward in Eden," which was the ancient symbolic way of saying the creative energies were moving forward but still in the prephysical plane.

It is from this ancient Zodiac lesson of the division of prephysical creative energies, rewritten as holy authority, that the devout religionists of our overpopulated world fashioned their excuse for unbridled and indiscriminate breeding.

The ancient Hebrews knew the constellation of Pisces as Dagim, meaning "the Fishes." The name shown for this constellation in the Egyptian temple at Dendera was Pisces Hori or Pi-Cot Orion, which translates as "the Fishes prolonged," suggesting the multiplication of the Life Principle into the endless expressions of life form. Since time out of mind fish symbols have served to express multiplication or the multitude of life.

The Old Testament story of Elisha, one of the many personifications used for the Life Principle, draws its presentation of Elisha's powers of multiplication from the Pisces lesson. Elisha allegedly fed a hundred men from meager substance, and increased the widow's barrel of meal and her cruse of oil to overflowing.

In the New Testament, because Jesus is used as the personification of the Life Principle, he too is made to "demonstrate" this multiplication action. With two fishes, the Zodiac symbols for Pisces, and five loaves of bread, he is alleged to have "fed the multitude." The two fishes and five loaves of bread add up to seven, which reveals the story's acknowledgment to the septenary elements, the elements employed at each plane of Involution.

The Zodiac sign of Pisces provided the source material for the story of Jesus' second outstanding "miracle" where he is supposed to have "fed the multitude." The "miracle" is said to have occurred at a Judean place, desert locale called Bethany. The name Bethany used in this story is strangely similar to the Egyptian word Bethanu, which meant "place of multiplying bread.

The fact is that there never was any such site named Bethany beyond Jordon. This was even noted by Origen, the second century Christian philosopher and scholar. This means it is not historically true that thousands of hungry people were miraculously fed there. This "miracle" is presented as having happened in a desert. The words desert and wilderness are used in occult scriptures for symbols of the Involutionary planes, where substance moves toward its matter form. The desert of this story is identical to the wilderness of the Moses tale, Involution.

In this story Jesus personifies the Life Principle's action in the fourth Involutionary plane. It is at this plane that primordial substance becomes infinitely divided into the monadic host. This is the Pisces lesson of the division of substance in the fourth plane.

Because Jesus is Christianity's personification of the Life Principle in action, and the ancient Watchers symbolized the lessons teaching this with the Fishes, Jesus also was symbolized by the fish.

The majority of Christians do not know, or choose to ignore the fact that the symbol of the Fish has been a savior symbol from time out of mind. Older cultures symbolized their saviors as fish-men. Among them were Oannes of the Chaldeans, Dagon of the Philistines, Phoibos of the Greeks, Vishnu of the Hindus and others. All were fish-men. Even the Hebrew Messiah was called Dag, meaning "fish." All these served to personify the Life Principle, the creative force within the primordial ocean which the Zodiac lessons presented with the Fishes.

In the secondary lessons given with the Lesser Zodiac of Signs which used the Celestial Man as its illustration, Pisces was associated with the figure's feet. This meant to illustrate that matter-expression stands firmly upon the action of the Life Principle involving itself.

*   *   *

The Band
or the Ribbon
first decanate of Pisces

This small constellation, although separate to itself, has traditionally had its stars included in the count of the constellation of Pisces. It is, however, a narrow band or ribbon of stars which binds the two Fishes of Pisces together by their tails. The peculiarity of this "tie that binds" is that it is also secured to the neck of the celestial Whale, Cetus, which is the second decanate figure of Aries.

The Egyptians knew this Band constellation by the name of U-Or, said to translate as "he cometh."

The lessons of Pisces represent the polarization of Divine Consciousness. Here was taught the division of primordial energies into two charged poles between which all creative energy is activated toward its intended form. The division of energies into two poles is commonly thought of as being in opposition. The divided energies are not in conflict, however, and this is the meaning of the fine Band that links the two Fishes. A singular intent binds them together, the intent to create.

The lesson of the Band constellation was simple and yet profound. It is the symbol of unity, "the ties that bind." These are ties that are not restrictive or confining, but which keep all things anchored in the Source. Although placement of the Fishes imply wide-range freedom, as symbolic representatives of the Life Principle they always remain bound in one Causation.

A number of Judeo-Christian mythologists have attempted to extend the interpretation of the lesson given with the Band hieroglyph as recording Israel being bound and oppressed by "enemies of god." If Israel is meant to symbolize primordial energies, these energies are bound together as an intention to create matter form. Matter is commonly presented by religious huckster as "evil," which figuratively makes it the "enemy" of their god. In this regard the claim is nearly correct. Most people, and especially the religious hucksters, are more inclined to take things literally and apply it to a people or a nation. Used in this manner the Israel-bound interpretation is but typical pulpit glitz.

This Zodiac lesson on the unity of purpose of the polar energies of Creation was cleverly incorporated into the New Testament where Jesus is quoted as saying, "I and my Father are one."

*   *   *

Andromeda

or the Chained Maiden
second decanate of Pisces

Pisces, as we have seen in these opening lessons in the Zodiac of Constellations, represents the multiplying action of the Life Principle. Its second decanate as the Chained Maiden therefore speaks of some detail in regards to this action. It speaks of the soul's consciousness.

In Egyptian representation this constellation was known as Set. This name became the source of much confusion, for in a long and sometimes contradictory history of various opposing priesthoods the name Set became a name of one of the Egyptian gods. The closest representation of this "god" to the Zodiac lessons has Set involved in the cosmic opposition of darkness and light. The lesson given with this constellation, which further explains the division of Creation's energies, is of the first stirrings of elementary substance being bound to Creative Consciousness. Light can be figuratively said to arise out of the void at this point as *intent* to create.

In Egyptian myth, interpreted by bloodthirsty priests, Set is therefore portrayed as having slain his brother Osiris. This is echoed in myths of other cultures as well, such as the Roman myth which told of Romulus killing his brother Remus, and the Greek myth of Herakles killing his brother Iphicles. The Bible has a couple of versions too, the more telling one being the myth of Cain murdering his brother Abel.

The consequence of all these myths was that the characters were chained to their consciousness/conscience for their acts. They were then banished from the plane upon which this took place and sent on their way to establish their lives elsewhere -- in matter.

To the Hebrews this constellation was known as Sirra, meaning "the chained." The name Sara, Abram's "wife," is phonetically similar which is also a clue to that myth. The Hebrews depicted this constellation as a woman, and female symbols and hieroglyphs, as we have seen, always symbolize prephysical substance. The meaning in this case of the chained maiden is that substance is to be bound to the soul's creative consciousness.

It is from Greek mythology that we know this constellation by the name Andromeda. In their myth, Andromeda was the daughter of Kepheus (Latinized as Cepheus), king of Aethiopia, and his wife Cassiopeia. Poseidon, god of the seas (primordial energies), became angered when Cassiopeia boasted that her daughter Andromeda was more beautiful than Poseidon's daughters. What the mythographer was saying was that Andromeda symbolizes refined substance while the daughters of Poseidon represent primordial or elementary substance. The story continued by saying that for this insult (of truth) Poseidon sent a devastating flood over the territory ruled by Kepheus, and placed in these waters a sea monster to terrorize the people.

Kepheus is said to have ruled over *Aetheopia*. This is not to be confused with the African nation of Ethiopia. Aetheopia means a region of darkness or mystery, and so refers to the primordial void. The flood is the pouring out of Causation's energies. Poseidon's wrath could be appeased only by the sacrifice of Andromeda so, for the sake of his people, which is to say uncommitted energy, Kepheus had Andromeda chained to a rock (matter) at the edge of the sea (primordial energies). Creation must continue however, so Andromeda was rescued by the hero Perseus, who symbolizes reason and is the name given to the third decanate of Aries.

The sea monster in this Greek tale is one and the same as the Assyro-Babylonian cosmic Dragon, Tiamat, which symbolized the tumultuous primordial energies collecting as prephysical substance. In the Assyro-Babylonian myth, Marduk (planet of crossing) slays the monster Tiamat by driving a cyclone-wind (the churning energies) into Tiamat's open jaw and thereby splits her in twain. These are the divisions of energies as told Assyro-Babylonian style.

Their myth continued by having Marduk creating heaven from one half of Tiamat's body and forming Earth from the other half. In this way the priests accounted for the division of cosmic energies, and it was from this version that the Bible mythographers drew their inspiration for verses 6, 7 and 8 of the first chapter of Genesis. In these verses the violence that attends Causation was masked over by having a "firmament" dividing waters from waters, and in this way giving explanation of how heaven and Earth came into being.

In much older Hebrew mythology which predates the writing of Genesis by Jewish priests, the tribal god Yahweh was presented as having battled with Leviathan the dragon in an identical manner as Marduk with Tiamat. This is what is meant in Isaiah 27:1. This is the meaning behind Psalm 74 as well, which reads, "Thou breakest the head of Leviathan in pieces, and gavest him to be meat to the people inhabiting the wilderness." Leviathan should be referred to as *her* in this verse, for it symbolizes primordial energy-substance, and wilderness, as ever, symbolizes the primordial/prephysical planes. The dragon "monster" Leviathan is also mentioned in the Apocryphal Book of Enoch and in the book of Job. The latter book happens to be of Chaldean origin.

Leviathan being portrayed as "meat to the people inhabiting the wilderness" is but priestly dramatics based upon the fact of Creation that all substance issues out of prephysical energies.   It is not something from Jewish history.   The young Chained Maiden portrayed with the hieroglyph of Andromeda presented a more refined illustration of creative intention. The hieroglyph figure alludes to the tumultuous energies of Causation as the antagonistic force but those raw energies are not the star of the story.

Whether in Zodiac lessons or in scriptural tales, it is important to remember that female symbols always stand for some aspect of prephysical substance. Since the Chained Maiden is depicted in the second Zodiac lesson of Creation, it indicates a prephysical aspect of substance in its movement toward matter form.

The symbol of this constellation is a maiden, which is to say the virginal, innocent, inexperienced, amalgamation of prephysical elements which offers itself up for the experience of matter-involvement. Andromeda stands for nascent substance, which is without form and void. This substance faces the monstrous and violent elements which are present within Creation energies.

The lesson given with Andromeda taught of the division of elements from the Absolute. In biblical verses this occurred on the second "day" of Creation. On this second "day," the nascent entity-form -- or prephysical elements of future substance -- is chained beside the "waters" or "seas." In scriptural jargon the term "seas" usually refers occultly to the three tumultuous planes between the spiritual and the physical.

*   *   *

Cepheus

a Crowned King
third decanate of Pisces

Cepheus is the Latinized name from the Greek Kepheus.
In Greek mythology Kepheus is presented as the king of
Aethiopia. This is routinely misinterpreted as meaning the
African nation of Ethiopia. Kepheus was the husband of
Cassiopeia by whom he was the father of Andromeda. Both
Kepheus and Cassiopeia were the Greek's version of the
figures used in ancient Zodiac lessons and so legend says
that both these mythological beings were placed among the
stars after their deaths.

The Egyptians knew this inconspicuous northern
constellation as Pe-ku-hor, which means "the one comes to
rule." This constellation lies partly in the Milky Way on the
side of the Pole Star diametrically opposite Ursa Major. Its
brightest star is Alderamin which is only third magnitude.
The name is from the Arabic *al dhira al yamin*, which means
"the right forearm." More important than Alderamin is the
fainter δ - Cephei which is the type star of the class Cepheid
Variables. δ - Cephei was the first variable star discovered
(rediscovered), which gives its name to the class.

In astrological placement Cepheus is surrounded by
the constellations Cassiopeia, Ursa Major, Draco, and
Cygnus.

In its common hieroglyphic presentation the figure is
of a crowned king, *partially* clothed in his royal robes. He
holds aloft a scepter in his left hand, and his left foot rests
just above the Pole Star.

The major clue here is that the figure is shown as
partially clothed, indicating some incompleted action. As
a part of the Pisces lesson on Creative Consciousness this
hieroglyph teaches of ideation not yet fully formed.

To understand this constellational hieroglyph correctly, remember that we have been influenced through
Greek interpretation of an extremely ancient presentation.
Greek legend inspires the notion that Cepheus referred to a
real king of the African nation of Ethiopia. This is not correct.

It was not the nation of Ethiopia over which mythic king Cepheus ruled, rather he reigned over the Greek Aethiopia which meant a region of darkness and mystery. In other words, here is the dominant element at work within the second Involutionary plane. It is here that the Creative Consciousness takes up its "scepter" of growing self-awareness. It is this self-aware element that is to be advanced and developed more fully in the next plane of Creative Ideation which is the lesson of Aries.

In summary of the ancient Zodiac lessons thus far, Divine Consciousness, taught with Aquarius, and Creative Consciousness, taught with Pisces, have reached the primary division of consciousness whereby it may truly "go forth and multiply." This is fulfilled in the third plane of Creative Ideation as once taught with Aries.

It is at this point in the scriptural account of Creation that the mythographers have their singular god suddenly and without warning say, "..let us make man in our likeness..." The earlier scriptural god is now, at this point, addressed as the Elohim. What is really being admitted here is that Creation is accomplished through the division of energies and these are shaped by the twelve Patriarchal Principles.

Aries
The Ram

*the third major sign of the Zodiac of Constellations
representing the prephysical plane of
Creative Ideation*

The constellation of Aries, Latin meaning "the Ram,"
is so named from the Greeks whose myth of the Ram of the
Golden Fleece was based upon this sign. With the Aries
lessons in the Zodiac of Constellations was taught the third
aspect within the primordial energies found in the singular
first cause of Creation. Together these constitute the
original and true trinity "mystery. The three-in-one aspect
will be touched upon later.

Creation can be said to figuratively begin with this
sign. All three aspects -- Divine Consciousness, Creative
Consciousness and Creative Ideation -- are really but
different facets of singular power. Aries, representing the
ideation of Creation, is the activating principle which, again
figuratively, impregnates Creation. For this reason the sign
was occasionally represented in more ancient times with the
symbol of Phallus Erectus.

With Aries presented as the symbol for the principle
of Ideation it became the logical place to begin the lessons
given with the Lesser Zodiac of Signs which used the
Celestial Man as the central teaching illustration. Ideation
implies creative mental powers and so in the anatomical
divisions of the Celestial Man, Aries represented the head of

the figure.

In both Zodiac texts Aries can be said to generate the action toward fulfillment. This is given added emphasis for us today by the fact that the most important reference point in the sky is in Aries. This is referred to as the "first point of Aries," and all heavenly bodies are measured from this point. Astronomy is indebted to the Alexandrian astronomer Ptolemy, the last great astronomer of ancient times, for this reference point. It was he who delineated the constellations from this point in his astrological study entitled **Tetrabiblos**. At that time the Sun entered the constellation of Aries at the vernal equinox.

The ancient Akkadians knew this constellation as Baraziggar, from *bar*, meaning "sacrifice" or "altar," and from *ziggar*, meaning "making right." The Hebrews referred to this constellation as Taleh, meaning "the Lamb."

In ancient Persia and Egypt when the Sun entered into the sign of Aries the event was celebrated with a sacred feast. This was prepared for prior to the full moon's occurrence at the spring equinox. In Egypt, on the fourteenth day of that moon phase, the nation celebrated in joy at the *domination of the Ram.* Here is a clue to consider in regards to the Jewish observance of Passover and the Christian observance of Easter. It is from this Zodiac lesson of Aries that the Jewish priesthood acquired their "Paschal Lamb," the lamb slain and eaten in honor of their mythical "Passover" out of Egypt.

In the lessons given with the ancient Zodiac of Constellations, Aries, symbolized by the Ram or the Lamb, taught of the creative principle in Involution at its point of Creative Ideation. In the long process of transmitting these Zodiac lessons into scriptural myths, this lesson of Aries became "the lamb slain from the foundations of the world."

The original meaning in the Zodiac lessons from which this was taken referred to prephysical substance, or so-called "dead matter," which is to reach its fulfillment as matter-form through stages of congelation. Prephysical substance congeals into visible-matter form at the seventh plane, the Etheric Plane, the lesson of Leo. In religious jargon this prephysical substance could be said to be "redeemed" so that the Life Principle may enter and reign over the dense-matter plane, the lesson of Virgo.

Cosmology made a lot more sense as explained with the Zodiac lessons than scriptural accounts or scientific theory. The Ram-Lamb sign explained what could be termed the ideation phase of planetary substance. Science now knows that matter is *congealed* energy, and this was the teaching of the Zodiac lessons. The elemental or primordial substance that would be formed into planetary matter was described as giving of itself -- energizing itself -- to move toward matter-form. Religion interpreted this necessary intentional involvement of energy for the purpose of achieving Evolutionary qualification as being a "sacrifice." This is an unfortunate interpretive choice of words. The intentional involvement of substance is simply a process, not a sacrifice, for the purpose of structuring conditions from which Evolutionary life might proceed.

This was too straight forward an explanation for priests who preferred to wrap everything in an enigma. The lessons given with Aries, illustrated with the hieroglyph of the Ram-Lamb, became reinterpreted in priestly explanations as the lamb "slain from the foundations of the world." Because the Aries lesson taught of Creative Ideation which is the foundation of everything, it was consequently the Lamb-Ram personified which was presented as having made the sacrifice. The priestly enigmatic claim, therefore, was true as far as it went. This clever half truth has left countless generations of seekers without knowledge of creation processes or the purpose and role humankind plays in it.

The Jewish priesthood, intent upon establishing a tribal-cult religion for political control, fashioned out of the Zodiac teachings a "history" of their people. All of the starring characters of the Bible books are but personifications of the Life Principle or Generative Principle in allegorical presentation. There is no supportive documentation from any legitimate cultures of the time periods involved that confirm the biblical characters as having been "historical" persons. Like good fiction today, genuine historical people are presented in supportive roles to give the illusion of authenticity. We will examine the character of Moses soon to illustrate the point.

The Christian fathers, in their turn, used the same process to fashion their religious claims. The Life Principle became personified as Jesus, and from the Aries lesson he was portrayed as the *Agnus Dei*, Latin for "Lamb of God." He was "sacrificed" that humanity might live, and this borrowed lesson from the Aries lesson of the Zodiac of Constellations became celebrated with Christian observance of Easter. This Christian "holy day" doesn't even have a proper or original name for the observance, but takes its name from the old Teutonic goddess of Spring, the "Pagan" goddess known as Eastre.

*   *   *

Moses and the Aries Connection

Because the Jewish scriptural character of Moses is claimed to be an historical person the western world has been led to believe this claim is true. It is not. The story of Moses is pure mythology structured upon the ancient lessons from the Zodiac teachings.

Moses is a larger-than-life figure, the personification of the Life Principle. His "history" really begins with him being cast adrift upon the waters -- prephysical energies -- which will carry him through the Involutionary planes toward matter fulfillment. This is said to be in the land of Egypt, and Egypt always symbolized the *matter plane* in occult writing. Beginning the story with a matter plane symbol was an artful blind designed to confuse anyone who might be familiar with the ancient lessons. It also added credence to the claim as "history" because the tale included many actual catastrophic events that happened to Egypt during the Venus-Mars encounters.

The father of Moses was said to have been Amram who lived without sin and died not of old age but from the effects of being poisoned by a *serpent*. The name Amram is but a variant of the name Abram who served as a symbol for the Creative Principle.

The name Moses is freely borrowed from the Assyrian myth figure of Mises. Because of the Egyptian setting for this story the starring character's name was reworked using the Egyptian *mo*, meaning "water," and *uses*, meaning "saved from water." This is a clear reference to the Zodiac lessons which taught of Divine Consciousness coming forth or being "saved" from the primordial waters of Creation.

The myth of Moses says that he had two mothers, meaning that he issued out of prephysical substance but was taken to be nurtured by dense-matter. This was not original with the Jewish priest mythographers for in an ancient Orphic hymn to Bacchus, Mises also bears the epithet of *bimater*, meaning "of two mothers."

Egypt, as the symbol for dense-matter, provides a cunning twist to this version. The rescuing aspect of this tale is the princess of Egypt who receives him from the waters. Female figures symbolize substance, so it is a foregone conclusion that substance will rear prephysical energy as her own son. This accounts for the spiritual -- or prephysical form -- to be dressed in the robes of the realm, meaning flesh. He becomes a prince of the dense-matter plane by adoption, which is a variation of the truth that the spirit must "die" to become matter.

Later in the long, involved tale of Moses this allegorical figure is presented as dividing the waters of the Red Sea (Sea of Reeds). This is done to "save" the Hebrews who are pursued by the Egyptian forces -- which is to say pursued by their intended matter form.

The Hebrews, symbolizing the prephysical energies, issue out of the divided waters to take up their sojourn in the "wilderness."

In the older Assyrian version of this story, Mises also divided waters, namely the rivers Orontes and Hydastus. Elsewhere he was presented as providing water to his thirsty followers by striking a rock causing water to gush forth, just as Moses was presented as doing.

Further admission that Moses is only a mythological character is in the claim that Moses was *seventh* in line from Abram-Abraham who had served as the personification of the Creative Principle. The scriptural claim of his six forefathers -- Abram, Isaac, Jacob, Levi, Kohath, and Amram- is further admission that this is taken from ancient Zodiac teachings. Moses, as the Life Principle symbol, proceeds through the planes of densifying energies to achieve "his" fulfillment at the seventh Involutionary plane.

Prior to the scriptural tale of Moses, the Assyrians were familiar with a popular myth fashioned around the legendary Sargon I (2750 B.C.E.). The resemblance between this tale and the account of Moses' infancy is suspect. Sargon I was portrayed as having been put in an ark of rushes after his birth and cast adrift upon a river where he was carried to Akki. This Assyrian version reads: "The river carried me to Akki, the water-carrier (Aquarius), it brought me."

Similar tales were common to all the ancient peoples of the Near East, with those of Assyria, Phoenicia and Arabia calling the character by the name *Mises*. Whether the name is Mises or Moses, it is certain he did not play any *historical* role in saving the Hebrews from slavery in the nation of Egypt. There is no reference to this person in any genuine records written in any nation in the time of his alleged wonderworkings. There is nothing anywhere except in scriptural myth of any mass slavery of Hebrews in the nation of ancient Egypt. The court of royalty kept meticulous records, and nowhere is a princess recorded as taking an abandoned baby as her son.

To place Moses in proper perspective, we should also note that the character of Moses was given only fleeting attention by the Jews until around the third century before our common era. It was in this period of time that politically minded priests revised Hebrew mythology and made it the foundation of a priestly religion. It was in this revision movement that Moses was recast into "savior" status and law giver.

As "law giver" Moses is Aries, a modified Phallus Erectus symbol. He carries with him two stones, symbolic of the testicles, upon which are written the "Laws" (of heredity). Any moral laws that came to be tacked onto these were drawn from the Hammurabic code, not from heaven. The "laws" were brought down from Mount *Si-nai* where Moses allegedly spent forty days. The number forty (again) represents the four prephysical planes.

We will dispense with Moses for now with a notation about the sacred mountain of Si-nai -- and the word "sacred" itself. In the oldest version of this tale the mountain was spelled Sina. The name is derived from combining the Babylonian god Sin, the moon god which was characterized as evil, and the Egyptian Seni. Mount Si-nai therefore symbolized Causation, the raw, violent and amoral energies from which all substance descends into matter. Here is additional proof that the "Laws" of Moses were not in regards to moral conduct of the Jews but in regards to the genetic laws in Creation.

We should be aware of what we mean by the word sacred. The Hebrew word for male is *sacr*, and so is one with phallus. Basically the male -- or phallus -- represents Creative Ideation (Aries), *god.* The female always personified substance-which generates secondly -- or at the side -- of creative energy. From this the three major western religions regard women as little else than second class citizens. Such is *sacred* writ.

*   *   *

Cassiopeia
the Enthroned Woman
first decanate of Aries

The Chaldean name for this constellation was Dat Al Cura, generally translated as meaning "the enthroned." The Arabic name, El Seder, means "the freed." The name by which we today refer to this constellation is Cassiopeia, mother of Andromeda and wife of Kepheus (Cepheus) in

Greek myth.

We have met Andromeda, the Chained Maiden hieroglyph for the second decanate of Pisces. She symbolized nascent substance, without form and void, which represented the first movement of energy toward maturing substance. We have also met Cepheus, second decanate of Pisces, ruler of the primordial void which represented the dominant element at work within the second Involutionary plane of Creative Consciousness. Now we meet Cassiopeia, the hieroglyphic figure which symbolized the lesson of substance in the process of bringing maturation, which is to say the first movement toward densifying action.

Properly speaking, Cassiopeia is the Chained Maiden which has now been released to its purpose. Turbulent energies are coming under the influence of substance-ideation. The lesson given with the Cassiopeia division of Creative Ideation concerned the first ideation within Creative Consciousness of its eventual substance form. In scriptural terms this is where Creative Ideation "adorneth herself with jewels." (Isaiah 61:10)

This Zodiac figure, like all others from the ancient Creation lessons has had its original meaning perverted so claims of religious "prophecy" could be said to be announced in the stars. This constellation has been pointed to as declaring a prophecy of the triumph of Israel, others say church, over their respective opponents. The stars of Cassiopeia foretell nothing of the sort.

The lesson of the first densifying action where turbulent energies are beginning to be shaped is cleverly worked into the epic tale of Moses. The three aspects of Causation's "law" of generation were personified in scripture as Moses, Aaron and their sister Miriam. Moses personifies the eruptive, ejaculating creative power, Aaron represents the conceiving or genetic energy, and Miriam personifies the first controlling influence of substance drawing from the turbulent energies within Cause. Miriam is therefore the personification of densifying action which was taught in the Zodiac lessons with the constellation Cassiopeia.

The name Miriam was derived from the name *Meriram*

who, among the earliest polytheistic Jews, was believed to be the chief of the "Turbulentos" -- the turbulent, raw, explosive energies at Creation's source. When Judaism was being shaped into a monotheistic faith by priest-mythographers of the 3rd century B.C.E., Meriram was reworked into Miriam, and presented as sister of Moses.

Miriam is but another element in a purely allegorical tale which became expanded and refashioned into a claim of Jewish "history." God allegedly destroyed Egypt in an orgy of malice while the "chosen" ones stole away to complete their destiny. If this was intended to show god's preference for the Jews and the consequent sense of morality and justice it implies then the tale is sadly deficient. Understood for what it really is, an allegorical tale telling of raw creative energy in the process of creating, truth is at last re-established to preside over sanity. False racial elitism is stripped away and genuine spiritual gain is the reward for everyone.

The Greek historian Zosimus (fl. around 450 C.E.) wisely suggested that the figure of Mary in Christian myth might be identified with Miriam who was presented as the sister of Moses. He knew what he was talking about for the names Miriam and Mary are diverse forms of the original name Meriram. They are identical in mythological content. This means that the Islamic claim that Mary was sister of Moses has basis which Christians, blinded by their own mythology, deride as absurd genealogy. Once we know what both mythical characters personify the claim has legiti-macy. Both characters represent substance that is using raw energy to shape intended matter-form. This substance density action has to accompany the Life Principle, which was personified by both Moses and Jesus.

*   *   *

Cetus

the Whale
second decanate of Aries

This is an equatorial constellation south of Pisces and Aries, and it is one of the largest. This bears the hieroglyphic figure of the Whale, and it is often referred to as "monstrous" but only because of its tremendous size.

In the tail of this hieroglyphic figure is the second brightest star in the constellation which is named Diphda, or Deneb Kaitos, which mean either "overthrown" or "thrust down."

This constellation also contains the star Mira, one of the largest stars known, with a diameter of 220,000,000 miles. Like the flickering light of a candle, the light emitted by Mira fluctuates. Ancient priest-astronomers were in awe of this star that appeared regularly in the sky every eleven months after which it would again begin to fade. In a period of about six weeks Mira would change in an astonishing range of brightness from a red star of second magnitude to a faintness that could not be detected by the unaided eye.

The reason for this star's performance is oscillation. At its maximum size this star is larger than the space in which our Sun and the four inner planets of its system orbit. No wonder the ancient astronomers called Mira "the wonderful."

At the mouth of this Whale figure is the star Menkar, which means "bound" or "chained." It is at this general area that the Band Constellation, first decanate of Pisces, is linked to the tails of the two Fishes of Pisces.

For the ancient Watchers the Whale constellation represented the monadic host in Involution. The ultimate unit, Causation, holds the potential of everything. That potential is symbolized here after three prephysical planes as expanded and ready to utilize the polarized energies for bringing ideation into defined purpose. This is why the Whale is shown as bound by its neck to the tails of the two Fishes of Pisces which taught the division of energies. This is also why ancient legends say that the Whale was the first *living* thing created by Jehovah.

The whale lives in the seas, has a fishlike form, but it is an advanced warmblooded mammal. It has developed to the point of giving off or disgorging defined ideation which is to be generated by Creative Energy. As the representative of Creation's potential the Whale can be said to be the original "ark" figure for it represents the vehicle of all life.

In biblical myth this is the third "day" of Creation, a presentation taken from this Zodiac lesson. Aries taught of the third plane, Creative Ideation, and primordial energies must pass from Causation through three planes to reach ideation of form. This accounts for the third "day" in the Genesis story.

This second decanate division of the Aries lesson, Creative Ideation, taught of the stage at which nonmoral nascent form is figuratively disgorged out of the amoral creative energies. No moral qualities are present or necessary in the Involutionary planes. Moral qualities become necessary and active *only* when form is achieved at the seventh plane. Until that plane is achieved there is no reason for qualification. Until that plane is reached there is only dynamic power at work creating. In other words, "god," (higher Wisdom Consciousness) does not dwell here.

This is where scriptural theology makes one of its greatest errors. At this point in the dynamics of Creation actions there is nothing even remotely resembling mercy, love, pity -- in short, no qualified or higher moral consciousness. There is only *nonmoral and an non-selfconscious Causation at work.* It is at this point where prephysical energy is "thrust down" or "bound" to its self-accepted physical potential. It was at this point of Creation that the scriptural authors declare that "evil" first appeared.

Priestly interpreters of this lesson, in branding this necessary process of Creation as "evil," had to conclude that matter-form was therefore something vile. In saying this they were actually accusing their "god" of instituting some monumental *blunder.* The blunder really lies in the priest-mythographers not knowing their Zodiac lessons. The negative interpretation of the necessary processes of Creation has resulted in condemning countless generations to the agonies of false shames, false guilts and fear.

The Whale is best known in the Bible for the whale-of-a-tale of Jonah being swallowed by a whale, and his living for *three days* within the whale's belly. Jonah personifies the Creative Principle present within Causation which, after dwelling at the third plane, is "vomited" forth upon the fourth plane of Creative Energy so that it may be activated. In the biblical account the Whale is not named to avoid reference to the Zodiac figure. In the **Shalshelet Ha Kabbala** account, however, the whale is called Cetos.

In Greek myth Hercules (Herakles) was said to have been swallowed by a whale and at the exact same place, Joppa.

The scriptural version disguised the knowledge that three prephysical periods have to transpire before substance can commence movement toward intended materialization. This is true for any and all matter formation, be it life form or planetary. It has to congeal from the "waters" of universal energies. Figuratively speaking it is as this point that "dry land" -- substance -- can be said to appear out of the waters -- out of the energies of Creation. It is upon this "dry land" that the Whale can then "vomit" up the Creative Principle that it may commence taking on its intended form. The Greek myth of the Titan god Cronus (Time) swallowing his own children and later vomiting them forth has the same meaning.

*   *   *

Perseus
the Breaker
third decanate of Aries

This constellation which we know by the Greek name of Perseus was known to the Hebrews as Peretz. Both names have the approximate meaning of "the breaker." In Egyptian it was known as Kar Knem, meaning "he who fights and subdues."

This constellation served as the source material for such biblical verse as "...the breaker is come up before them; they have broken up, and have passed through the gate, and are gone out of it; and their king shall pass before them, and the Lord on the head of them." (Micah 2:13) In this example "they" refer to the primordial energies which are going out of the "gate" of Creative Ideation. These are to become activated as Creative Energy (subject of Taurus). The "king" passing "before them" is in reference to the Creative Principle. The "Lord" is Divine-Creative Consciousness at the plane of completed ideation which is to be activated. The "Lord" is said to be "on the head of them" and alludes to Aries in the Zodiac of Signs which is symbolized by the head of the Celestial Man.

To the prehistory Watchers who first fashioned the Zodiac lessons of Creation, this constellation presented as its subject the emergence of reason out of the violent aspect of Creation-power. Reason is not moral intellect, it is simply *motive*. Perseus personified reason which induced ideation to subdue primordial energies into its first movement toward intended form. This is why in Greek myth Perseus, son of the divine father, was immediately sealed into a chest after his birth and cast into the sea. Perseus was saved by the Dictys, which means "five," -- a reference to the five lower Involutionary planes.

In classical Greek myths Perseus (as reason) -- armed by Athena (wisdom) and by Hermes (swift thought), and hidden from the physical senses by Hades (invisible prephysical elements) -- can alone gain victory over the Gorgon named Medusa (the physical senses). This myth is a blend drawn from Aries in both the Zodiac of Signs and of Constellations.

The Gorgon, a Greek word meaning "grim," is better known by the name Medusa which means "queen." This mythological character represented more that present day interpretations have offered. The head of Medusa, pictured as surmounted by hair of writhing snakes, symbolized the *medulla oblongata.* This is the widening continuation of the spinal cord forming the lowest part of the brain and containing the vital nerve centers for the control of breathing, circulation and similar functions. These register only *physical impressions,* not the soul's monitions. This is the reasoning behind the story that the Gorgon's head renders humankind insensate with its stony charm. For this reason also, Medusa was regarded as a mortal figure although born of divine parentage.

The principle story of Medusa, as we received it from Greek sources, was of the hero Perseus slaying her. The victory of Perseus (reason) over the Gorgon symbolized the overcoming of importunate demands of the physical senses. In life lessons of the Zodiac of Signs this illustrated the betrothal of reason with the soul's consciousness -- which was personified as the divine maid Andromeda.

Located within this constellation of Perseus is the star named Algol, which is an Arabic word meaning "destruction," from *ghala,* meaning "to destroy." This star has always borne an evil reputation, and has been traditionally associated with Golgotha (Hebrew, meaning "skull"), the place of skulls. The word *algol* -- or *algor* -- signifies a cold or rigid state, and suggests the stony charm by which the mythical Medusa destroyed her victims.

The ancient Watchers also presented a kind of footnote symbol for this variable star with the hieroglyph of the "Evil" Eye. This was not to say that this binary star radiated evil. The hieroglyphic footnote meant to stress that to eye matter-life solely in a sensual view is to deliver the death sentence to the finer or spiritual nature which is temporarily suspended within it.

The meaning of the "Eye" hieroglyph became lost through millenniums of confusion. All that was remembered of it was that it represented some aspect which threatened life's purpose. The result has been that the star Algol has had traditions of malign influence heaped upon it while its vital meaning was lost.

We have noted before that the star Algol has been traditionally associated with Golgotha, which means "skull" in Hebrew. It is out of this that we received the Christian myth of Jesus being crucified upon a hill known as Golgotha. The Latin word for "skull" is Calvary.

With the constellation of Perseus was taught the point of completed ideation of intended form as taught with the Zodiac of Constellations. In the Zodiac of Signs which used anatomical divisions of the Celestial Man as illustration, Aries was represented as head-mind-skull. The ancient Watchers taught that it is at this point in Creation where spiritual nature willingly propels itself toward or commits itself to -- or crucifies itself upon -- the experience of physical matter senses. This was presented as the mount of crucifixion for prephysical substance.

This was one of the most important lessons of the Zodiac lessons of Creation, that spirit willingly takes upon itself the experience of dense-matter expression. In other words, *the spirit willing crucifies itself upon intended matter form to further its own divine knowledge.*

Upon this pivotal lesson priests of various religions constructed their ideas of savior-gods who were physically crucified so his people might live. Crucified "saviors" include Mithra, Tammuz, Attis, Thules, Odin, Hesus, Krishna, Indra and others. Jesus is just one of many portrayed in this manner. Personifying a cosmological-spiritual truth in this manner allows the priests of such a religion to act ticket takers to approach and be "saved" by this being. The truth is that we have all accepted our being and it is we who must save ourselves.

Most all crucifixion myths of a heavenly representative who was sent to "save" the people contain references to a skull or a mount of the skull. When we know the Zodiac connection we understand why. Algol, traditionally associated with Golgotha-Calvary, became the "mount" upon which Jesus was allegedly crucified to "save" mankind.

This serves to show why there has always been so much perplexity over the physical site of the claimed crucifixion of Jesus. There have been countless theories and arguments over why the crucifixion site was known as the Mount of the Skull. Bafflement has never been eased by the fact that if such a place of execution had ever really existed it would be referred to somewhere in records of the time. There are no legitimate records to confirm such a site.

Religious scholars have offered numerous fanciful suggestions as to why the "Mount" was so named. Some have maintained that the site was known as Mount of the Skull because the hill resembled a skull-like formation. Others have insisted that the name was due to the many skulls found there of executed persons. The precise location of this site continues to elude and frustrate Christian scholars. Some have claimed it was located within the present walls of Jerusalem, but most agree that the site was somewhere outside the Damascus Gate -- to the north of town.

They have always searched -- and will continue to search -- for this earth-bound site in vain. Deceived by myth, they do not understand that the real crucifixion is at the beginning of Involutionary movement, and is found symbolized in the constellation of Perseus far above their heads.

*   *   *

Trinity Mysteries

Aquarius, Pisces and Aries represent the three active aspects present within the primordial source. The Creative Principle at this point becomes motivated with intent. These three combined aspects -- Divine Consciousness, Creative Consciousness, Creative Ideation -- present within the source, unfold -- or bud out -- as the Quaternary. "Spirit" begins here, with the blending of the three aspects at the cusp of the third and fourth Involutionary planes, its intention of becoming matter-form.

In religious interpretations these three active aspects or attributes within the ejaculating primordial energies is the basis for various trinity "mysteries." The great mistake of religious interpretations is to worship and adore the three amoral aspects of primordial energy as "spirit" -- implying

Divine Wisdom is present and is the cause. Wisdom, however, is the highest quality of Evolutionary development, which means priest-class religions have been worshipping the wrong end of Creation.

The next four planes into visible matter, far from representing the "fall" of spirit or man, represents the first steps of making that spirit *hallowed.* The spiritual three constitute the *will* to move into denser expression, which means the densifying into material form is the concretion of the spiritual three. No one "fell" and nothing was lost. Quite the contrary.

Theology generally distinguishes "Three Persons" within the godhead, which echoes the ancient Zodiac teachings. Reduced to personifications the means by which the primordial energies first move to create are rendered into figureheads that explain nothing. Once that happens the three-in-one attributes within the source can only be viewed as a "mystery."

The Judeo-Christian concept of a Trinity Mystery without a feminine aspect is comprehensible only in association with the ancient Zodiac lessons of primordial energies. In the ancient Zodiac lessons of the three aspects within the single creative source was taught with Aquarius, Pisces and Aries.

Properly, there should be a feminine (substance) attribute as part of this triune activity, and which was subtly present in the Zodiac lessons with the subconstellations of Andromeda in Pisces and Cassiopeia in Aries. These represent the seed within itself.

Jewish priests who first formulated their Trinity concept did not fully comprehend the subtle meanings in the Zodiac lessons with which they may have had some access. The tribal priests understood only that there were three major attributes present within the source. This triune nature, present "in the beginning," was represented as a male creator because the hieroglyphic figure of Aquarius shows a male figure pouring out the waters. From this lack of comprehension errors proliferated.

The much maligned Pagans all knew there had to be

some feminine aspect present within the creative power in order for substance to be made manifest. All Pagan trinities, therefore, always had some feminine aspect. In their myths these were generally personified as the wife or the consort or the concubine of the highest god.

The Pagans also well knew that the raw, amoral creative forces at the point of beginnings were not concerned with ethical or moral behavior. This is why their creative gods were forever involved in sexual or romantic intrigues and lusty behavior. It was not moral shortcomings of the Pagans that inspired these myths, but their superior under-standing of the primordial energies at the source which caused them to picture the gods that way. This points up the pathetic lack of understanding which the Judeo-Christian Trinity presentations offer. These faiths insist on trying to establish moral and ethical refinements at the onset of Creation where it does not and could not possibly exist. Morality and ethics are purely epigenetic refinements.

Knowledge of the three attributes present within Creation's source is the key to the riddle of all Trinity mysteries. Based on ancient Zodiacal imagery the first "person" is always seen as male. The Aquarius Man symbolizes Divine Consciousness -- or the Creative Principle out of which the passive or androgynous* Life Principle must arise.

In this understanding we see why the feminine aspect first issues -- *only symbolically* -- out of the male. This was personified in the tale of Eve being fashioned out of the side (not a rib) of the androgynous Adam. ("Rib" has been commonly translated from the word *tzala*, which more correctly translates as "side.")

---

*This common understanding of the androgynous nature within Creation's source explains why peoples of classical Pagan time openly accepted persons of homosexual nature. They were seen as being a physical echo of the three combined powers of the androgynous First Cause. Religious institutions, of course, saw that likening to the First Cause as a possible threat to their power and so have always condemned homosexuals.

The Jewish Trinity concept came to be shaped upon a "vision" attributed to the prophet Ezekiel. We will see more later of what Ezekiel's "visions" were based upon. In this case the Jewish Trinity constitutes the three elements of the Tetrogammaton, the "incommunicable name" of the Supreme Being. This "name" is made up of *Yod*, which is the letter of the phallus; *He*, representing the passive principle; and *Vau*, the product of will. The passive *He* is repeated, making the name Ya-he-vau-he-or Yahweh.

In Ezekiel's Trinity, the "First Person" was the All-Father, the "Let there be light" Creator. The second "Person" was the "Enthroned Man," or spiritual man in "god's" image. The third "Person" was the "spirit moving upon the face of the waters," which personifies the Life Principle. In this version the third "person" could be regarded as either androgynous or as a virgin with child. The Christian version never allowed this much leeway.

Any religious trinity "mystery" is simply a confessed lack of comprehension of the unfoldment of Creation actions at the source once taught with the Zodiac of Constellations.

Taurus
The Bull

the fourth major sign of the Zodiac of Constellations
representing the prephysical plane
of Creative Energy

The constellation of Taurus is known by the Latin name which means "bull." This marked the fourth lesson division of the ancient Zodiac of Constellations, and was the second lesson presented in the Lesser Zodiac of Signs. The second Logia section of the teachings in the Zodiac of Constellations began with Taurus and this, together with Gemini and Cancer, taught of the densifying substances within the prephysical planes.

In the more familiar Zodiac of Signs used today in astromancy the presentation concentrated upon the figure of the Celestial Man to present life lessons. In this use Taurus represented the neck and throat area. To the ancient Watchers this symbolized the epitome of utterance for it marks the area where the creative brain finds expression through speech.

In both ancient Zodiac instructions the hieroglyph used was of the forequarters of the Bull only. This served to indicate that creative action within this prephysical plane is still in the process of formation. The figure has always been presented as if in fast, forward movement, as though rushing and/or pushing.

The hieroglyphic figure of Taurus is shown southeast

of the Pleiades, below them in its rising. The giant red star
Aldebaran, nearly a standard first magnitude star, is the
Bull's fiery eye. Aldebaran comes from the Arabic, *al*
meaning "the," and *dabaran* meaning "following." This star
is the bright star in the group of five called the Hyades. The
constellation of Taurus also contains numerous double stars
and the crab nebula, so named from its crablike appearance.

The Chaldeans recognized the Bull-figure constellation as the harbinger of spring, and a symbol of the creative
cosmic phase where the primary Sun is conceived as form.
The Sumerians referred to Taurus as the "Bull of Light" who
maintained the cycle of seasons. Out of this understanding
the Bull constellation came to symbolize the renewal of the
world after winter's "death," and its appearance was honored
with annual resurrection rites. Not so coincidently the
Christians celebrate the resurrection of Jesus at this same
general period of the spring equinox, and the Jews celebrate
their Passover. The lessons from Taurus has shaped belief
even into present day religious usage. The Jews received
their word Torah, meaning "a law," from Taurus, "Bull of
Light," who maintained the order of cycles. From Taurus also
we received many names out of classical antiquity such as
Tarshish, Tartessos and others.

Around the fifth century B.C.E., in the Persian period
of Achaemenes, priests presented Taurus as the sacred Bull
which the god Mithra had to slay (sacrifice) before the Sun
could rise. This interpretation was based squarely on the
lesson of Taurus where it was taught that the Creative
Principle must shed the primordial aspects to conceive itself
as luminous life force.

The Bull, as the symbol of the first prephysical plane,
marks that point in the creative process where "spirit" is
temporarily laid aside so that energy substance may proceed
toward its intended matter form. Figuratively this is where
the Life Principle "cuts" off spirit's influence temporarily. For
this reason the bloodthirsty Persian priests presented the
image of the god Mithra, symbol of the Life Principle, slitting
the Bull's throat, the organ of higher utterance.

In Greek legend, Zeus, the "father of the gods,"

symbolic of the Creative Principle, assumed the form of a white bull to carry the beautiful Europa (symbol of energy-substance) over the sea (first three primordial planes) to the isle of Crete. There Zeus made her the mother of Minos, Rhadamanthus, and Sarpedon (Aeacus), who became the judges of the dead (matter). In this myth the sons decided the worthiness of each being's soul. The virtuous and heroic were assigned to the Elysian Fields as a reward, meaning they were allowed to proceed in Evolution. The wrong-doers were assigned to Tartarus -- a name derived from Taurus -- which is to say that they were not yet ready to proceed beyond the fourth prephysical plane into Evolution-ary development. The Cretan Minotaur myth is the celestial Bull, Taurus, concealed in the labyrinth of stars.

From the Bull hieroglyph used in the ancient Zodiac lessons the Egyptian priests fashioned their incarnated divine savior Osiris who took the form of a bull, Apis or Osiris-Apis, known in classical times as Serapis. The sacred Apis was regarded to be the incarnation of the god Osiris, which was the personification of the Life Principle.

Because Taurus marked the beginning of *spirit's commitment* to physical life form, it symbolized *the entombment of spirit in its destined physical form*. It is for this reason Taurus came to serve as a symbol of a sepulchre or tomb.

In the ancient lessons of the Zodiac of Constellations, Taurus symbolized the fourth prephysical plane of Creation. The Sumerians understood the cosmological truth behind the designation of Taurus as the "Bull of Light." They understood it represented the elemental energy approaching the Sun-stage in the process of Creation.

In the Genesis account of Creation this is presented as the fourth "day" during which god whips up the geocentric Sun to give light to the older Earth (matter-form).

*   *   *

Taurus and the Pleiades

The group of stars known as the Pleiades, located within the neck of the hieroglyphic figure of Taurus, are among the earliest mentioned in literature on astronomy. For example, these stars were specifically regarded in Chinese annals that date back at least 2527 years before our common era -- or around 4530 years ago.

Earlier Chaldean myth implied an intimate connection with these stars to the story of the Deluge. When it is remembered that the primordial energies of Creation were symbolized as waters, and Taurus was the lesson of the emergence of creative energies, we discover what the flood-deluge really signified. It was not some worldwide inundation, it was the outpouring of energies sweeping into substance planes where it would bring forth matter-life forms.

A high percentage of the most ancient cultures regarded the Pleiades as their central focus and based their symbols, myths and religious calendars upon the constellation of Taurus. The stars of the Pleiades were regarded as indicating the center of the universe, and it was considered the fountainhead from which humankind's ancestors had issued. This is not too great a misinterpretation when we remember the lesson of Taurus in the Zodiac of Constellations which concerned Creative Energy. It is at this plane that is activated the formation of elemental substance toward matter fulfillment.

Various ancient cultures maintained that personages from the Pleiades had made random visitations to Earth during which they openly communicated with Earthlings. These visitations were said to have been due to concern over cataclysmic events which this planet's inhabitants suffered. This type of association did not occur until around the time of the Venus-Mars-Earth encounters, a time when much of the ancient Zodiac teachings were lost.

Homage to the Pleiades has been worldwide. Most of it dating from the encounters mentioned above. There was an almost reverent regard for this particular group of stars ranging from India to Mexico, from Peru, Brazil, Samoa,

Hawaii, Easter Islands to South Africa, Egypt, Greece and others. A great many Grecian temples, such as the Acropolis, the Parthenon, Asclepieian, Hecatampedon, and the temple of Bacchus, were all oriented to the Pleiades.

The Pleiades are regarded by astronomers as "young" stars since the cluster has many high mass main-sequence stars. The Hyades, another cluster of stars within the constellation of Taurus, contains no high mass main-sequence stars for they have burned out, indicating they are older.

There are some two hundred and fifty stars in the Pleiades, but only seven have been held to have special significance to life on Earth. The Pleiades are mentioned by name twice in the Bible, both in the book of Job. This book of Job, included in what is alleged to be the word of god, is not even Hebrew in origin, but is a modified Assyrian work. In its canonized version we now read in Job 9:9 of Job acknowledging god as that "which maketh Arcturus, Orion and Pleiades, and the chambers of the south." Again in a later verse, Job 38:31 the ever-verbalizing "Lord" is quoted as asking, "Have you fitted a curb to the Pleiades?"

The Pleiades are not mentioned by name in the Book of Revelations, but the seven "seals" on the book held by the "lamb" pertains to the seven stars known as the Pleiades. Revelations, attributed to the fictional John, the personification of light, is presented by Christianity as being a predictive text. It predicts nothing. It is but an altered and reworked account of creative actions and energies within the seven prephysical planes which in ancient Zodiac lessons were known as the Involutionary planes.

The seven angels who, in the Revelations account, come forth to sound a trumpet in unison and pour their vials upon the Earth are really symbols of loosened cosmic energy as taught with the Taurus lessons. These stars are in the neck of the Celestial Bull, the area of utterance -- in this case *trumpeting*. The Revelations account pictures the seven vials poured out upon the Earth as causing the seven last plagues bringing humankind's destruction. This is not a worthy interpretation of the Involutionary planes. Neither is it a worthy example of what a loving god would do.

All the references to seven stars, seven angels, seven vials and so on are but ugly echoes of the lessons presented by the ancient Watchers regarding the seven planes of Involution. There will be more detailed examples of what the symbols used in Revelations were built upon in the chapter on the Capricornus lessons.

From the Watchers' lesson presented with Taurus, the lesson of the fourth prephysical plane, we are privileged to discern the process of a congealing prototype for every matter-form.

*   *   *

Taurus and the Missing Mass in the Universe

An accent to the Taurus lesson on Creative Energy is found in the creative activity that is known to be going on in this celestial region. The dark clouds of interstellar gas in the Constellation of Taurus are known to be a stellar nursery. This is a region were condensation is still taking place giving "birth" to star babies. Most of these observed stars are not stars in the true sense of the word since they are not sufficiently massive to compress their cores enough to keep fusion reactions continuing.

Because of their insufficient mass these "stars" cool rapidly, becoming too dim for observation. In other words, as far as our searching telescopes are concerned they transform into nearly invisible matter. This pretty closely fits the hypothetical type star that astronomers have long predicted and which they call a "brown dwarf." The probability is that millions upon millions of these exist in the universe and may make up the bulk of the so-called "missing matter" in the universe.

Astronomers have known by observing the way visible bodies move through the heavens that those objects account for only about ten percent of the mass in the universe. Where is that mass? -- or more correctly, of what is the other ninety percent composed? This infamous puzzle only proves that most of what we regard as "reality" is not visible to us. With these ancient Zodiac lessons can be found a better understanding what composes the planes of Reality.

*   *   *

Orion

or the Belted Knight
first decanate of Taurus

The Orion constellation is the brightest and most brilliant in the heavens, and it has been mentioned in the legends and literature of many ancient people. We know this equatorial constellation just east of Taurus by the Greek name Orion. The Hebrews knew it as Shemhazai, and the Persians called it Nimrod.

Pictorial charts of this oblong constellation commonly show a figure of a great man as a hunter who stands with a sword hanging from a belt or girdle. This lusty hunter is shown standing with an uplifted club and wearing a lion's skin.

Three bright stars lie in a diagonal line across the approximate center of this constellational figure and these represent his belt. What appears to the eye as the middle star in Orion's belt is really a great diffuse nebula, known in astronomy as the Orion Nebula. A nebula is made up of clouds of gas in which new stars are beginning to form. This is a clue to the lesson given with this figure. Three fainter stars align south of the belt and are regarded in modern hieroglyph depiction as his sheathed sword.

Orion's left shoulder is marked by one of the brightest stars in the heavens which is called Betelgeuse. The name is from Arabic and is said to mean "the shoulder of the giant." In modern astronomy this is designated as Alpha Orionis. Diagonally opposite is the blue-white star Rigel, from Arabic

Rijl meaning "foot." This star is designated in modern astronomy as Beta Orionis.

In Hebrew legend the giants Shemhazai and Azael, portrayed as "angels" who were in god's confidence in the "days" of Creation, are quoted as chiding god, saying, "...did we not warn you on the Day of Creation that man would prove unworthy of your world?"

The word "unworthy" is inappropriate but carefully chosen by the priestly authors of this tale. The "day" of man's creation began with ideation moving into the plane of Creative Energy from which man would be conceived. The only reason man could be termed "unworthy" on the Day of Creation is because he is not yet fully conceived.

Once the priests established man's unworthiness they proceeded to present these "angels" to be no better than the creatures they so scorned. It is unlikely the authors meant to show that those who find fault in others are usually prone to the faults they find. The tale continued with these two angelic confidants of god finagling permission to inhabit Earth themselves in order, they tell god, that they might "sanctify Your name."

For Shemhazai sanctity hit the fan as soon as he cast eyes on the "daughters of Eve," by whom he lustfully produced two monstrous sons, Hiwa and Hiya. Eventually, of course, Shemhazai repents, and in self-punishment sets himself head-downward in the southern sky between heaven and Earth. This demonstration of angelic repentant submission was not lost on the Christian fathers who spun the tale of the mythical Peter having himself crucified upside down because he felt unworthy to be slain in the same manner as his savior.

The Greek myth of Orion, older than the Hebrew myth of Shemhazi, not surprisingly, shared several of these plot elements. Orion was a giant, unusually handsome, and a hunter. Enamored of Merope, daughter of Oenopion, and offended at her father's refusal to consent to their marriage, Orion took her by force. For this rape, Orion was blinded by Oenopion. Orion regained his sight by exposing his eyes to the rising Sun. In this myth Merope personifies primordial substance, Oenopion personifies the plane of Ideation, and Orion, the conceiving Creative Energy, must *ravage* substance to activate it. Orion renews his sight, which is to say Creative Ideation is activated, by instigating the movement of substance into the first visible stage of matter. Cosmologically this is the gaseous, luminous stage before dense matter allegorized as the rising Sun.

There are other tales of Orion's lusty nature. In one tale he was said to have attempted to ravage the seven virgin Pleiades. Orion also loved and was loved by Artemis, goddess of the Moon and wild life. After his accidental death caused by an arrow shot by Artemis, Orion was placed in the heavens as the constellation bearing his name. His lusty nature is the prime ingredient, the telltale clue to the meaning of this Zodiac lesson.

In scriptural myth, Nimrod, son of Cush, is presented as a mighty hunter (Genesis 10:8,9), he is offended by his god, and he rebelled by building the Tower of Babel to reach heaven. The name Nimrod in this Hebrew myth is the same as the Persian name for the constellation of Orion. Nimrod is derived from the verb *marod*, meaning "to rebel" It is not coincidence that the name Mardon is given as the name of Nimrod's son in scripture myth. Through priestly oversight the connection goes undisguised. This name, as well as the anagramish Nimrod, are probably cacophemisms of the Babylonian god Marduk.

The scriptural Nimrod tale and the Tower of Babel has its counterpart in an older Greek myth. In that version the giant Aleoeides pile Mount Pelion upon Mount Ossa in an attempt to establish a position to attack Olympus, the heaven of Zeus. The Hitties also had a version of this where Kumarbi plans to launch an attack on the seventy gods of the heaven from the head of the towering giant named Ullikummi. Adding zeros to a number was an occult way to disguise its true meaning, so drop the zero and you get the reference to the seven Involutionary planes leading into the matter plane. The stone head indicates the dense-matter plane.

Present day chartings depict Orion as mentioned previously, with a sheathed sword, uplifted club, and wearing a girdle and a lion's skin. The emblemic figure generally shown carved upon the hilt of the sword is of the head and body of a lamb. This symbolizes that Creative Ideation is to be activated through Creative Energy. The sword, in its sheath, is commonly shown to hang at an angle down across the groin, so the hilt rests in a most peculiar placement for use as a weapon. The original hieroglyphic figure for this constellation displayed a less subtle reference to the Aries lesson.

The illogical placement of the sword hilt is a much later imposition dictated by false shames. Remember, this lesson taught of the continued Life Principle's action in the prephysical planes. The original figure for this constellation was of the standing giant figure in the state necessary to propagate, his erect phallus thrusting upward where the sword hilt is now represented. This symbolized Creative Energy as a generative force in an unshamed acceptance of natural arousal. This explains why in all the myths and tales based upon this constellation -- Orion, Shemhazai, Nimrod and the others-they were always presented as rebellers and ravishers.

The Watchers were not morally perverse in this hieroglyph presentation. They knew that the primordial Creative Energy -- or Generative Energy -- is a totally amoral function which brings forth out of Etheric substance the first flickering of its intended matter-form. The "lust" displayed in this figure and in the myths is but the necessary dropping of spirit in order to generate-conceive prephysical substance into its intended matter form. The lion skin, borrowed from Leo, the lesson of visible matter, indicates the "animal" nature it will be assuming.

*   *   *

Aaron, the Judaic Orion

With the Aries lessons was shown the source material for the biblical characters of Moses and his sister Miriam. With the Taurus lesson presented with Orion is to be found the source material for the "brother" of Moses, Aaron. Even the names -- Orion-Aaron -- are phonetically similar.

The name Aaron is said to derive from the word *harah*, which translates as "to conceive." The name, the meaning and the Zodiac teachings from which this mythical character was drawn opens new understanding about this alleged first high priest of Jehovah. The power hungry priests who fashioned this story were careful to give themselves the divine right of their office, so much was made of the prestige of descent from him. An admission of his Taurean origin lies hidden behind the references of Aaron making the golden calf and of his "rod" budding indicating Jehovah's choice of him as his priest.

If you are of the opinion that the Bible is short on graphic sexual content then be prepared for a shock. The first thing to understand is that Aaron personifies the generative principle within Creative Energy. In terms of cosmology he personifies the planetary genetic.

As in the Orion lesson, Aaron represents the *ideation* or *conceiving* of substance form through energy action. He is active genetic ideation, so in effect Aaron is the one "to conceive." This is the action-power at the plane of Creative Energy, so this is why the scriptural tale says that only Aaron and his sons could perform the rites and ceremonies for women giving birth. As "sons" of Aaron the priest-class acquired their mythical right of authority.

Aaron, the conceiver, is required to clothe himself with sacred garments to perform the rites and ceremonies of conceiving, the "garments for glory and for beauty." These garments included a *breastplate* and an *ephod*. It is these "garments" which expose naked occultism at work. The word ephod comes from the Greek word *ephebos*, meaning entering upon early manhood. As such the ephod is the *erect phallus*, the same as in the original hieroglyph for Orion.

Breastplate is used as the symbol for the female. This means that what is required to be put on in the rites of conceiving is the physical flesh forms of male and female.

That this is the true meaning of the "garments" is found in the continued instruction of what Aaron is to wear in the rites of conceiving. In Exodus 28:9 it says, "And thou shalt take two onyx stones, and grave upon them the names of the children of Israel" These two onyx stones remain the objects of attention through verse 14, where it is stressed that names of *all the children of Israel* are to be engraved upon them. It is clear that millions of names could not be engraved upon two small stones. What is being referred to is the productive means within Creative Principle, and this is the "garment" of the onyx stones which symbolize the *testes*. It is a biological fact that millions of "names", sperm cells, are encoded there.

The instructions continue that the "onyx stones" are "to be set in pouches of gold." Gold is always a symbol for high regard or sacred respect, and the symbol of respect here is the *scrotum and its contents.* From this sacred regard of these "onyx stones" the custom arose when swearing an oath of truth to reach under the robes of the man sworn to and grasping his testicles. From this practice we have received the holy word *testament,* and such legal terms as *testimony, testate, testator, testify* and others.

Elsewhere in the story, Aaron is instructed by god to speak to the "children of Israel," which means the overshadowed people, about a "holy anointing oil" Knowing what the ephod and the onyx stones represent we discover the "holy anointing oil" is *seminal fluid.* This alone can account for god-Creative Principle -- declaring "... This shall be an holy anointing oil unto me throughout your generations." Additional verses state that there is to be no other composition like it, which hints that this is the means of transferring the special genetic codes for reproduction.

Aaron was charged by god to carry these "garments" and ritual items whenever he entered the "holy place ." There is some spiel of binding the "rings" of the breastplate "unto the rings of the ephod," and Aaron is to bear the names of the children of Israel when he "goeth in unto the holy place..." The "rings" of the breastplate symbolize the generative female organs, particularly the womb where conception and gestation occur.

In verse 30 it then says, "And thou shalt put in the breastplate of judgement the Urim and the Thummim..." These are symbols for light and perfection. Since this story revolves about the personification of the generative principle within Creation, the Urim and Thummim express the ascertainment of divine intent within Creation. It refers to genetic purity which is set apart that each form may reproduce only its own kind. It has nothing at all to do with human sexual morality, purity, chastity or the like.

With this priestly double-talk decoded we will be able to see through all the ravings in Leviticus, third book of the Old Testament. This is the favorite book for perverted interpreters who want everyone to tremble with guilt for what are natural sexual joys.

The mythical character of Aaron as the conceiver was borrowed from the Zodiac lessons on Creative Energy given with the constellation Orion. Moses personified the Life Principle and for this reason Aaron was portrayed as the brother of Moses.

*   *   *

---------------------------------- **Eridanus** ----------------------------------
the River or the Judge
second decanate of Taurus

This constellation derives its name from the Greek river god Eridanos son of Okeanus (vast primordial waters) and Tethys (primordial substance). This southern constellation stretches in a meandering course from near the star Rigel at the heel of Orion almost to the South Polar Circle. Its principle star is Achernar (02-Eridani) with a faint double satellite. Achernar, a star of first magnitude, is approximately one hundred and fourteen light years from Earth.

This constellation is regarded as having been "discovered" by the ancient Greeks only because the first known cataloging it was presented by Ptolemy. It is unlikely Ptolemy could have himself charted such a southerly line of stars from Alexandria where he made his observations. It is more likely he "discovered" the River in ancient reference books in the library at Alexander.

The star name Achernar comes from the Arabic *akhir al-nahr*, meaning "the end of the river," which refers to the star's position in the constellation. There is strong association with this star's name and the river Acheron in Greek myth, a river of the "underworld." Acheron translates as "woeful," and in the myth it was one of the four rivers of Hades which separated the living (spirit) from the dead (matter). This is another myth of four rivers built upon the Watchers' teachings of the prephysical elements flowing downward through the quaternary. In ancient Greece a number of rivers were called Acheron. All of them bore that name due to some peculiarity such as mephitic gases, or others with black or bitter waters.

The Greeks, of course, always put their own interpretation on everything. By using the name Eridanus for the celestial River's name they did not step too far away from the ancient Watchers' lessons of Creation. This is the River of Life, just as the river of Eden in the scriptures. In the Watchers' presentation this celestial River is channeled by Orion's great phallus, and the "waters" flow toward and into its density of prephysical substance. Only for this reason is it "woeful". It has moved -- or has discharged itself away from creative spirit to activate and nurture the gathering or embryonic matter form. Being still a lesson of action within the prephysical planes, this is where primordial energy, growing darker in etheric substance, approaches its first vaporous form. The celestial River therefore symbolized the first flow into etheric substance. This is the period of Involutionary development presented in religious interpretation as the time when spirit entered its so-called "conflict" with matter.

Eridanus, as the River of Life, is one with the primordial waters of the Aquarius lesson, the waters moving downward through the Involutional planes. The River has issued from the fountainhead, that is to say out of the Creative Trinity aspect at the source (Aquarius, Pisces, Aries). From the Trinity aspect it pours forth as the stream of the fourth watch where it is to divide into the "four waters" of the Quaternary.

Eridanus represents the headwaters where Creative Energy begins in earnest to fulfill Creative Ideation and the division between the spiritual and the material elements commence. Because the spirit commits itself to immerse in dense matter, Eridanus came to be regarded as the "River of Woe." This lesson was reworked in scriptural myth where it was said to flow from Eden into the Garden where it also divided into four.

The four substantive energies of eventual matter-form issue out of the flow of primal energy which Eridanus symbolizes. From this point the prephysical energies take on distinctive action.

In scriptural myth these prephysical energies were presented as having been actual world rivers which has led billions of people into the erroneous belief that the tale had historic basis. The names given to the symbolic four rivers were given as Pison, Gihon, Hiddekel, and Euphrates, all of which coursed through the Mesopotamia region. Knowing the meaning in the names makes one wonder if the rivers were named from the Watchers' lessons.

The name Pison means "a multitude," as could be applied to atoms, the building blocks of Creation. Gihon translates as "to break forth," as the emergence of the life-force. Hiddekel means "rapid action," descriptive of the unencumbered Creative Energy. Euphrates means "fruitful" suggestive of the intended multitudinous expressions of Creation.

Elsewhere in scriptural myths the River of Life is presented as the River Jordon. It symbolizes the life-essence flowing downward through the Involutionary planes to water --energize -- matter expression. Again the priest-mythographers deliberately used the name of a real river, this one the principle river of Palestine, to give the illusion of historical reality. Little that is claimed in scriptures to have happened along the River Jordon ever really transpired as genuine history. It is ninety-nine percent mythology.

In Judeo Christian scriptures the waters of the River Jordon are said to come "down from above," which represents the free flowing elements moving from prephysical planes toward matter fulfillment. The descending waters symbolize the Involutional processes which culminate in the archetypal human. That archetype is "soul" the aspects of self-awareness and self-directed energy. It is these which take up its physical intention at the mental plane, the lesson of Gemini.

In Christian mythology Jesus is presented as having been baptized in the Jordon River. Jesus, as we have noted before, personifies the Life Principle, so it is only natural that the Life Principle would be submerged in the River of Life. Jesus was allegedly baptized by John the Baptist. The word "baptism" originally meant "to plunge under the waters of the world." The Life Principle must be plunged into the primordial waters to fulfill its intention of gathering matter-life. John the Baptist symbolizes that first movement.

*   *   *

———————————————————— **Auriga** ————————————————————
the Charioteer, or Wagoner, or Shepherd
third decanate of Taurus

The hieroglyph given for this constellation is as old as the Zodiac itself, and yet its occult meaning has been among the most difficult for students of the Zodiac or occult lore to unravel. This constellation has always been depicted in a peculiar form which is complete only by "borrowing" a star from the tip of the Celestial Bull's horn. This, of course, has meaning. The name of the star at the tip of the Bull's horn is El Nath, which means "wounded." We will come back to this shortly.

The hieroglyphic figure for this constellation is of a seated male. He is sitting on the Milky Way. He is holding in his left arm a she-goat, and in his lap are two very small goat kids, probably newborn. The mystery of this figure is compounded by what have been interpreted as "reins" held in his right hand. Even in the oldest known Chaldean astrology charts this figure appears in this manner-goat, kids, "reins" and all.

The Greeks called this figure Haeniochos, which translates as "charioteer" or "driver." We know this constellation by the Latin name Auriga which translates as meaning "coachman," a variation of the charioteer interpretation. From this, in its interpretation as "coachman," arose more confusion which resulted in the figure being called the "Wagoner." It by this incorrect name, Wagoner, that most modern atlases have listed this constellation. Even known as Auriga more confusion was gendered for the word Aurgia in Hebrew is said to mean "shepherd."

The name of some of the major stars in this constellation hint broadly at the original significance of this figure. The brightest star is named Alioth (also called Capella), which means a "she-goat." This star is the heart of the goat figure. The second brightest star is named Menkilinon, meaning "the chains of the goat." Another star in this hieroglyph is known as Maaz, which translates as "a flock of goats"

The strange male figure which has gathered up the goat and her kids is not a charioteer, a wagoner, or even a shepherd -- although shepherd is a closer approximation of its intent. The male figure is again symbolic of the Creative Life Principle. With this lesson was taught the Life Principle *releasing* the "reins" from the she-goat, a substance symbol, that she may give forth the twin actions needed for material-matter creation. Those twin actions are *undefined conscious-ness* and *impersonal energy*.

The she-goat gazes at her two kids resting in the lap of the Creative Principle -- or upon the loins of the Modadic

Host, as it were. She looks upon them with a mixture of accomplishment and regret, for the two newborn kids represent the active presentation which is to activate dense-matter expression. Both the tiny kids are male, as they are to mature to represent *two generative aspects of the First Cause* which are *Consciousness* and *Energy*, the subjects of the next Zodiac lesson.

The goat mother, symbolic of etheric substance, has been "barren" until now for up until this point etheric substance has not been endowed with genetic ideation. This is a strong clue why such scriptural substance symbols as Sarai, Martha, Rebekah and the like were said to be "barren" until god, meaning the Life Principle, activated their capability. Every one of the "barren" women of scriptural myth are symbols for primordial or etheric substance not yet endowed with genetic ideation.

The twin newborn kids resting in the lap of the Creative Principle represent the rudimentary double-natured composition or constitution that propels all life-form, which are consciousness and energy. It here, at this point of Involutionary development, that spirit becomes "wounded" upon the horn of Creative Energy. We see the meaning of the borrowed star. This could also be said to be spirit on the *horn of dilemma,* for it must submerge itself to experience its matter destiny.

The lesson of spirit moving toward its densifying matter substance form is further explained in the next major lesson taught with the constellation of Gemini.

Gemini
The Twins

the fifth major sign of the Zodiac of Constellations
representing the prephysical plane
of Mental Matter

The Zodiac sign of Gemini, Latin meaning "twins," is the fifth major division of the ancient Zodiac of Constellations which continued the lessons concerning the processes of Creation. This constellation was also used as the third sign in the Lesser Zodiac of Signs depicting the Celestial Man and which was concerned with life lessons. The Sun is in the constellation of Gemini at the time of the summer solstice.

In the Zodiac of Signs presenting the Celestial Man, Gemini marks the hands and arms, representing dual function. Because of this dual function the hieroglyph of twins is an apt symbol. In the life lessons given with this sign there was presented the principle of fermentation or renewal as expressed in childhood. It served also to illustrate in both Zodiac teachings that the bringing in of new order is always the confusion of the old. This is an important point in understanding the activity within the Involutionary planes, and it is an important factor in matter-life expression.

The constellation of Gemini is located on the side of the Milky Way opposite from Orion (first decanate of Taurus). This constellation's most prominent features are two bright stars, Castor (Alpha Geminorum) and Pollux (Beta Geminorum). These stars represent the heads of the twin figures.

Human infants or child twins or grown human males or a pair of peacocks -- the Arabian symbol for this sign -- are not the original or proper symbols for this star grouping. The more ancient hieroglyphic figures for this constellation have not been discovered, but evidence has already been given as to what the proper figures should be. The logical figures for this lesson division would be the maturing twin male goats that were presented in the third decanate of Taurus as newborn kids. This is given additional support by the fact that astronomers of ancient Egypt symbolized this constellation as a pair of young goats. The twin goats, as focus for the Gemini lessons, are at this stage just approaching "siring age." This is where Mental Matter, the subject of Gemini in the Zodiac of Constellations, is to bring forth a mental concept of its eventual dense-matter form.

The Hebrew name for this constellation was Thaumin, which means "united." The Coptic name, Pi-mahi, also meant "united."

The most luminous star in Gemini is Pollux, meaning "judge" or "ruler." Near the center of this star group is the star named Wasat, meaning "put in place." The star named Al henah in this constellation means "afflicted." All these names used with this grouping emphasize the content of the lessons taught with this Zodiac lesson. With this lesson was explained the preparatory actions of spirit as soul substance which is at this point of elementary self-awareness and self directed energy. With these, at the Mental Matter plane, is shaped the concept of its eventual dense-matter form. The lessons of Gemini taught of the plane were dexterity within prephysical energy begins its movement as assertive self-expression.

In terms of cosmological action this is where primordial elements move to unite into a planet's eventual luminous gaseous cloud state.

Upon this constellation's hieroglyph of twin figures were based the Greek tales of the twins Proteus and Acrisius, and their struggle within the womb. This myth properly represented the action that takes place within this *prephysical* plane. The Greek myth of the twins Iphicles and Herakles

-- better known as Hercules -- is also story-form action demonstrating the action within this Involutionary plane. The Romans had a similar tale of Castor and Pollux, twins who are often referred to by the Greek word *Dioscuri*, meaning "Sons of Zeus." The scriptural tales of the twins Jacob and E'sau, and the twins Pharez and Zarah are also based upon this ancient Zodiac hieroglyph.

In the book of Genesis, the Hebrew-Judaic myth-version of generative actions of Creation, we are presented with the twin characters of Jacob and E'sau. This means, bluntly, that these were never real flesh-and-blood histori-cal people any more than were Herakles and Iphicles or the rest. Like the twin characters in the other myths, Jacob and E'sau simply personify consciousness and energy within the "womb" of space.

This particular Genesis tale, taken from the Gemini lessons symbolized by twins, therefore represent the dual aspects of the first cause at the Involutionary plane of Mental Matter. One of the twins would have to be older, and symbolically the dominant one. E'sau personifies primordial Creative Consciousness in this myth so he is older than Jacob who personifies Creative Energy.

The main conflict in this tale is over "birthright" which brings with it their father's blessing. The scriptures neglect to explain just what E'sau's "birthright" was, except the vague suggestion of the broad rights of primogeniture. In this tale Jacob, following after E'sau at birth "...came out and his hand was holding onto the heel of E'sau; so they called his name Jacob..." (Genesis 25:26)

This account of the twins' birth is but an allegory of natural sequence. What was being explained was that spirit, in its movement toward becoming matter, must forfeit its nature to the energy that pulls and holds it down in dense matter.

Later when it is told of E'sau's "birthright" being bargained away -- for a mess of pottage, yet (Genesis 25:21-34) -- what is being said is that spirit domination is forfeited when entering into the dense-matter plane. This story simply personified the dual nature at work within Creation,

which is why the story is given in Genesis. The dual nature
is, at this point, still undefined and impersonal.

Upon this personification of prephysical consciousness and energy, scholars incapable of abstract thought
have regarded this narrative as reflecting the history of the
Edomites, represented by E'sau, and the Israelites, represented by Jacob. The truth is that the story is not historical
in any sense.

In still another story of twin rivalry in the book of
Genesis (38:27-30), twin sons sired by Judah are born to his
daughter-in-law Tamar. Again this female figure symbolizes
prephysical substance. "Twins were in her womb," we are
told typically, and they were named Pharez and Zarah.

The events which allegedly occurred at the birth of
these twin sons are a bit odd to say the least. One son is said
to have thrust his hand out first, to which the midwife
attached a scarlet thread, saying, "This came first." Spirit,
of course, must come first. But then, if we are to take this
tale literally, an unnatural -- or is it supernatural -- thing
is declared to have happened. The babe on his way out of the
uterine tract then pulls back his hand, retreats, and his
brother pops out first.

This is not reality. For any mortal woman to live
through such an unnatural internal scrambling would be
impossible. This is not a story of the birth of any mortal twins.
Occurring as it does in the book of Genesis, it is but another
tale personifying the creative actions and its order within the
Involutionary planes. It is from this myth, however, that the
world has been presented the claim that Judah was a mortal
man who sired twin offspring through which sprang an
historical line of the "House of David."

We have every right to ask why a supposed moral god
would honor such an immoral union as a man' sexual
involvement with his own daughter-in-law? What kind of
pervert deity would look so favorably upon the sordid affair
that "he" would happily establish a whole "royal line" from
their relationship? Such a blessing could not be based on
morality, ethics or justice. It does, however, make sense
when it is understood that these are but personifications of

energies, actions and substance in the prephysical planes. The only conclusion left open once this is revealed is that those tales of Creation's actions have been presented by manipulative priests as being "history." The saddest part of it all is that a gullible world would fall for it.

In Christian mythology, "doubting" Thomas is another character drawn from the Gemini lesson on consciousness and energy, for he personifies in a distilled form the same dual nature of Creation. There was thoughtful and implied meaning in the name, Thomas Didymus, given him by the Christian myth-makers. The name Didymus comes from the Greek word *didymos*, and referred directly to the Zodiac twins. In doing this Thomas personified the dual nature at work in Creation, and as such he is therefore the undivided or bisexual genetic energy. This means that his intelligence of order certainly was not of a doubting nature. What would be in doubt theoretically once energy prevailed as temporary life-force, is where is spirit? At the plane of dense matter the generative force he represents is therefore indiscriminate in the sexual aspects it creates.

In the earliest days of the Christian movement, there were sects whose writings were presented in a manner which could be interpreted that Jesus had a twin brother. In Gnostic "gospels" at the time, such as **The Gospel of Thomas**, the first line reads, "These are the secret words which the living Jesus spoke, and which the twin, Judas Thomas, wrote down."

Whether this was intended to be understood in the same vein as the Hercules-Iphicles myth -- where Hercules is the Divine Son and Iphicles is the mere mortal -- is open to conjuncture. Hercules, too, was called god's "only begotten son." On the other hand, the reference given in the first line of the Gnostic "gospel" could just as easily mean that Thomas was indeed a twin, but not necessarily that of Jesus. The opening line could also be interpreted as expressing a oneness in spiritual unity.

In another Gnostic book, **The Book of Thomas the Contender**, the text reads in such a way that each reader is led to accept himself as a twin of Jesus. Needless to say, this was not a popular theme for the men who sought to set up the religious power structure of "orthodox" Christianity. The one incontestable point remains that regardless which myth is addressed, Thomas is the personification of Gemini, sign of the Twins.

One of the main points given originally with the Gemini lessons was to express the truth that *the norm of spirit is androgynous*. This means that development of spirit-soul is made not only with characteristics of both sexes, but that it is composed of all universal elements. This the Pagans understood clearly, and this is the meaning behind the hermaphroditic figures displaying both male-female sex organs which so embarrass the sniggling religionists of our era. The double-sexed figures were not intended to excite with lustful fantasies, but symbolized the total spirit -- the spirit in balance.

Everything in Creation must contain duality within itself in order to generate and sustain its matter form. This duality is reflected in human physiology. No man is ever one hundred percent male, and no woman is ever one hundred percent female. The vestiges of the "opposite" sex are always present in various levels of dormancy in every being who lives. In human physiology, if we approach it with a lack of bias, there are far more similarities in composition between "opposite" sexes than there are differences. It is a habit of thought born of ignorance which leads us to concentrate upon differences and negatives of the two sexes rather than admit there are actually more similarities and positives.

In the human species during the first four months after conception the embryo cannot be termed as being either male or female. It is, in actuality, both. It carries within itself both the male and female potential. Only gradually does a geminated life-form (this is not yet self-aware conscious-ness, it is only energy-potential) take on what will become its external characteristics. The underlying fact here is that each and every one of us commences our life-form experience with the potential of becoming either sex.

Human physical development follows the same gen-eral processes as given in the Lessons presented with the ancient Zodiac of Constellations. The fetal child -- the ideation of human physical form -- is a concentration of dual energies, which is to say it is a bisexual creation in the beginning. About four months, reminiscent of the fourth plane, ideation is energized toward its physical type. At this point it still is not self-consciousness. Development from this point on to birth can be likened to Mental Matter-Astral Matter involvement, with birth symbolizing the entry out of the Etheric Matter, the visible formation period.

The lesson of Gemini with its hieroglyphic figure of twins taught of the two poles through which all Creation is energized. Just as a battery unit produces energy by use of the positive and negative poles, so too is the universal power activated. *Everything in Creation holds this duality within itself.* In the Lesser Zodiac of Signs, Gemini is symbolized as the arms and hands of the Celestial Man. They can operate independently or together, functionally or destructively.

In the greater Zodiac of Constellations this duality was symbolized properly as twin kids, equal in all respects but disposed oppositely for balance. This is not like the division of energies as in the Pisces Lessons, but is the balance of energy with consciousness which is to energize itself as self-consciousness. The balance of these two poles of being has been interpreted by most religions as a conflict of "good" and "evil." The flaw in this good-evil interpretation is that nowhere in all of Creation is there anything that is demonstrably all good or entirely evil.

Everything in Creation exists only because they represent balanced degrees of positive-negative energies. For this reason any fanatic attention bestowed on one or the other poles as being a "god" or a "devil" inevitably leads to imbalance that shines forth as hypocrisy, prejudice, irrational actions and all their attendant ills and violence.

If god is good and good only, devotion to that god should have brought about world peace long ago. It is a historical fact that no god-based religion has ever brought humankind any kind of peace. Peace will be achieved only through understanding that it is through the interaction of positive-negative factors, not rejection of that balance, which assures genuine harmony.

Because the ancient lessons given with Gemini taught that the spiritual essence is, in a sense, sacrificed for the benefit of matter experience, a number of superstitious practices arose when the meaning of these lessons became lost. A notable example was the priest-inspired tale of Leviticus upon which was instituted the ritual of an annual sacrifice of two goats. One goat was sacrificed upon the priest-flanked altar in an effort to coerce from god another year of favor. The second goat was sent into the "wilds" -- to Aza'zel. This poor goat allegedly bore the "sins" of the people which, the priests claimed, would be eradicated when the hapless goat was torn apart and devoured by beasts.

A slightly different version of this sacrifice ritual was carried out annually near Jerusalem. Some three or four miles southeast of Jerusalem there is a desert cliff from which was thrown the "scapegoat for Aza'zel." The superstitious Jews led by politico-priests believed the sins of Israel were in someway transferred to a selected goat. This poor hapless goat was then hurled to its death by the merciless priests to provide them with their "Day of Atonement." (Leviticus 16:8-10)

From this double-goat sacrifice we received the tradition and the slang expression of "scapegoat." A "goat" has come to be regarded as one who takes the blame for another. The practice of a scapegoat sacrifice was simply a priestly ploy offering the false notion that personal or national responsibility could be passed on to someone or something other than oneself. It profited the priest-class considerably to provide their flock with their "Day of Atonement."

In typical misuse of this constellational grouping some Christians have claimed to see the prophecy of some future great marriage-union of "Christ and his bride Israel." This is imagined to take place at the close of the present world order. This mixed marriage, apparently, is regarded as some kind reward to Jesus for taking on the "sins" of the world.

*   *   *

Lepus
or the Hare
the first decanate of Gemini

Modern atlases refer to this constellation as Lepus, from Latin meaning "hare." This is not the hieroglyphic figure representation assigned to it by the ancient Watchers who conceived the Zodiac lessons. The same is true of the other two decanates of this sign. The Zodiac of Constellations told with the lessons of Aquarius through Cancer of the prephysical planes of Creation energies. The hieroglyphic figures given as chapter headings therefore symbolized various aspects taking place within each plane. To understand the subject matter of specific lessons we must refer to more ancient Zodiac figures.

The Persians showed this constellational figure as being a Serpent. In the Egyptian temple at Dendera it was also shown as being a Serpent, upon whose back stood a bird. In later lessons we will find a similar image where the Raven, third decanate of Leo, sets upon the back of the Hydra, Leo's first decanate. The name given in the Dendera representation in reference to this decanate of Gemini was Bashti-beki; *Bashti* translates as "confounded," and *Beki* translates as "falling."

In the Egyptian depiction the Serpent hieroglyph appears below and in front of the right foot of the figure representation of the constellation of Orion, the first decanate of Taurus. The Orion figure is shown with his left foot upon the head of the Serpent. In modern atlases Orion's foot rests upon the head of the Hare.

Among almost all people in ancient times the Serpent was commonly understood as being the symbol of divine wisdom and the Creator/Cosmocrator. In ancient Egypt, for example, the Serpent, known as Kneph, was the symbol for the Creator. In their version the Serpent impregnated the cosmic waters by breathing upon them and in this way produced matter and life. The "waters" breathed upon were understood to be inactive prephysical energies. Egyptian hierophants, the expositors of sacred mysteries, were accustomed to reciting, "I am a serpent, I am a snake," meaning that they were students and pursuers of divine wisdom.

The Orphic Greek Cosmocrator, too, was said to be a Serpent named Ophion -- or Ophioneus. As late as the first century of our common era Ophites believed that the world had been generated by the cosmic Serpent (Cosmocrator). In Orphic art Zeus, as the Cosmocrator, was identified as a serpent-god. Other lessons given later will also have a variation on the Serpent figure, a reminder that Cosmic Intelligence is the guiding principle at work. These variations will range from the serpentine shaped spermatozoon -- capable of active spontaneous movement -- as symbol for Cancer, to Serpens of Scorpio and Draco of Sagittarius.

This understanding of the Serpent figure as symbolic of the Creative Principle at work was worldwide. This is the meaning behind such mysterious mound construction of serpents found around the planet. The one thousand foot long serpent-shape near Peebles, Adams County, Ohio is an example. In this structure the Serpent holds between its open jaws an egg-shaped mound. This is symbolic of Divine Wisdom/Cosmic Intelligence bringing forth the world..

Judaic mythmakers refashioned this and relates that Moses made the Brazen Serpent (Numbers 21:8-9) at god's command. This is a clear suggestion that among the early Hebrews the tribal god Yahweh had been identified with a serpent-god. The Druids revered the Serpent as symbolic of Divine Wisdom-Knowledge. Early Indian Buddhism honored the Serpent. Legend has it that a great serpent defended the citadel of Athens. The Romans had their *genius loci*, the guardian spirit of a place which was believed to often take serpent shape. Even in Christian myth Jesus is quoted as saying, "Be ye as wise as serpents."

All of these associations came through the ancient Zodiac lessons where the Creative Principle is presented as activated by higher Wisdom-Consciousness. With the Zodiac lessons this had been symbolized as the Serpent hieroglyph which represented Mental Matter forces within the prephysical planes. This is why in John 3:14 it says, "As Moses lifted up the serpent in the wilderness..."

With the Gemini lesson in the Zodiac of Signs dealing with life lessons and spiritual guidance, the Serpent decanate taught of *the manifesting reason* within self. It is this which allows for rational self-evolution by which self is to identify itself with the universe. This can be said to be seminal reason or the potential intellect of being. In the Zodiac of Constellations, the Creation/cosmology lessons, the Serpent lesson taught of the Creative Principle manifesting itself as the organic principle of the universe.

The spirit soul, *energy as self-awareness*, is now at the position to choose the direction of its experience. The Serpent symbol for this lesson was representative of the Creative Intelligence which accompanies the forming substance-matter. The desire-mind is being shaped at this plane and it is more binding to the ego than is any of the lower plane desires. This is the stage where desire manifests within Mental Matter, and is therefore the *captivity* which will lead to *bondage* in matter. For this reason the Serpent was said to be more subtle than any beast of the field.

The idea presented in the Judeo-Christian faiths that the Serpent personifies evil is therefore far from universal. The acceptance of the Serpent as evil comes as the result of the priests of Judaism overthrowing rival priests of Yahweh who had honored the Serpent as representative of Divine Wisdom.

In ancient Egypt, after Ra, Lord of the Planet of Crossing, was transformed by rival priests into Ra god of the Sun, the Serpent figure was, as a matter of course, inverted to become their symbol of evil. This vilification of Divine Wisdom has been standard priest-class procedure for the western world's religions ever since.

The priests of Ra, god of the Sun, then named the Serpent Apep or Aaapef, which is better known to us by the Greek adaptation Apophis. Presented as Apep the Serpent then became mind-desire of lower nature, the adversary of higher qualities. This was true as far as the interpretation went but the priests were limited in their understanding of Zodiac lessons which by then had become fragmented. With this limited understanding, Apep was understood to be a form taken by the Egyptian god Set whom they imagined ruled over evil and darkness. Set-Apep was therefore portrayed by the Egyptian priesthood as the archenemy of the sun-god Ra when properly it is Creative Principle manifesting out of the dark void of prephysical planes.

The priests of Ra, as the sun-god, had muscled their way into controlling influence over those who had understood the real meaning of the Serpent as being symbolic of Divine Wisdom. This is apparent in the Ra priests' "Book of the Overthrowing of Apophis" (Apep). The concept of the Serpent as symbolic of wisdom was ancient even then, and it posed a constant threat to the Ra priests. The priests therefore recited the Book of the Overthrowing Apep as a daily ritual. In this was catalogued in great detail all the alleged horrors thought to befall Apep-Apophis in his nightly battle with the Sun. Apep was described as having an undulating body and that "his voice goeth round the Tuat," meaning the underworld (prephysical planes).

The Zoroastrian priest-class of ancient Persia, following the lead of Zoroaster (625-551 B.C.E.), cast the Serpent of Divine Wisdom into their wicked Al Dahaka. The Serpent then became one of the evil spirits, the *daevas* or *divs*, which made up a kind of army at war with the good spirits headed by Ahura Mazdah. The "war" between these representative images of Creation's planes is the subject matter of a fully developed cosmogony and eschatology of Zoroastrianism.

That Zoroastrianism drew from some of the ancient Zodiac lessons is likely. The source material was probably fragmented and perhaps consisted only parts of the first lessons in the Zodiac of Constellations. With Zoroastrianism was presented the entire history of the universe, past present and future. This was taught as occurring in four periods, each of three thousand years. The first period was thought as being when there was no matter. The second preceded the coming of Zoroaster. The third period was to be when his faith is propagated. The fourth period was to be the triumph of good over evil which the Zodiac lessons taught as the evolution of soul into Wisdom Consciousness.

Zoroastrianism considerably affected Judaism, especially during the time of the Babylonian Captivity. It also affected Gnosticism. In its turn Christianity drew heavily upon both of these sources for its foundation material. This is reflected in the religion's quasi-dualistic aspects where both poles are recognized, but good is predicted as ultimately triumphant.

The changes in regarding the Serpent as evil are all traceable to the putting down of the older understanding taught with the Zodiac lessons. The Serpent in the Zodiac lessons taught of where Creative Intelligence accompanies and activates the forming substance-matter with desire-mind. This necessary plane or stage of development was cast as being the influence of evil by priests more intent upon establishing their power structures than in teaching honest Creation processes. To accomplish their true purpose the rival they sought to overthrow had to be cast as evil. The result was that the Serpent emblem which once symbolized higher wisdom was reversed to become the symbol of evil and darkness.

The Serpent is still regarded by much of the world's population as emblemic of wisdom. This crops up even in the Judeo-Christian cultures where, for example, serpent symbols suggest the knowledge embodied in the medical profession.

In ancient times the Serpent figure was accepted worldwide as symbolic of higher wisdom because of its association with the lessons from the Zodiac of Constellations. In the lesson given with Lepus, first decanate of Gemini, this higher creative wisdom was presented as encountering the idea of generative production. This is to say as the plane where Mental Matter, the subject of Gemini, considers the means of future matter-life production. It is probably because of this association that the Hare came to be substituted as the symbol for this constellation. The Hare is an extremely potent reproducer.

What is the symbolism of Orion standing with his foot on the head of the Serpent -- or on the head of the Hare? Orion, the first decanate of Taurus, taught of Creative Energy. He stands as the First Cause symbolized by his erect phallus, and his left foot is shown as upon the Serpent's head. Orion is not attempting to crush it or bruise it as commonly presented in religious propaganda. The figure's stance and his turgid state of arousal indicates that Divine Wisdom is to be temporarily held down and dominated by the gnawing energy which is forming as dense-matter. It is at this point where spirit soul, developing as ego, is said to be "dragged down" into its dense-matter form. In scriptural verses this where Eve, *the polar twin of Adam*, is tempted by the Serpent which leads to them being aware of their "nakedness" In another version this is where Jacob "took hold of E'sau's heel," his twin -- or spiritual -- aspect, dragging it down, when coming into the matter plane.

It is in the context of matter dominating spirit while experiencing action on this dense matter plane that many of the stars in this constellation received their names. The most luminous star in the Serpent constellation was known by the Hebrews as Arnebo, said to translate as "enemy of him that cometh." The Arabic name Arnebeth translates similarly. Other Arabic names of stars in this constellation include Rakis, meaning "the bound;" Nibal meaning "the mad;" and Sugia, meaning "the deceiver." All these reflect the ancient Zodiac lessons of spirit being submerged and bound in its self-activated densifying form.

*   *   *

Canis Major
the Greater Dog
the second decanate of Gemini

Canis Major is a constellation of the Southern Hemisphere southeast of Orion, which includes within it the brightest star in the sky, Sirius. The hieroglyph of the Greater Dog for this decanate of Gemini is of recent origin and its modern recognition as Canis Major comes from the Latin word *canis* meaning "dog." The source for this depiction is from Greek assignment. The Persians knew this constellation as Zeeb, meaning "leader," and pictured it as a wolf. In Hebrew too it was known as "leader." To the Egyptians this constellation was known as Apes, meaning "the head," as signifying a leader, and pictured it as a hawk.

In considering the names that were given to stars in this sign it should be remembered that the subject of Gemini is Mental Matter. This sub-constellation of Gemini represents the synergistic efforts which produce matter form, which in the cosmology given with the Zodiac of Constellations indicates planetary form.

The second brightest star in this constellational group is Mirzam, from Persian *mirza* which means "ruler" or "prince." The star Adhara means "glorious." Aschere means "who shall come." Abur, Hebrew, means "the mighty." Muliphen, Arabic, means "leader" or "chief."

The most prominent star in this constellation is Sirius. The Egyptians gave considerable attention to this star. Its name is derived from *seir*, meaning "prince," "guardian," or "victorious." This is the star referred to as the "Dog Star," from Egyptian association of its prominence as seasonal burning heat and its accompanying pestilent conditions. Sirius was regarded as the "Dog Star" only when in midsummer it rose at dawn. Midsummer is still known as canicular days -- or "dog days." Other ancient cultures did not regard this star to be associated with disaster or discomfort. To the Akkadians this star was known as Kasista which meant "leader."

The star Sirius, the brightest star in the heavens from Earth's point of view, has long played a major role in the religious beliefs of the Dogon tribe of west Africa. Their traditions and understanding of this star have never been submerged by either the Christian or Islamic religions.

The Dogon *officiates* -- (a word used in place of the term priests out of respect for the Dogon's devotion to truth) have long known secrets about Sirius that weren't even discovered by the West until relatively recent times -- 1862. The officiates of the Dogon people have known for centuries -- without the benefit of telescopes to observe it -- that Sirius had a satellite. This satellite is invisible to the naked eye, and is known to astronomers today as Sirius B. The Dogons have known as far back as can be recounted that this satellite orbits Sirius *in an elliptical orbit*, not in a circular one. They also knew that the satellite's orbit took fifty years to complete.

How this accurate knowledge was imparted to them remains a mystery. They declare that the knowledge was given to their ancestors in a far distant time by visitors to Earth -- visitors from that selfsame planet that circles Sirius.

It is from the Egyptian word *seir*, meaning "prince," and the Egyptian word *naz seir* (or *nazer*), meaning "the sent prince," that the Jewish priest-mythographers fashioned their *netzer* -- better known as David.

The word *netzer* is commonly translated as meaning "the branch" since it was derived from *seir*. Judaic scriptures claims that the "Rod", called *netzer* in the Hebrew writing, came forth from the stem of Jesse, the name given for the father of the mythological David. Jesse translates as meaning "to be," which is the concern of Gemini. David's "father" is therefore the personification of a prephysical formation action. Jesse, the personification of the preparatory period in the prephysical plane, is the "stem" from which the "Rod" issues as Netzer personified as David, "the sent prince. What is being said occultly is that David -- or *netzer* or "branch" -- simply *represents the Involutionary King of Earth*, not some pretended historical one.

Because the character known as David has played such an important role in western religious propaganda we should take a close look at this alleged founder of the Judean dynasty.

The proper form of the name David should read Dod. This was, in ancient times also written as Dodo with the vocalic suffix of the niminative. Dod or Dodo is the masculine form which corresponds to the Phoenician goddess Dido whose name meant "the beloved one." This was the same Dido who was consort of the Babylonian sun-god Tammuz, "the beloved son."

Tracing the name through ancient variations can be found curious resemblances arising from the names Hadad, Dada, Adad, Dido, Dod, Dodo and David. Hada or Dada are the abbreviated forms of Abd-Hadad. These abbreviated forms were more current in the northern Middle East nations. In the southern areas Dada was confounded with the Semite word which Assyrians wrote as Dadu, meaning "dear little child." Hadad was regarded as the supreme Ba'al or sun-god, his worship extending south from Carchemis to Edom (Idumaea) and Palestine. His Assyrian name was Rimmon.

The Israelites of the northern Babylonian kingdom worshiped a deity Dod or Dodo, adoring the supreme god under that name as well as under the name Yahweh. Some versions regarded Dod as being at the side of Yahweh -- in the same way that Christ is regarded as being at the side of god. This is what is meant in Isaiah 5:1 where Jerusalem is described as the tower of the vineyard that the Lord had planted in Israel and calls him Dod-i, meaning "my beloved." Out of this, the name David was developed of whom it was said in I Samuel 18:16 "all Israel, and Judah loved him."

The similarities of David's "life" are suspiciously like that of other scriptural figures such as Adam, Abraham, Moses, Joshua, Samson and others. The similarities are inescapable since the stories are all about the same thing; Involutionary development. David, as others, tends his father's flocks just as Moses was said to have tended the flocks of Jethro. The "Lord" speaks to him during these shepherding duties, as he did in the Moses version. David slays four lions, symbolic of the four prephysical planes, therefore outdoing Samson.

David personifies the prephysical Earth in the occult cosmology known as "scripture." If David had been an historical person what a monster he would have been. A murderer, thief, bandit, adulterer, voyeur, deceiver, lecher, blackmailer, a mutilator of bodies; but we are supposed to believe that this was the "prince" loved by all the people. Even more incredible we are supposed to believe that the "Lord" chose him for temple building and to pass on a "royal line."

Seen as "history" this is insane. Recognized as a personification of creative energies in the Involutionary planes it restores sanity to the "sacred."

If David were an historical person there is not a shred of morally redeeming quality in any of the despicable acts attributed to him. A slayer of holocaustical proportions, he allegedly killed tens of thousands of Philistines. He was a lecher of monumental proportions, acquiring wives and concubines by the dozens. He married Michal, King Saul's daughter, as a prize for performing an act of needless butchery which we will relate in case you don't recall.

Saul had, understandably suspicious of David's nature, sent David off on a mission to secure one hundred foreskins of slain Philistines. This makes Saul pretty questionable too, but on with the tale -- or off, as case may be. This quest would have certainly deterred any man of reason. The story relates, however, that David returned from his bloody chore with double the amount requested. For this he won the hand of Saul's daughter, poor girl.

The second wife of this treacherous "hero" was acquired after first attempting to blackmail an honest man, the hard working Nabal who was told to forfeit tribute or suffer death. (Remember the name Nibal, a star in the previous constellation Lepus?) David was sorely envious of Nabal's wealth and when Nabal refused to be blackmailed David planned to have him murdered. David was spared this little inconvenience for the *loving* god did it for him. David thereupon married Nabal's wife and acquired Nabal's fortune.

David's next target was the lovely Bathsheba whom he took to spying on while she took her bath. To get rid of Bathsheba's husband Uriah, David instructed his general, Joab, to put Uriah in the front lines of battle so he would be killed off. The rest was sexual delight. Even in his old age David reportedly took virgins to bed to keep himself warm and in an attempt to resurrect his flagging sexual abilities. This is what is claimed as the foundation of a historical "royal line." Even the "royal" family of England claim heritage from David!

It should go without saying that the Psalms, credited as being from the pen of David, were not composed by this character either.

This is scriptures' much honored *netzer* -- David-"the sent prince." In the New Testament this same root source *naz seir, nazer, netzer* -- was used to fashion the royal character of Jesus as their "sent prince" and their "leader," the "king of the Jews." Christian myth makers placed a great deal of importance upon the imagined genealogical lines which "proved" the mythological Jesus was descended from the mythological David. Knowing that *occult cosmology is the true theme of the biblical tales* we know that Jesus is not descended but simply another version of the personified Creative Principle.

All of these "holy" contortions simply disguise and echo the lesson which had once been given with this second decanate of Gemini. This lesson taught of the fidelity of spirit to the progressive involvement with densifying substance and intended matter experience.

*   *   *

Canis Minor
the Small Dog
the third decanate of Gemini

This constellation consists of only fourteen stars which in itself suggests the combined seven planes of Involution and the seven planes of Evolution. This number is arrived at by counting the matter plane twice as the goal of Involution and as the springboard of Evolution. The fourteen stars of this constellation therefore serve as a reminder of the intent of the Zodiac lessons about the planes of Creation.

This decanate of Gemini, as did the previous decanates, has had its original name and hieroglyphic figure altered. The result is that vital clues to the lesson given with this decanate were lost. Being a sub-constellation of Gemini

which symbolizes Mental Matter this division too was given
to add emphasis to this stage of Creation.

In Egypt in the temple of Dendera this constellation
was known as Sebak which means "conquering" or "victorious." It was portrayed as a human figure with the head of a
hawk. This figure, Sebak, should not be confused with Sebek,
the Egyptian crocodile god. The hawk symbolizes the intelligent soul, and in conjunction with the Gemini lesson we
can discern this part of the lesson. The spirit-soul is now
ready to enter the Astral Plane, having at this point achieved
the direction of self-awareness.

Again it is the star names which express the older
occult cosmological meanings. Procyon, the brightest star in
this group, means "redeemer." Al-Gomeyra means "who
completes." Al-Gomeisa translates as "burdened" or "loaded
down." All of these indicate the continuing process within
the Involutionary planes. At this prephysical plane, Mental
Matter is energized and self-awareness becomes active to
direct the form of its dense matter expression.

Part of the purpose of this small constellation was to
serve as a reminder of the seven planes of Involution into
matter and the seven planes of Evolution that are to follow
the qualifying action of the matter plane. Matter-life is a
refining process. The quandary of all life, most especially of
youth, is the abstract concept of virtue and vice. The future
always depends upon the choices which are colored by both
of these magnetic attractions. In the life lessons given with
the Zodiac of Signs this decanate stressed this point, and
taught that all these choices must later be considered or
weighed with the lessons of Libra.

The last decanate of Gemini contained the lesson of
the spirit-soul's expanding awareness as it approaches the
threshold into the Astral Plane. Here, energy-consciousness
involves itself as self-awareness, which will provide the
means of exercising *choice* in matter experience. This lesson
of spirit-soul out-budding became dramatically reworked in
the book of Genesis where Job "wrestles" with an "angel."

The so-called religious "mystery" of the *Scala Coeli*,
which means "ladder of heaven," is better known as Jacob's

ladder. Jacob is one of the Gemini twins, the symbol of energy which pulls down spirit. At the point of the story where prephysical substance arrives at the Dense Matter plane it is the final or seventh plane of the Involutionary process. It is the seven Involutionary planes which make up the seven-runged ladder that Jacob sees at this point of the Genesis tale.

The "angels of god" seen moving up and down upon this "ladder" are but the symbols for the creative forces in action at each of those prephysical planes. The "vision" is but a condensed revision of the seven "days" of Creation. The "angel" with whom Jacob wrestles is his own spiritual self which must be submerged to experience matter. This is why when the wrestling match is described it is impossible to discern which of the contestants is meant when it says "he," "his," "him." In cosmological formation this is the stage where Mental Matter enters its self-determined ,planetary-Earth form. After Jacob and his other self wrestle, Jacob sleeps. He rests his head on a stone, which symbolizes the matter plane he is to enter. When Jacob, symbolizing the prephysical energies, reaches the Dense Matter plane this is signified by having his name changed to Israel.

Cancer
The Crab

the sixth major sign of the Zodiac of Constellations
representing the prephysical plane
of Astral Matter

With this Zodiacal constellation of Cancer, Latin meaning "the Crab," was presented the sixth lesson of the Zodiac of Constellations, and the fourth life-lesson in the more familiar Zodiac of Signs.

There have been some doubts expressed that the Crab was the hieroglyph used by the prehistory compilers of the two Zodiacs, but this figure is used also in the Chinese and Hindu Zodiacs which indicate agreement of the original celestial figure.

The Greeks knew this northern constellation by the name of Karkinos, which means "hiding" or "encircling," and figuratively this can be said to be the fuller descriptive meaning of the Latin word Cancer. The Syrians called this constellation Sartano which means "who binds" The Arabian name Al Sartan has similar meaning. The Egyptian representation in the temple at Dendera called this constellation Klaria, translated as meaning "the folds" or "the resting places" This clings most closely to the teachings which the Watchers presented with this star grouping.

This constellation has no stars more luminous than the third magnitude, and so is one of the faintest to be seen from the perspective of Earth. The faintness of this group makes it seem strange at first that it should be used as a life lesson heading. This apparent insignificance is itself symbolic of that necessary fading or forfeiting of spirit power at the stage of Involutionary development where soul-ego begins to direct its dense-matter form. The lesson of Gemini taught of the soul's "captivity" or dedication to its matter fulfillment. For this reason Cancer can be said to be the plane of "bondage". It is here at the Astral Plane where ideation is bonded with densifying substance which is to be expressed as matter-form for the soul's experience. This is the "house of bondage" mentioned in Exodus 13:14.

It is at this general point in the Exodus myth also that the Lord (the Life Principle) allegedly instructs Moses to sanctify all the firstborn, "whatsoever openeth the womb..." In other words, prephysical substance is set apart within the void of space to have imparted to it its intended form. The instruction adds it is to be the firstborn "both of man and of beast: it is mine."

In this chapter also is found the injunction, "Seven days thou shalt eat unleavened bread..." The Jews in devout literalism eat unleavened bread during Passover observances. It is not eaten in honor of the alleged mass Passover of the Hebrews out of the nation of Egypt, for genuine history records do not validate the claim of mass Hebrew slavery in ancient Egypt. What is being eaten is the symbol for primordial energies which pass over into destined matter form. Unleavened bread symbolizes only lifeless and soulless substance, which is all that the Life Principle draws upon at Creation's source. The seven day diet is merely in reference to the planes or sub-planes of Involutionary activity.

None of this symbolism of unleavened bread is original with the Hebrew-Jews but is traceable to Sumero-Akkadian usage as is so many of their observances. The rituals in use at the Bel-Marduk temple in Babylon became the model for those observed in the temples of the Jews. At the temple of Marduk -- known in biblical form as Merodach -- there was conducted the morning and evening sacrifice, the meat and drink offering, and the "shewbread." Shewbread gets its name from the Greek *shaubrot,* and is unleavened bread. In Exodus 25:30 the Lord allegedly commands, "And thou shalt set upon the table shewbread before me always." The Creative Principle is always at work creating out of the lifeless, soulless primordial energy. The Jewish priests set up the ritual where twelve loaves of unleavened bread were placed at the altar before Yahweh every Sabbath. These were eaten by them alone at the end of week, a seven day period based on the seven Involutionary planes.

The constellation of Cancer together with its three decanate groups advanced the lesson regarding the last of the "invisible" prephysical planes. It is at the Astral Matter plane that the actions take place which prepare spirit-energy to involve itself as visible matter form. It is at this plane that the pressures of densifying substance stimulate the forming egos. The ego is entering the falsity of matter reality, the "bondage" to slower, sluggish energy patterns that temporarily densify as matter.

The hieroglyph of the Crab for this sign served to symbolize the lessons presented with both Zodiac texts. Crabs are noted for going forward by moving sideways. The Zodiac lesson of Cancer is of the turning aside from spirit-energies to enter as spirit consciousness or *soul* into dense-matter experience. It is spirit-energy which is being likened to the crab movements, the implication being that the spirit moves sideways -- or turns aside temporarily -- from the higher energies that it may move toward its experience in matter.

At the center of this faint constellation is one of the most luminous nebulous clusters in the heavens. It is commonly referred to as "the Beehive" in modern astronomy. This cluster is composed of a multitude of little stars. The formal name given to this cluster is Praesepe which means "the multitude" or the "innumerable seed." The ancient Watchers presented this entire constellation as the celestial Manger, and with it taught the lessons of entity life being made ready for its material-matter form. In cosmological terms, this is where the Sun of the Creative Principle becomes energized to blaze forth in visible light at the next plane of

Etheric Matter. From this cosmological explanation of the luminous or Sun period religion drew its "Son of God."

Many star names in this constellation still echo the ancient understanding of Cancer as being representative of the final prephysical plane before beginning its entrance into visible matter form. Some among them seem to act as review material of earlier lessons. One star is called A1 Hamarein, Arabic, which means "lambs" or "the Kids" Another star, Ma'alaph, Arabic, means the "assembled thousands." Other stars hint of the preparatory plane just before taking on matter-form, and this aspect is further accented in the three decanates associated with this constellation.

In the Lesser Zodiac of Signs concerned with life lessons, Cancer, as the fourth sign, was presented as the breast and stomach of the Celestial Man. Pagan wisdom recognized in the sign of Cancer the cosmic illustration of life nourishment. In this understanding the sign of Cancer was regarded as being where all matter-forms and all persons, individually and collectively, enter their final stage as undefined substance toward their visible-matter experience.

In the holy writings the Hebrew word *shaddai* -- properly it should be *El Shaddai* -- has been traditionally translated as meaning "Almighty God." This is something of a contrived interpretation for the Hebrew word *shad* means "breast." El Shaddai should translate to something closer in meaning such as "nourisher," the strength-giving elements personified as god. Shaddai, the almighty nourisher, was drawn from the Celestial Male figure where the Cancer lesson is symbolized by the breast.

Because this Zodiac lesson taught of the spirit at the threshold of its animal or matter-life form, this constellation was symbolized as the manger where life-essence is nourished and housed. At this Astral Plane is accomplished the mystery of incarnation which will result in "birth" at the matter plane. Because of this lesson given with this constellation, Cancer was regarded as being where spirit begins its descent toward matter. Because the lessons of Cancer taught of the plane of the incarnating spirit, Cancer came to be referred to as the "Gate of Men" or "the Northern Gate."

The ancient Egyptian symbol for Cancer was the scarabaeus, a nearly black dung beetle, shown with its wings folded and encased. This substituted symbol was more comprehensible to more people of the region. The scarabaeus served as a studied analogy to the spiritual powers being held in bondage within each matter form. The encased spirit, fettered with the thrall of flesh, must throw off that low form before each being's metamorphosis is accomplished. Only in outgrowing their matter bonds can soul mount into higher planes of being where the mystery of their grub-life is solved.

The lesson given with the Cancer constellation served as the foundation for all the numerous myths of divine infants and their "savior" status. It was well known that the constellation of great length which is known as Hydra always arises with the sign of Cancer. Hydra is the "monster" symbol of greed and desire, and is the first decanate of Leo which presents the lessons of dense-matter form. The common priestly interpretation of this was of a divine infant slaying the serpent or dragon of desire while still in their crib. Herakles (Hercules), Mithra and many others were depicted as having done this. There were also early myths of Jesus doing the same.

This was simply the mythologist's means of expressing an Involutionary truth -- that the monster of desire and greed is inherited with dense-matter life. Desire and greed assails the child from the start, symbolically in the cradle. For this reason divine beings or spiritual teachers were routinely characterized as having slain or mastered this aspect of mortal experience in their infancy. The implication to be drawn from this was that these savior beings lived solely for the benefit and advancement of humankind.

The founding fathers of Christianity borrowed heavily upon this aspect of the ancient Zodiac lessons which had also spawned numerous other "savior" myths. They did not fully comprehend, just as the earlier priests of Judaism had not comprehended, the full spiritual and cosmological meanings of the lessons. The result was a jumbling of their myth symbols.

From the lesson of Astral Matter was drawn the material of Jesus being born in a manger to fulfill the incarnational traditions. The Astral Plane is where each great cycle begins its incoming movement. The alleged "guiding star'" which led the "magi" to the scene was symbolic of the constellation of Cancer itself.

The lessons of the prehistory Watchers taught that in every incarnation of life the offspring is of divine issuance -- meaning fathered by Divine Consciousness -- but is mothered by Nature. The ancient Watchers also understood and taught that every child upon arrival in this matter plane was "wrapped in swaddling clothes" of the flesh, and that it was placed in the manger of physical expression. It is here that spirit really takes up its cross of matter, and does so voluntarily in order to develop the qualities necessary for proceeding into the Evolutionary planes.

*   *   *

The Manger of the Ascelli

In the sign of Cancer, in the vicinity of the constellation of Leo, is located the Manger of the Ascelli where is found the two celestial asses known as the Ascelli. Out of this celestial depiction came the many myths and scriptural tales wherein asses play an important role. The ancient Egyptians drew their red-haired ass-eared god Set upon it. The cult of the ass-eared Set was well established within the boundaries of ancient Judea.

The Ascelli asses served as story material in numerous myths such as in the Roman tales where Bacchus and Vulcan were depicted as riding upon an ass. In Orphic myth Dionysus rode upon an ass. Numerous ancient cultures had myths of their solar heroes or saviors riding upon these asses to their (spiritual) deaths (in matter).

The lessons of the Watchers taught that the Life Principle must be "buried" in dense matter expression before it may rise into the higher planes of Evolution. The Asses of the Ascelli symbolized the lower nature upon which spirit is to ride. The lower nature is stubborn but still capable of being directed by one's sense of higher purpose.

The lower nature was what was being referred to in Jewish legend where the Lilim, the children born to Adam by his first wife Lilith, were said to be ass-haunched. The ass plays a role in many scriptural tales and always indicates the lower nature to be overcome.

In Exodus 4:20, as one example, Moses is said to have taken his wife and sons, placed them upon the back of an ass and returned to the land of Egypt. All our symbols are here. Moses personifies the Life Principle; the wife and sons are symbols for substance and energy; the ass is the lower nature ridden upon while moving into matter, which is symbolized as Egypt.

Abraham, a personification of the Life Principle, is presented as having an ass with him when he prepared to sacrifice his son Isaac. Abraham is accompanied by lower nature when he willingly prepares to sacrifice the spiritual elements which are symbolized by Isaac.

Samson, one of several Judaic solar-savior figures, uses the jawbone of an ass to slay a thousand Philistines. This is a variation on the teaching that lower nature is to be controlled and used to overcome the unqualified lower elements of being. From this jawbone of the ass which Samson had used to slay his thousands water springs forth. The waters of life.

Saul, Hebrew for Sol-Sun, was chosen king while in search of Kish's lost asses; and he came riding back upon an ass to take up his kingship -- to take up his planetary matter-form.

The ass of Balaam spoke with a human voice. Balaam was an alleged prophet hired by Balak, king of Moab, to curse the Israelites who had invaded the Jordon valley. On his way there an "angel of the Lord" appeared before Balaam, and the ass upon which the prophet was riding saw the angel and turned aside in terror. Balaam, not seeing the angel beat the ass three times, whereupon the beast "spake with a man's voice, and stayed the madness of the prophet." None of this is history, of course. The Israelites, as usual, symbolize lower disciplined mental qualities and so are "chosen." The Jordon valley is nourished by the River of Life and so must be inhabited. Balaam is elemental undifferentiated ideation, a "prophet" whose curses turned to blessings for the Israelites. Elemental ideation could not see angelic presence, lower nature might be aware of it.

According to Islamic myth, Muhammad, while standing upon a bridge, was raised up to heaven upon a fabulous animal. Depending upon which version one leans to -- a winged horse (Pegasus) or an ass -- it is but another version of a savior-like hero riding to their sacrificial death or their reward out of Ascelli manger.

In Christian myth Jesus is said to have ridden upon an ass accompanied by her colt when he rode into Jerusalem on his way to his sacrifice. The ass and colt symbolize lower nature, the colt represents new form in Nature.

*   *   *

Ursa Minor
Small Bear
the first decanate of Cancer

In this constellation of Ursa Minor (Latin, meaning little bear") is found the present Pole Star, Al-Ruccaba. The name is Arabic and its meaning is "ridden on" -- as on a pivot or a hinge. Some seven to eight thousand years ago, however, the Pole Star was Alpha Draconis. Due to gradual recession Alpha Draconis is considerably removed from its former position as the apparent "gate" or "hinge" of Earth's motion.

The ancient Watchers were so accomplished in celestial knowledge that they knew the star Al Ruccaba would eventually take up a position as Earth's Pole Star. There was nothing of prophecy in regarding this star as "the turned" or "ridden on." The meaning of this star's name simply indi-

cates that their scientific understanding of celestial mechanics was advanced enough to know that it would someday
be in place as the Pole Star of Earth.

Ursa Minor is probably better known to most people
as the "Little Dipper." Our modern atlas references of this
constellation as a Bear is due to Greek interpretation. In
more ancient celestial charts such as from the Chaldean,
Egyptian, Persian, East Indian and others, bear figures did
not represent these two constellations. Nor did the ancient
Watchers use any figure that might suggest a bear. The
celestial hieroglyphs they inscribed upon the constellations
were always of either obvious mythological creatures or else
fully natural life forms. No bear species has ever had such
an elongated tail as is depicted in the Greek interpretation.

When we understand the lessons taught with this
Zodiac group we see that the Bear is a *fair* substitute as a
lesson heading, but the broader meaning is lost. Bears have
been used traditionally as symbolic of basic passions which
accompany the experience of life.

For the more ancient peoples this constellation was
most often regarded as a "fold," meaning a place where
domesticated animals, especially the younger animals, are
penned or confined. What we know as Ursa Minor was more
properly presented with the lessons as the Lesser Sheepfold.

This subdivision of the Cancer lesson on the Astral
Matter plane gave further example of the actions and
purpose of this prephysical plane which immediately precedes spirit's full immersion into visible matter. This is
accented by the names given to some of the stars in this
group. For example Al Pherkadian, an Arabic name, translates as "the calves" or as "the young." The star Arcas or
Arctos is interpreted as "a traveling company." Kochab is
said to mean "waiting for him that comes."

The Zodiac lessons taught that it was at this
Involutionary plane of Astral Matter that the prephysical
energies, symbolized as sheep, begin to take on densification
and virtues. In this sheepfold the sheep are tended, nourished and made ready to go forth on their own. Sheep
symbolized qualified energies which develop as *being*. The

Life Principle activates the qualified (chosen) elements toward its life form.

This is what is meant when it is said in the book of Matthew 25:33, "..and he shall set the sheep on his right hand, but the goats on the left." Goats, the symbols for the Gemini lessons of Mental Matter, represent the lower attributes of self-awareness, desire, instinct and passion. The full verse from which the above was quoted also speaks of separating "nation from nation" according to merits. This is not meant in terms of historic nations but in reference to the planes of Involution and Evolution.

From the names of the stars mentioned earlier various religious spokesmen have interpreted biblical verses as being "prophetic." Some evangelical astromancers say that Genesis 22:17 is tied to these star meanings and promise that Israel is to "possess the gate of his enemies." Others have preached that the stars of this constellation foretell of "Christ's little flock" which, they assert, is to be whisked off to heaven just prior to his "second coming."

Sad to say, they look for some physical reappearance of what was but a personification of a Principle. The single line from which this interpretation is taken is allegedly a direct quote from Christ. They do not understand that Christ is but a personification of the Life Principle as it enters the planes of Evolution. The qualities gained in the Evolutionary planes are to be held and developed as Divine Wisdom. That is why the line in question, in Chapter two, verse 25 of Revelations, the Life Principle says, "But that which ye have already *hold* fast till I come."

The fact remains that the star groupings and the star's names were never delineated to be used as tools for prophecy, either religious or personal. The Watchers who first charted these constellational groups did so only to present the lessons of Creation/cosmology and life purpose.

With the constellation of Cancer and its subconstellations, the lessons were of the creative actions that take place in the Involutionary Plane which precedes visible matter. The Life Principle at this plane grows denser in energy-substance and it is from here that it will shine

forth as emanations of the Creative Principle. The emanations are the true *Is.Ra.El* which does not refer to any person
or nation, but refers to the "overshadowed people." That
means all of us.

*   *   *

Ursa Major
the Great Bear
the second decanate of Cancer

This is probably the best known of all the constellations due largely to its conspicuous shape which gives rise
to it being popularly referred to as the "Big Dipper," or as in
Britain, the "Plough." There are eighty-seven stars in this
arbitrary group. Out of these there are seven major stars
which outline the "dipper" shape. They are so complimenta-
rily matched in luminosity that the constellation is easily
and quickly recognized. Another factor contributing to
familiarity with this group is that Ursa Major never sinks
below the horizon in latitudes higher north than forty
degrees.

This second subdivision of the Cancer confederacy is
known to us today by the Latin name, Ursa Major, meaning
"Great She-Bear." From this have come the modern celestial
charts depicting the constellation with the hieroglyph of the
"Great Bear." Some scholars have suggested the Greek
interpretation of this constellation as a Bear sprang from
some confusion in association with the name Dubah, the
brightest star in the group. There are other reasons for the
Greek interpretation of this constellation being symbolized
by a bear, as was noted in the previous decanate. Bears
symbolize the basic passions which activate life. The Greeks
referred to this constellation as Arctos, and sometimes as
Hamaxa, meaning the "wagon."

In Roman times this constellation was sometimes
referred to as Septentriones, meaning the "seven plowing

oxen." The seven major stars being referred to as "plowing oxen" contributed to the pattern of stars being known as the Plough in Europe. Among the Hindus the seven major stars represent the seven *rishis* -- the holy ancient sages.

Of the seven stars constituting the bowl-shape, six are of the second magnitude and one is of the third magnitude. Two of the second magnitude stars forming the "dipper" wall opposite the "handle" point directly to the Pole Star, or North Star. For more than three thousand years these two stars have been called "the Pointers" by navigators. For the past five thousand years the pole star has been Polaris, otherwise known as alpha Ursae Minoris.

The brightest star in this group is named Dubah or Dubhe, which translates as "herd of animals," or "a flock." This name reaffirms the lesson material given with both the first and second decanates of Cancer. The Arabic name for this constellation, Al Naish or Annaish, means "to gather together," as animals are gathered together in a sheepfold.

The names of other stars in this group still whisper of the original intent when they had been named in association with the Creation Lessons presented with the Zodiac of Constellations. Most of these names were not understood by the religious mythographers of western cultures, and so names bearing the same meanings were retained. To the Watchers this star group represented *the assembly of energies for spirit's descent into matter-form.* This is still echoed today in names such as Benet Naish, from Arabic, meaning "daughters of the assembly." Daughters, female reference, symbolize substance. This same star is also called Al Kaid, meaning "the assembled."

The second brightest star in this constellation is known in Hebrew as Merach, meaning "flock." In Arabic this star's name translates as "purchased," suggesting the temporary forfeiture of spirit for the purpose of acquiring dense-matter experience. Other names also suggest references to a multitude, assemblage, flock, herd, redemption, company of travelers, coming and going, and similar lesson association.

At the point at which the handle of the dipper bends

is located the star known as Mizar or Ursae Mapris. Mizar is one of the earliest double stars known, and consists of two components having magnitudes of 2.4 and 4 respectively. The name is from Arabic *mi'zar* which means "cloak" or "veil."

In the lessons of Creation/cosmology this sub-constellation of Cancer taught of the assembling astral energies in readiness for their entry into the next plane of Etheric Matter. At the next plane matter-form reaches its first visible or luminous form, but is not yet dense-matter. The actions and energies taking place in this Astral Matter plane still are not what could be termed as being *qualified*. They are still amoral creative processes and nothing more.

For this reason the Watchers symbolized this constellation as the Greater Sheepfold. The prominent squarish bowl shape seen in the heavens was held as symbolic of the enclosure from which the flocks go out from the fold. It is from this plane that all substance-matter expressions descend to enter into their individual or self-aware entity-form.

Of course religions have attempted to use this star group as prophetic for their propaganda. These stars do not announce some prophecy of a savior gathering his flock, as some proclaim. The Life Principle is active on the Involutionary plane gathering and activating energies into combination where they will be discharged into visible form at the Etheric Plane. Neither do these stars testify, as others suggest, a covenant giving Israel, the nation, the rights to the region of Palestine.   The celestial forms and star names do not speak of any ego-god's promise, and this constellation is not successfully reworked this way.

*   *   *

Argo

or Arco, the Ship
the third decanate of Cancer

We know this southern constellation as Argo from the Greek legend where the ship Argo was used by Jason and the Argonauts in their quest for the Golden Fleece. In legend the Argo was said to have set in its prow a beam cut from the divine speaking oak tree of Dodona which held the power to foretell the future.

The Golden Fleece is symbolic of Creative Ideation taught with Aries whose hieroglyph is the Ram. Jason is the Life Principle and his shipmates, twelve in number, symbolize the Patriarchal Principles which set out upon the deep to fulfill the ideation of life. This is regarded as only myth, but Jason is identical to Moses, Jesus and other scriptural characters.

The Argo constellation is exceptionally large, extending north almost as far as the equator, and south almost as far as the Pole. This constellation sometimes had parts of its mass named in accordance with parts of a ship. In modern celestial charts astronomers have tended to follow this example and broken down the huge grouping into several smaller ones which have retained the names of ship parts. Now considered as separate constellations in their own right we have Puppis, meaning "the stern;" Carina, meaning "the keel," Pyxis, meaning "the binnacle;" and Vela, meaning "the sails" All these were originally included in the total Argo constellation.

Argo, the last decanate of Cancer, represents the final substance-energy concentration as Astral Matter from which spirit-soul is launched into the experience of matter-form. The Watchers taught with this hieroglyph of the *multitude* of in-coming (Involutionary) travelers. The name for this constellation reflects this teaching, for it means "company of travelers."

Star names, as usual, give us clues of the original intent of the constellation lessons. The star name Sephina, for example, translates as "the multitude" or "abundance."

The star name Asmidiska means "the released to travel."
Canopus -- or Canobus -- means "possession of him that
comes." Other star names echo these meanings.

With the Argo lesson was expressed the preservation
of individuality. Self-awareness now arises to direct its
experience as densifying form. At this point all primordial or
unqualified energies are left behind, gone with the primordial flood, as it were. With this understanding we can see
that the lesson given with this constellation is the source of
all the world's "Ark" stories, such as the Ark of Noah and the
Deluge that bore him *to the peak of matter.*

Argo symbolizes the preserving vessel of spiritual
things -- *qualified elements* -- which are to be carried into
their matter fulfillment. There was never any historical
person who built an ark at the direction of god. There was
never any world-drowning deluge from which only one man's
family survived. The flood upon which the in-coming travelers were/are borne were/are the waters (energies) of life. In
cosmology understanding this is the all-inclusive planetary
genes just beginning to form as visible matter. Planets are,
in turn, the "ark" of all life forms.

The scriptural "Flood" of Noah is only allegorical. It is
symbolic of Creative Consciousness riding upon the violent
aspects of the world's creation. To give added evidence that
this is only myth, the name Noah is taken directly from the
Chaldean word *Nuah* which served to identify the third
person of the Chaldean Trinity as well as the third sign of
their Zodiac.

The forty days and nights of flooding during which
Noah and his family were safely preserved in the Ark
represent the four prephysical planes from the "flood"
source, the Aquarius lesson. These are Creative Consciousness taught with Pisces, Creative Ideation taught with Aries,
Creative Energy taught with Taurus, and Mental Matter
taught with Gemini. These bring us into the Astral Matter
plane where the "flood" recedes leaving matter to be exposed
upon the Etheric Plane as visible matter.

Adding zeros to disguise their source material was a
common practice with scriptural mythmakers. The Flood

coming forth in Noah's "six hundredth year" (Genesis 7:11) brings the Life Principle into the Astral Matter plane, to the boundary of the sixth plane, the Etheric Matter Plane, subject of the next Zodiacal lesson given with Leo.

A different presentation of this constellation was used in the Egyptian temple at Dendera. There the hieroglyph was of an Ox from whose neck was suspended a cross. It must be stressed again that the cross symbol, from time out of mind, was the symbol for matter. It was never, as Christians interpret it, a symbol of immortality and life. In the Egyptian interpretation this constellation as the Ox, active Genetic Energy is symbolized. It is agreeably depicted as in the process of taking upon its neck its Etheric Matter form.

*   *   *

A Visit to Sodom and Gomorrah

Here at the close of the lesson on the Astral Matter plane we are poised upon the next lesson in Leo concerning Etheric Matter. The lessons have brought us down through the Involutionary planes, and with the next plane will deliver us to the plane of visible matter. Without even knowing it you have visited "the Cities of the Plain" mentioned in Genesis. You have visited Sodom and Gomorrah.

Sodom and Gomorrah have been used by religionists to fan hatred, misunderstanding, prejudice and absurdity for thousands of years. The truth is that the "Cities of the Plain," mentioned in the book of Genesis, never existed in the southern portion of the Dead Sea. They never existed anywhere on this planet. They were used by priest-mythographers as a camouflage device for the Involutionary planes. Where do we read of them? In Genesis. Who is the star of the story in which these Cities are mentioned? Abram, who personifies the Life Principle on his its way to Egypt, matter.

Sodom comes into the story by means of a subplot which involves Abram's "nephew", Lot. Both Abram and Lot personify the Life Principle, which is why their "seed" must be saved--at any cost. The name Lot is from the Hebrew, and it translates in meaning "wrapping." The Life Principle is being wrapped by the energies at each Involutionary plane to take on matter-form.

The city of Sodom was said to be "east," and Lot is said to have traveled "east" to reach Sodom. In all occult Creation/ cosmology accounts "east" always means *toward matter.*

Lot is interwoven with the Abram story, and he dwells in Sodom. Abram fights the kings of Sodom and Gomorrah, the prephysical planes of Astral Matter and Mental Matter. The royal wars involving "four kings with five" simply mean that the lower planes of Involution are wiped out as substance moves toward matter. The Life Principle must "fight" through the five prephysical planes to reach Dense Matter. The five Cities of the Plain are named as Admah, Zeboiim, Gomorrah, Sodom, and Zoar. These are in reference to the Involutionary planes of Creative Ideation, Creative Energy, Mental Matter, Astral Matter, and Etheric Matter.

Sin, the priestly excuse for everything, is claimed to be the reason for the destruction of Sodom and Gomorrah. The reason favored most by religionists for the destruction of Sodom was that its citizens were addicted to anal intercourse. The idea speaks more of priestly obsession than anything else. It was not wrongdoing which brought down Sodom and Gomorrah, it was the natural involvement of energy forming as substance. The city of Zoar was declared to have been spared. Zoar represents the next plane of Etheric Matter and Abram, at that point of the story, has not yet passed through it. When the Lower or matter planes come into formation, then the former Involutionary models are erased. The "cities" are destroyed.

Forewarned of Sodom's destruction, Lot asks of god, "...Behold now, this city (Zoar) *is* near to flee unto, and it *is* a little one: oh let me escape thither, (*is* it not a little one?) and my soul shall live."

At the time for Sodom's destruction, Lot fled from the burning city with his wife and daughters. We understand that it was the Life Principle with elementary substance. Lot's wife goes unnamed in the scriptural tale because she personifies only elementary substance which is left behind at the Astral Plane. She looked back and was turned to a pillar of salt. Some serious students have even theorized that this was due to an atomic blast. Atomic elements are involved, but not for bombing. The two daughters represent advanced substance, those elementary particles that accompany the Life Principle to produce matter-forms with consciousness. From this the priests treated the devout with the scandalous story-twist of Lot's incestuous unions with his "daughters."

The last mention of Sodom appears -- where else? -- Revelations. In the wording used there we find added proof to the true meaning of the Sodom symbol. In chapter eleven, verse eight it says, "...the great city which is spiritually called Sodom and Egypt where our Lord was crucified."

Every Christian knows that Jesus was not crucified in Sodom and Egypt. He was crucified on a hill at Jerusalem. Well, they are wrong. Sodom still represents the Involutionary plane where the illusion of matter takes on form, and this is where it crucifies itself upon its destined matter experience. Egypt, as always, symbolizes the Dense Matter plane where the illusion of life is experienced.

*   *   *

And a Visit with the Moon

In ancient cultures the Moon, or Luna, served as a fitting symbol for the enlightened mind. The Moon represented for them the negative or receptive principle which is the means of mental discernment, for neither the Moon nor the mind shed their own light but only reflect what they borrow from a higher light.

Throughout antiquity humankind was commonly symbolized by the Earth itself, for many obvious reasons. In association with the Moon a more intense understanding was offered. Earth in its rotation turns from the Sun, and consequently brings upon itself its periods of non illumination. This seemed symbolic of humankind in its repeated turning away from the Cosmic Intelligence. In turning away, humankind obliged itself to depend upon the reflected light which intellect offers, just as the Moon reflects light offered by the Sun. Without the light of the Sun to give it purpose (visibility), the Moon would be virtually invisible to our sight.

Like the Earth in its turning, half of one's human nature receives illumination while the other half resides in apparent darkness. The enlightened mind perceives its cosmic unity rising above the horizon before it is capable of illuminating humankind's night.

To the Watchers every phenomenon of the visible world held significance which they studied and interpreted. For them, every position of the Moon, just as every feature of Nature, held symbolic expression. The first quarter of the Moon, for example, was seen as having issued from its conjunction with the great illuminary. That is to say, with the fecundating principle of life. Luna thus typified the gestive attributes of Nature, the first quarter representing first growth and the issuance of higher wisdom.

It is for this reason that the crescent Moon was often used on the robes of Pagan-age wizards, priests, and priestesses. Druids are a good example. This is the reason also why it is a symbol of the goddess honored by Witch-Nature covens. This accounts, too, why the crescent Moon is held to be the attribute of Christianity's Virgin Mary, which personified Nature impregnated for spiritual expression on this dense-matter plane.

The crescent Moon being regarded as Mary's aspect was brought into Catholic thought during the Middle Ages. The crescent Moon in its waxing stage had stood as the symbol of the young maiden from the most ancient of times. In Pagan sources the Moon's three phases -- the waxing, full and waning -- served as the receiving representative of intellect, hence it was regarded a feminine aspect. These three phases were commonly presented as maiden, mother, and crone.

The Moon, as a passive receiver, was adopted in ancient times as a goddess figure, and the three aspects became a trinity mystery. This is the triple aspect adored by many in Witchcraft. (True Witchcraft, by the way, is a spiritual respect for all that is natural and not evil or dedicated to Satan as organized religions falsely claimed.) The Moon in its triple aspects came to represent the "Great Mother," and in this capacity was often referred to as the "White Goddess."

Students of ancient cultures often find it curious that the ancients regarded the Moon to be a separate and independent member of the solar family and not merely a satellite of Earth. This is usually shrugged off as ignorance on their part even though the ancient world habitually kept close scrutiny on the heavens. The secret of their regard for the Moon as an independent entity can be found in the oldest known "myth" tablets.

Fragments from Sumerian astrological tablets give an account in mythological style -- with planets personified as gods. These tablets assert that in the formative period of our solar system the densifying mass that was to become our Moon was at that time a planet-to-be in its own right. The account tells of a series of "battles" where an incoming "lord," a large planet (it was made clear that it was not an asteroid or comet) struck the forming planet and broke it in two.

One half of the forming planet was thrust into a new orbital pattern to form as Earth, and the other half became a belt of shattered asteroid material which now occupies the area between Mars and Jupiter. Pretty wild science fiction? Well, the band of asteroids does exist in that area. How did they know?

A satellite of the invading planet interacted with the planet which was destined to become our Moon. The "battle" resulted in the *forming* planet losing its atmosphere and radioactive elements which resulted in its shrinking in size. The drained planet was then thrown from its orbital path to become a companion of Earth, sharing its orbit. Scholars chalk it off to wild imagination. An inquisitive mind will still want to know, how did they know the Moon had no atmosphere?

In Sumerian-Babylonian myths this invading planet came to be known as the god Marduk. The not-yet-formed planet with which Marduk "battled" was depicted as a "monster" due to its being a huge mass of molten, eruptive, gaseous material. The name they gave to this unformed planet was Tiamat. In the epic tale, the planet that was to become our Moon was known as Kingu.

In this mythic account Earth developed from one half of the material left after the break up of Tiamat. For this reason it was said that Marduk established the Earth and the heavens; he was *not* deemed the Creator. The "heavens" was considered to be the celestial regions that lay beyond the band of asteroids. This debris is a line of demarcation which separates the smaller inner planets from the massive and gaseous outer planets. It is from this Sumerian-Babylonian account that the scriptural version has god making heaven and Earth. The scriptural god is cast, erroneously, as Creator. The region of space within the band of asteroid debris is what was referred to when scriptures speaks of "firmament." Heaven is anything beyond the belt of asteroids.

*   *   *

The Interaction of Cancer and Leo

The sign of Cancer, the breast of Celestial Man, is inseparably connected with the action of the heart. The heart is symbolized in the Celestial Man with the next sign, Leo. Cancer, as the Crab, symbolizes the inspiring and expiring functions by which the life stream is aerated and kept pure. The Crab stands as the symbol of this actions for the reason that the whole mechanism of this crustacean is virtually little more than a breathing apparatus.

Seasonally the Zodiacal sign of Cancer dominates July, and in northern latitudes this is Nature's respirational period during which she is absorbing the Life Principle into all her air vessels. The annual period is aptly symbolized, for July is commonly the season of atmospheric disturbances.

*   *   *

The Conjunction of Cancer and Leo

When Creative Consciousness moves from Astral Matter (lesson of Cancer) into the plane of Etheric Matter (lessons of Leo), the invisible energy-elements are transfigured at last into visible form. In planetary formation this is the gaseous stage, not yet solid. Aggregation begins in the gaseous state, adhering to the characteristics of the nuclear synthesis (astral prototype). During the gaseous stage of development the solids and liquids of a planet would be in the form of gas. In this stage the energy being generated causes the forms to be luminous.

From this fact of Creation processes taught with the Zodiac of Constellations we have received a number of scriptural embellishments. Personifications of the Creative Principle, such as Noah and Moses, were said to have been *transfigured* at birth, with the light of their new presence "flooding the whole house." This special light was always a factor of savior birth stories

In Christian myth, Jesus has credited to him as his sixth major "miracle" -- which corresponds to the sixth Involutionary Plane -- his own Transfiguration. Correctly, this should represent the close of the sixth plane action where energy-substance moves into Etheric Matter. He would be shining at his birth. Jesus, at this later point of the myth, is departing dense-matter to be transformed into the Evolutionary Christ. He would not be shining as a Sun at this advanced stage. The myth makers did not understand the Creation processes and so had him shining brightly as a Sun at his *departure* from the Dense Matter plane.

Neither spirit-energy nor the soul essence proceeds into the higher Evolutionary planes as a luminous gaseous entity. That occurs only upon its entry into the Etheric Matter plane.

Leo
The Lion

*the seventh major sign of the Zodiac of Constellations
representing the plane
of Etheric Matter*

The constellation of Leo, Latin meaning "lion," east of Cancer, is the seventh lesson of Creation/cosmology which was given with the Zodiac of Constellations. This is the fifth sign in the life lessons given with the Lesser Zodiac of Signs.

The emblem for Leo is another phallic one. It is no longer the Phallus Erectus of Aries for now, having achieved intended visible matter form, it is flaccid.

We know this constellation by the name of Leo through association with Greek mythology. In that myth Herakles (Hercules) performed the first of his twelve labors, which was the slaying of the Nemean Lion. The name Nemean comes from the name of the valley Nemea in Argolis, Greece which in classical times contained a sacred grove and a temple to Zeus.

Herakles was a divine son of Zeus, a savior figure, who strangled the enormous lion which was terrorizing the valley. It is undefined prephysical elements which are "terrorized." The Lion was said to be the offspring of Echidna and Typhon, and these are the symbols of raw primordial elements. The Lion symbolizes matter form to be taken on, so naturally Herakles wore the pelt of the Lion as proof of his prowess until his death.

This constellation contains the first magnitude star known as Regulus, which means "a pretty king." Another name for this star was Basilicas, implying royal or kingly. Among astronomers this star is more commonly referred to as Alpha Leonis. This star is regarded as the "heart" of the Lion hieroglyph.

Nearly as bright is the star of second magnitude, Denebola, which is known by astronomers as Beta Leonis. The name Deneb comes from the Arabic *dhanab al (asad)*, meaning "tail of the Lion."

Many of the star's names in this constellation speak clearly of the Life Principle's movement toward its intended matter-form. Among them is the star Sarcam, from the Hebrew, which means "the joining." The star Al Giebha, Arabic, means "the exaltation." The star Zosma, located on the Lion's lower spine, means "shining forth."

A curious phenomenon related to this constellation is that there radiates from it swarms of meteors through which the Earth moves in November. These are known as the Leonids. The greatest numbers of these meteor showers occur at intervals of about every thirty-three years. Is it coincidence that this is the same amount of earthly years allotted in Christian myth to the matter-life "ministry" of Jesus, "the king of the Jews"?

The hieroglyph for this constellation, the Lion, has been the same for all peoples and cultures of the world. The Hebrews knew it as Arieh, one of six words for lion in Hebrew, which broadly translates as "lion bringing down its prey." It is from this constellation that one of the mythical twelve tribes was claimed to be the "lion of the tribe of Judah." It is from this constellation also that was derived the characteristics of the mythical David, who was also a "pretty king."

One name in Egyptian for this constellation is Knem, which means "who conquers." The Syrian name for this constellation, Aryo, means "rendering lion." The Arabic name, Al Asad, translates loosely as "the lion comes vehemently." All these names are suggestive of ideation coming into its visible matter form.

In the Lesser Zodiac of Signs, which served as

instruction using Zodiacal signs as components of the
Celestial Man, this sign symbolized the heart and back. The
heart, we know, pumps out the physical streams of life in all
directions to nourish life. Because of this it was said also that
the heart gave life to all the emotions, affections and desires
which feed and sustain spiritual life. It was in this regard
that the Watchers taught that the heart, symbolized by the
lion, nourished and ruled over the "beasts" of emotions,
affections, passions and desires. The phrase "lion hearted"
did not originally mean animal strength and courage, but
meant to imply that one is to be guided by spiritual
understanding in their matter experience.

From these ancient associations the heart has traditionally been regarded as the seat of emotion, desire, passion
and aspiration. It was held that the attitude of the spirit was
also the attitude of the heart and vise versa. The heart organ
was seen as the dominating factor of both physical and
spiritual life, and so is "king." This sovereign function of the
heart dominates the whole of the animal kingdom, and this
is why the Lion has always been known as the "king of
beasts."

From this understanding given with the Leo lesson
where spirit enters its visible matter stage, the lion symbolized the *lust of life.* For this reason mythological and
scriptural figures were often depicted in some life-death
struggle with a lion. This is the meaning in East Indian art
where the Yogi is shown in combat with a lion. This is why
Herakles-Hercules could slay the lion only with his hands
and not some weapon. The meaning of this lesson accounts
for Samson's life-death match with a lion, and why David
took on not one but four lions.

The lion, whose parched thirst has passed into
proverb, is a symbol of the Life Principle which thirsts for the
springs of matter-life. It is not accidental then that the sign
for August, the period of "dog days'" heat when Nature is also
athirst, is given to the Lion. In August the Sun descends upon
the standing grain, its heat bursting every fetter and casting
forth with the ripened seed another cycle of ideation into
form.

It is in the Zodiacal sign of Leo, representing the formation of Etheric Matter, that all visible physical form begins. From this understanding we received all the legends that speak of the Age of the Lion, or the Heart Age, where, mythically speaking, was brought forth all the "deathless" gods of yore. It is with those actions also, represented by this sign, where originated the Is.Ra.El which signifies "the overshadowed people." That is to say all human life.

In the greater Zodiac of Constellations, Leo marked the unfoldment of the Creation process as it moves from Astral Matter into Etheric Matter. It is at this point where spirit must temporarily "die" in order to enter the Dense Matter plane to begin its qualification procedures. Spirit prepares itself at this visible point with the task of putting on form -- or "takes up its cross" of dense matter experience.

The lesson of Leo taught of life assuming its visible matter form. This is the means of taking on matter form whether it is planetary, organic, inorganic or life form. It is built up out of planes of gathered energy. The submerged energies of spirit are temporarily submerged, and will be eventually reclaimed -- or in religion's vernacular it is to be "redeemed" when spirit consciousness continues into the Evolutionary planes.

Leo, representing spirit-ego's movement into Etheric Matter with all the unfolding possibilities of matter form, is *figuratively the maker of matter.* In Leo's cosmological instruction was taught the actions in the Etheric Plane which literally brought prephysical elements forth as the "light of the world." This lesson gave instruction on the formation period, the gaseous stage in planetary formation, which announces itself to matter by radiating light. The Sun is an example. It is not now anywhere near being a dense matter form, but someday, eons away, it will be.

It is this self-radiating light-to-be-form which was first personified as Lucifer. The name is from Latin *lux, lucis,* meaning "light," and *ferre,* meaning "to bring." This is the same light that such biblical characters as Noah, Abram, Moses and Jesus allegedly manifested at their birth. Usually though, because this light announces visible matter, priest mythographers personified it as an evil being. Later the name Lucifer was applied to the new light of the new planet Venus when it appeared as the morning star. Technically, Lucifer in both cases is the Son (Sun) of the Morning -- or *first perceived light.*

The first light of matter-form is the point where religionists abandon all reason. This is the *necessary* stage for the qualification of Lower self so it may advance into Evolutionary purpose as refined self-aware consciousness, but it is viewed as unequivocally evil in religious concept. The reference to Lucifer in Isaiah 14:12 is a prime example of misinterpretations and erroneous deductions. It reads, "How art thou fallen from heaven, O Lucifer, son of the morning! how art thou cut down to the ground, which didst weaken the nations!"

This was a direct statement regarding the then-new planet Venus which no longer "raised hell" on Earth. Biblical scholars, ignorant of the part the planet Venus played of world affairs, decided that Lucifer was used figuratively for the king of Babylon, but was misunderstood as a fallen angel. The name Lucifer then passed from there into tradition as a name for the imagined devil.

In Christian myths this same stage of Creation, first visible light form, was personified as Jesus' loving disciple John.

*   *   *

The outermost planets of our solar family -- Jupiter, Saturn, Uranus, Neptune and Pluto -- are composed of lighter elements than the chemical components of the innermost planets -- Mercury, Mars, Earth and Moon. The exception is Venus which is not, comparatively speaking, in their solid weight classification, being more gaseous than the other inner planets.

The outermost planets are repositories of hydrogen, helium, methane, ammonia, and even water vapors. In a real sense, these planets are nearer in composition to the universe at large than are the more densely compacted inner planet forms. This fact seems to stand as a visible confirmation of the lessons from the Zodiac of Constellations. The outermost planets illustrate the stages or planes of development. The planets are not fully developed but have within themselves all the elements needed for the production of organic molecules. In other words, they are not yet fully involved but hold the potential to produce life-elements.

The Sun is *the Etheric consciousness* of our planetary family-group. It is itself the active, gaseous hub of stupendous primal energy. Just as we, as individual points of self-aware consciousness, have the Astral and Etheric Matter in our Dense Matter form, so too does the unit of our planetary family. These planes of energy can be seen in the panorama of space which is not evident in viewing ourselves. This shows that the Earth and the denser planets are more involved (older) than the Sun. This means the Earth is older than the Sun.

Unscientific? Blasphemy? Not at all. Even the elementary biblical account of Creation based upon the lessons of the Zodiac says that Earth was made before the Sun. Look it up. Genesis 1:9-10, "dry land" appears and "God called the dry land Earth..." This was the "third Day" of Creation. Not until verse 14 through 19 is the creation of "two great lights," one being the Sun, accounted for. This was the "fourth Day." The Sun is in its Etheric Matter form. The Earth is in its Dense Matter form.

The Sun as the Etheric consciousness of our planetary family-group, radiates its aura out to embrace the whole planetary group. The solar system exists within what could be termed a bubble of turbulent gas which the Sun spews out at a rate of a million miles per hour. This turbulent gas is what is called "solar winds." Its field of influence extends out to beyond the orbital range of the planet Pluto, our solar family's outermost planet. This field of influence -- or the heliosphere -- does not diminish gradually as its turbulence reaches the outer edge. It ends -- or more precisely *confines itself at a distinct boundary*. This boundary is defined by the impact of the solar winds and the Sun's magnetic field upon the interstellar gases and magnetic field. It is beyond this aura-boundary that true interstellar space begins.

Our solar system, in the true sense, makes up a body -- *a living body* -- within which we are each a necessary living part. All the ancient Pagan cultures believed the universe to be a living thing. We see now, they were right.

Like the Sun, all living things have an aura, an emanation of light-energy about them. This is not mystical nonsense, science knows that there is a field of energy which surrounds every material thing. This aspect of matter-form is not ignored in scriptural story either.

Probably the most famous bit of men's apparel in any literature is the strange "coat of many colors" given to Joseph by his father Jacob-Israel. Bible students have always puzzled over this special "garment," wondering such mundane things as was it made of wool? Was it fashioned in stripes of color or was it made in a patchwork method? Once again the story elements are taken literally and students of scripture are blind to allegory.

To take the story literally raises a sticky problem. The time setting generally given for this alleged historical being is c. 1700 B.C.E. The problem is that in that time the Hebrews knew of and used only about three dyes, those being indigo, purple and scarlet. This fact shows conclusively that the "coat" in question was not in reference to some handmade fabric.

Joseph personifies the Life Principle at the Etheric Matter plane on its way toward the Dense Matter plane which is symbolized as Egypt. The meaning of the name Joseph gives additional clue to what the coat symbolized, for Joseph means "he shall add." In cosmological terms Joseph personifies the *forming planetary aura* which occurs following the Astral Matter plane in the formation of stars and planets.

The famous "coat of many colors" is only occult terminology for the Involutionary stage where the many-hued aura *displays its intended or destined matter form.* The

story-plot of Joseph's brothers, who symbolized the Patriarchal Principles, selling Joseph into "slavery" and bound for
Egypt, is standard occult story form. *This* is what is claimed
as "history" of the Hebrew-Jews.

*   *   *

It was not the intent to dwell at length on any of the
fictional biblical characters such as Abraham, Moses,
David, Solomon or others. This cannot be avoided, for the
belief that they were all real historical beings has played an
inordinate role in shaping religious thought. In turn this has
shaped world policy.

Here, with the lesson of Leo, some of the biblical
characters who either are at the visible-matter plane or who
personify the Sun will be touched upon.

In the story of Moses approaching the Involutionary
stage of visible matter formation there is given a sly twist to
the plot. Moses comes upon the "burning bush," which
"burned with fire, and the bush was not consumed." From
this bush god, the Creative Principle, spoke to Moses and told
Moses what was expected of him. He was to go into Egypt
-- symbol of Dense Matter -- and bring forth the "Children
of Israel" (the overshadowed people) out of Egypt. The
"burning bush" is the first light of visible matter. What is
meant by god's instruction is that Creative intention must
be delivered into the Evolutionary planes where it will be
qualified. The Evolutionary planes are where is accomplished the release from "bondage" in matter.

The story of Joshua, the alleged successor of Moses,
is neither historical nor a sequel to Exodus. The book is but
a parallel story with the same subject -- the delivery of the
Life Principle into the bondage of matter. In this version
Joshua is the personification the Life Principle at the visible
matter plane, and in this understanding he was originally
honored as a solar deity among pre-Judaic Hebrew tribes.
Because Joshua was a personification of the Sun, it is

understandable that he alone accompanied Moses up the
mountain. It is understandable that he is credited with
stopping the course of the Sun. The highlights of the Moses
tale are duplicated by Joshua, from parting waters (this time
its the Jordon) to leading the people into their battle with
matter. It is from the name Joshua (Hebrew, Yehoshua) that
the name Jesus was derived.

One more example is Solomon, the alleged son of
David. This one requires a bit more detail. The name Solomon
is derived from the Roman *Sol*, meaning "Sun," combined
with the Hindu *Om* (or *Aum*), a mantra characterizing the
Supreme Power, and the Chaldean-Egyptian *On*, always
associated with the Sun.

The books of I and II Kings were not penned in the age
when Solomon allegedly lived. These books were written
centuries after the alleged events by the scribe of Jeremiah
(the prophet was himself illiterate). The scribe's name was
Baruch ben Nerian, and his sources for I and II Kings' stories
were other than genuine Hebrew or Jewish history.

There are no records or documents from any nation of
the presumed time of Solomon's life that ever mentioned him.
If we are to believe the scriptural tales, however, "...all the
kings of the Earth sought his presence" (Chronicles 9:23).
The time of Solomon is routinely given as being c.972-c.932
B.C.E., placing him slightly ahead to the age of Homer and
Hesiod. Strange to say neither of these widely read Greek
poets of historic events ever devoted so much as a line to
Solomon. Neither did Herodotus (484?-425? B.C.E.) who is
regarded as the "father of history." This is a peculiarly blind
oversight if Solomon had been a genuine worldly influential
person. On the other hand, to be fair, Herodotus never
mentioned the Jews as a people either.

All evidence shows that this "richest and wisest of all
kings" obviously was not an historical Jewish king. What we
read in scriptures is a fictional "history" tacked upon Zodiac
lessons where Leo rules as king over matter. The Sun is Leo's
orb of authority over this planetary system -- its Etheric
Consciousness. It is only in terms of a solar hero that this
scriptural character makes sense.

The name of Solomon's mother is given as Bathsheba, the one David loved to spy upon in her bath when she was the wife of someone else. *Bath* means "daughter" (substance); *Sheba* means "seventh," and seven happens to be the plane of visible matter, Leo's concern. The name Sheba is a direct borrowing from a Hindu book of poetry, the **Maharharata**, circa five hundred years before our common era. All of the proverbs attributed to Solomon came from similar sources. Later in the story Solomon is said to have brought the Queen of Sheba into his house. This means the Creative Principle brings its intention (substance) into the seventh plane -- into Etheric Matter, its first visible form.

Solomon is credited with enjoying innumerable wives and concubines -- 700 wives and 300 concubines, if you believe the tale. What mortal man could enjoy all that sensual privilege and still retain wisdom? Understood for what it is, the tale makes sense. Solomon, the Sun, symbol of primal energy in visible form, can cover all substance without exhaustion. The scribe Baruch ben Nerian modeled the Solomon story upon the god Krishna of India who also had innumerable wives and concubines (twice the amount of Solomon's). In the Krishna tale, as in all occult symbology, females symbolize substance, that is to say, material elements. This *must* unite with genetic principle to bring form to the physical world. This fact of the Creation process is what is claimed as Jewish "history."

The story continues that Solomon's heart (symbol of Leo in the Celestial Man) turned from spiritual to material devotion. This is the lesson of Leo. The priest-mythographers, of course, pronounced this to be an "evil" event. Even so, the Lord continued to love Solomon -- in spite of acts of murder, fratricide and other assorted gross "sins." So much did god love Solomon that he even commissioned Solomon to build a "holy temple."

Solomon's temple is another myth and myth only. This is clear by the assertion that it was a "temple not made with hands, eternal in the heavens." What we have here is the ancient Zodiac lesson being reworked as "historical" happenings. Solomon personifies the Sun, Leo's emblem, and this "rules" over the Etheric Matter plane where primal energy comes into visible form. This story is occult cosmology, so the Sun -- Solomon -- is figuratively the planetary maker. The "temple" that is being built is therefore the Earth itself, and not some insignificant little edifice in Judea.

The temple of Solomon is said to have taken seven years to build (Creative Consciousness moving through the seven Involutionary planes). Solomon's own house, on the other hand, took thirteen years to build. Does this mean that Solomon regarded himself better than the Lord? No. This is occult cosmology, not history, so the reference is to the cosmic house. "His" house means the Creative Principle. The cosmic house means all the combined creative planes of Involution and Evolution. Together these comprise thirteen if the physical plane is counted only once. The "temple" is the Earth being created, and represents only one half of the cosmic house, the Involutionary half of Creation.

The details of the temple's building (as in I Kings 7:32-33) are but disguised Zodiacal-astrological references which are presented as specific dimensions of the temple. Solomon's temple is Involutionary fulfillment of cosmological matter -- the Earth. This is why the priestly myth goes on to say "Satan came also" standing on Solomon's porch. Since Baruch ben Nerian based this story on the Hindu god Brahama, Solomon is presented in the part of Brahama the builder and then in the part of Siva, the destroyer.

Solomon's fantastic wealth is only natural when it is understood that he personifies the Sun. According to I Kings 10:14, "Now the weight of gold that came to Solomon in one year was six hundred threescore and six talents of gold." This adds up to the occult number 666. This is regarded as being god's number, since it is the Hebrew letter *yod* (god) repeated three times as a trinity mystery. (So now you know what the beast 666 in Revelations is; it is *god*.)

In historical terms the riches attributed to Solomon defy all logic. Six hundred and threescore and six talents of gold would weigh in at approximately five and one fifth tons of pure gold a year. By today's value this yearly take would be in the neighborhood of something like sixty four million dollars. Not likely. Most of this wealth is credited as coming from King Solomon's mines. For generations adventurers have searched in vain for these mines. They have never found them because they are only occult symbols for the benefits of the Sun.

Legend says that Solomon gained much of his wisdom from the **Book of Raziel**. This "book" is declared to have been a collection of astrological secrets cut on sapphire which had been kept by the angel Raziel. Jewish tradition has it that the Book of Raziel was given by the angel to Adam, and had been handed down through Noah, Abraham, Jacob, Levi, Moses, Joshua, and finally Solomon. The concept of a divine book upon which was revealed cosmic secrets was an idea shared by many peoples of the ancient world. The legends are obviously based on reactions of the celestial book, the Zodiac, with which the Watchers had once taught the lessons of Creation/cosmology.

The final comments on Solomon is in regards to the "Star of David," also known in magic circles as the "Seal of Solomon." This consists of two equilateral triangles superimposed upon or interlocked with each other to form a six-pointed star. This emblem of Judaism is taken from the ancient lessons on Involution and Evolution taught with the Zodiac lessons. The downward pointing triangle was used in the ancient lessons as the symbol for the Involutionary planes. The upward pointing triangle was used as the symbol for the Evolutionary planes. With the points of the triangle symbols touching, the whole Creation process was indicated.

This figure was often displayed in a shorthand version which looked like the figure 8. This was used all around the world as symbolic of eternity.

The overlapping of the two triangles symbolizing the planes of Creation and fulfillment was used as a kind of summation of Creation and its purpose. This was the meaning of the "Star of David" and the "Seal of Solomon" -- ultimate fulfillment of purpose which is Divine Wisdom. This "star' belongs to the Zodiac lessons which explained with stars the purpose of Creation.

*   *   *

Hydra
the Water Serpent
the first decanate of Leo

The long, slender, winding constellation known to us today as Hydra is from the Greek which means "water serpent." The constellation is depicted in charts as a dragonlike serpent with its head near Canis Minor, and its tail some one third distance across the southern heavens, pointing toward Libra. It is with the lessons of Libra where the experience in matter-senses is "weighed" for evolutionary advancement. Pictured as riding upon the Hydra's back, side by side, are Leo's other decanate constellations -- Crater (the Cup) and Corvus (the Raven).

Hydra is located almost entirely within the southern hemisphere of the heavens. Its northern extremity crosses the celestial equator between Canis Minor and Cancer. Its brightest star is Alphard, from Arabic *al fard*, meaning "the solitary one." It is a second magnitude star located just south of the celestial equator.

The ancient Watchers regarded the Hydra's head as symbolic of awakening self-awareness -- or self love and the many issues that such self-regard can cause. The hieroglyph of the Hydra in association with the constellation Leo served as the lesson regarding the multifarious issues of the heart. The Hydra appearing on the horizon served to illustrate the submergence of spirit within the delusions of the forming physical senses.

In Greek myth the Hydra was a monster that ravaged the country of Argos, and it dwelt in a swamp near the well of Amymone. The Hydra had nine heads (some versions vary from nine to one hundred heads), and whatever ones were cut off two more grew in its place. The central head was immortal. Herakles had to destroy the Hydra as the second of his twelve labors. He did so by having his friend Iolaus sear the neck stubs of the heads with a firebrand after Herakles had cut off the heads. The immortal head was also cut off and buried under a great rock (matter-Earth). Herakles used the blood of the Hydra to tip his arrows which made the wounds inflicted by them incurable.

The Hydra is a water serpent. The waters are the energies of creation and life, and the serpent at this point represents the lower mind. It is the lower mind which expresses the desire impulses in the hu-man being, which is only slightly removed from bestial instinct. These ride upon and within the primal energies. This meant to show that wisdom is seeded to develop and to mutate the hu-man soul above beasthood. The potential for higher purpose is presented, but at this early point is not made manifest.

This constellation did not escape being used for scriptural myths or "gospel" tales either. It is this constellational hieroglyph, for example, which is referred to as "the Great Dragon, that old Serpent, called Devil and Satan, which deceiveth the whole world" (Revelations 12:19). "The whole world" is, at this point, just coming into visible matter form, and is the point where religion insists "evil" entered. The Hydra and Draco, third decanate of Sagittarius and the true Dragon of Zodiac teachings, are mixed up in Revelations and presented as synonymous. Of course this perverts everything.

It is from the formation of prephysical elements into visible matter that we received the scriptural fiction of the "chief angel," Satan, falling from grace and who "kept not his first estate." Prephysical substance is the "first estate" of all matter. To fulfill Involutionary form and Evolutionary purpose, the "first estate" cannot be kept. There could never be any Evolutionary advancement. Priests in their cunning used this as their meal ticket by declaring free will was used to "rebel" and humankind had to be saved from the "sins" of that rebellion. Their hobgoblin Satan-Devil-Lucifer had been the first to "rebel" and was responsible for leading all humankind into evilness and "sin."

The Hydra as symbol of the developing material senses was refashioned as the scriptural serpent who "seduced our first parents." Religion's conclusion, of course, is that these natural sense-perceptions symbolized by the Hydra, are passed on in our species as "inherited sin."

The Serpent, as we have already noted, stood as a

symbol for higher wisdom throughout all the ancient world. The Hydra, as a *water* serpent, is Creation-wisdom using creative energies in matter formation. The means for acquiring wisdom of the higher self can only be achieved through the experience of the physical senses. There is nothing evil about this. It is the wisdom of the amoral Creative Principle coded into the hu-man species. This is the only way by which spirit can be propelled through the matter planes to achieve the wisdom needed to advance into the Evolutionary planes.

The Hydra is an incredible symbol of the life-force entering the first stages of its eventual matter-form. It is not coincidence that this hieroglyph bears a striking resemblance to the microscopic "serpent" of the male germ -- the spermatozoon (sperm cell). It is the sperm cell that activates the egg of life in all the animal kingdom, including humankind.

The Hydra, the symbolic sperm cell of all matter creation, is the figure mystically alluded to as "the worm that never die" That this was more honestly presented in antiquity (as opposed to the "source of sin" version of priest-religions) is seen in their Serpent myths. In Egypt the Creator- Serpent, Kneph, produced matter and life by encircling a vessel of water and breathing upon the water. In Buddhist myth the Creator-Serpent, Naga, is depicted as having seven heads, indicating the seven planes of Involution. On the other side of the world the Mayan Naacl version presented the Serpent of matter-creation as also having seven heads, and with fierce determination guarded its eggs of germinal life. To further prove the worldwide knowledge of this Zodiacal lesson, the name of the Mayan Naacl Serpent was identical to the Buddhist's -- Naga.

With this Hydra lesson, the Watchers reminded us again of the source and cause of all Creation, Divine Consciousness. That Consciousness has encoded itself in all things, but is mixed with higher purpose in the hu-man species. Divine Consciousness is with us at all times because we are a part of it.

*   *   *

Science now knows that there are two dense groupings of galaxy clusters located in the direction but beyond the constellations of Hydra, first decanate of Leo, and Centaurus, second decanate of Virgo. The center of mass of these superclusters exists in a region estimated at 150 light years from Earth. Our own Milky Way galaxy along with twenty or more galaxies of our group speeds toward this supercluster region, drawn by the gravity exerted from there, at about 370 miles per second. This huge mass which draws us toward it has been dubbed "the Great Attractor." (This information is based on work conducted by Alan Dressler of the Carnegie Institution in Washington, D. C., and Sandra Faber of the University of California at Santa Cruz.)

That the Creation lessons given with the Zodiac of Constellations are rooted in accurate knowledge is further indicated by additional discoveries concerning this celestial region. What studies have revealed is that our galaxy is not flowing directly toward the Great Attractor. Our galaxy is being deflected in a direction roughly coinciding with Virgo. Like the Crab we skitter a little sideways toward the constellation Virgo, and Virgo is itself rushing toward the Great Attractor.

When we remember that the Virgo lessons are concerned with spirit's attraction to its Dense Matter experience, the implications are awesome.

*   *   *

Crater
the Cup
second decanate of Leo

This "cup" which the ancient Watchers suggested with the hieroglyph for this decanate of Leo, bears within it the water-wine of life. It is logical that it should ride upon the back of the Hydra, the symbol of the physical senses of animate life. As a subconstellation of Leo, which taught of the first visible light of energy-matter, this continues the explanation of visible matter creation.

The small constellation Crater lies just south of the celestial equator, and has no bright stars, the brightest being only of the fourth magnitude. The astronomer-geographer Ptolemy is credited with re-introducing it to the constellational line-up. Although small in size the influence of the Crater constellation has been disproportionately large upon myths and legends.

The cup has always symbolized higher fellowship or communion with spirit. In the use of the common cup all class or caste distinctions are lost. The cup served to symbolize that our most common usages hold a double expression, the spiritual as well as the physical. For this reason Mithra, Jesus and all other similar "savior" figures -- personifications of the Life Principle -- were said to have passed the cup to their disciples to demonstrate the communion and fellowship between "higher" and "lower."

The cup is mentioned in the Old Testament at least thirty-eight times, and in the New Testament there are thirty-two references to the cup. A good amount of these refer to the cup as the container of woe and evil because they are based on this Zodiac lesson of the taking on of first visible matter form. The taking on of intended dense matter experience is necessary for the soul's evolutionary advancement, but the priest-class always insists it is somehow wicked or evil. That we are expected to pay *them* to pardon us for being here may be the reason for this interpretation.

Are our souls really being served when we are force-fed such "holy" verses as found in Psalms 11:6? There it says; "Upon the wicked (the spirit entering its dense-matter experience) he (the Creative Principle) shall rain snares, fire and brimstone, and an horrible tempest (the sensual pains of life): this shall be a portion of their cup, and the wine (of life) is red: but the dregs thereof, all the wicked (all the dense-matter plane) of the Earth shall wring them out, and drink them."

Of course we drink them! The whole purpose of spirit's involvement with matter experience would be lost without "drinking" from the cup of life (experiencing with the five senses).

Other examples from biblical interpretation can be found in Revelations 14:10 where it refers to this constellational lesson as "...the cup of his (the Creative Principle's) indignation." The *amoral* Creative Principle is incapable of being indignant. Rationality is never the forte of religionists so it goes on in 16:19 "...the cup of wine (life) of the fierceness of his wrath..." We are supposed to believe that the pains of life experienced through the physical senses is all bound up with an angry god.

In the New Testament myths Jesus , the personification of the Life Principle, is quoted as saying, "...take this cup from me..." The Life Principle would never consider such a thing. Although in this part of the story Jesus is facing his sacrifice, it is not death of physical matter that is being alluded to. It is self-aware consciousness taking on its intended physical matter form. This is the crucifixion of the spirit *upon its intended matter form.* The whole process is being told backwards. The reference is to the cup filled with the waters (or wine) of sometimes painful matter life.

About one thing the priest-class is right. *We need deliverance.* But it is not from "sin," it is from their dedication to keeping us all in ignorance.

In Christian tradition the cup or chalice has been used as the attribute of the "beloved" disciple of Jesus known as John. John personifies light, so he is Leo, and this Leo lesson is what the church knows as a "saint." Because the stars affirm that the sign of Leo contains the chalice (heart) which holds the sacramental wine of life (blood), John the Beloved is given the cup as his attribute.

The Cup -- or the chalice -- is also regarded in Christian legend as the attribute of Joseph of Arimathea (also known as a "saint"). It was often referred to as his "divining cup." The name Joseph means "god will add," so take this story accordingly. Medieval legend had it that Joseph of Arimathea, who gave the body of Jesus a decent burial, was the founder of Christianity in Britain. He allegedly brought the Holy Grail -- used by Jesus at the Last

Supper -- into Britain. Tradition relates that the Holy Grail appears and disappears.

In a similar vein, the cup attribute is also given to Britain's legendary King Arthur where it is also called the Holy Grail.

When it is understood that this "Grail" refers to the cup hieroglyph of Leo's second decanate, the basis of the legends is exposed. It is then understandable why and how this exquisite chalice is caught away to heaven and disappears in a material age.

*   *   *

For thousands of years before our common era, the use of "prophet's herbs" was common. There were numerous plants which could be used singularly or in combination to stimulate clairvoyance, hallucinations, and mental illuminations. Many of the "visions" of the revered biblical "prophets" were induced in just this way.

The use a these "prophet's herbs" generally served in some initiational capacity in the majority of the "mystery" religions such as in the Assyrian, Phoenician, Pelasgian, Samothracian, Phrygian and others. These religions all borrowed from and influenced each other, and it was through the Samothracian influences that the Celtic mysteries were derived. The Celtic Gwyon, for example, was the combined Apollo-Cybele.

What does this have to do with the Holy Grail?

It was noted that initiational potions were common in the mystery religions. In ancient Celtic texts the vessel of Koridwen (meaning the primordial or virgin night) was thought of as containing a mixture (primordial elements) which was known as *greal.*

The composition of this greal, it was said, evoked the *six* colors of the rainbow. This was a symbolic way of saying that both spiritual and energy-substance was developing in concert in the six prephysical planes. Initiatic potions were

considered to be an imitative action of this which aided the
initiate to experience a deeper union with that higher action.

When the more materialistically oriented Christians
moved in to usurp and dethrone the Celtic religion, this was
all seen to be evil. The Celtic understanding of the cosmic
vessel as being the primordial night which contained the
holy greal was reworked as the Holy Grail containing the
blood of Christ -- the Life Principle elevated.

To conquer the "Grail" would be the same as to
conquer Eternal Truth. It would be the attainment of
understanding of the purpose and pattern of Divine Wisdom
which humans tend to view as chaos. This cosmic understanding was reduced through Christianity's influence to
personifications such as King Arthur.

It was through poetry attributed to Taliesin, a legendary Welsh bard said to have flourished in the sixth century,
that the fantasy of a wondrous vessel was presented.
Taliesin, like the biblical characters, is probably a mythical
character around whose name have collected a series of
traditional poems The works do, however, reveal information
that served as an important part of the Druidic religion. The
bard sang of a magic cauldron (primal night) endowed with
miraculous powers (creative force), and which the gods
(elements) endeavored to possess (to use at the Dense Matter
plane).

It was out of Celtic interpretations of these same
bardic tales that Britain received its legends surrounding
King Arthur and his search for the "Holy Grail."

*   *   *

Corvus
the Raven or Crow
the third decanate of Leo

This small constellation, consisting of only nine stars,
is situated just south of the constellation of Virgo. It is
hieroglyphically presented as a Raven riding upon, and

pecking at, the back of the Hydra, the Water Serpent. We know this constellation as Corvus, which is from the Latin and means "raven." In Hebrew it is known as Areb, which also means "raven."

The position and the action of the Raven holds a double meaning. Used in Creation/cosmological teaching the Raven symbolized the Involutionary stage of development where primordial elements are removed -- pecked away -- from forming matter. In this capacity the removal of elemental or primordial energy substance brings matter into form. The Raven marks the courser part of matter -- or total fulfillment into visible matter form. We will touch upon this aspect again soon.

The second meaning was more in keeping with the life lessons given with the Zodiac of Signs. In this use the Raven represented the torment of the physical senses which accompanies matter-life's experience. It is through the physical senses that the developing soul-ego will experience the means of qualifying itself to advance into the Evolutionary planes. The star names in this constellation refer to this prodding and pecking of the physical senses.

The star Minchar al Gorab, Arabic, means "the raven tears to pieces" The brightest star in this group, called Gienah in modern atlases, was known earlier as Al Chiba, which is Arabic and means "the cursed inflicted." These names undoubtedly inspired priestly interpretation that the taking on of matter form was "evil" which brought "sin" with it.

In its association with Leo, which rules over the flow of life, the celestial Raven served not only as representative of that which is the guardian and preserver of humankind, but also represented that which can be humankind's destroyer as well. In this understanding among ancient nations the raven was commonly borne upon the banner of conquerors.

The raven has always been known as a carrion bird. It was seen as capable of flying directly to its prey from afar by means of its acute power of perception. Because of this apparent perceptive ability the raven was regarded as symbolic of the expression of the higher foresight or perception which is of the spirit rather than of mental vision or reasoning. In truth, it was the physical sense of smell which attracted the birds to their carrion prey.

No matter: the ancient world believed there was a great spiritual correspondence in odors, and recognized smell as a potent means of elevating spiritual perception. This is the reason for the common use of incense in many religion's rites.

The raven, it was said, usually destroys the eyes of its prey first. This was regarded by the ancient peoples as expressive of the fact that the surrender of physical vision is generally the first step toward the putting away of animal nature.

Because of the significance placed on the raven by the ancients, it was often incorporated into scriptural tales. The Raven of this constellational lesson is one and the same as the raven which was "sent out" in all the world's Deluge stories. The raven was sent out to see if Earth was yet visible from the (Creation's) receding flood waters. In the Genesis account Noah sends out birds to find land (matter). The dove returned to Noah bearing an olive branch, indicating dense matter is not yet formed although it is in its potential form. The raven which Noah sent out later represented the courser elements, so it did not return (into the Etheric Matter plane).

Another example of raven representing this prephysical stage of development is in the mythical Elijah who was fed by a raven while "in the desert." That Elijah, one of the outstanding figures in the Old Testament, is mythical and not historical is found in his name. Elijah is derived from *Eli* which means "god," and the suffix *jah* signifies "life." His character therefore symbolizes the Involutionary action moving into the Etheric Matter stage of being, the subject of Leo. The "desert" is the same desert or wilderness so many of the scriptural characters got lost in, namely the intermediate planes between Creative Ideation and Dense Matter. The raven in this tale guards and preserves Elijah because it must if spirit is to proceed into the next plane of matter.

What we read of the miracle of Elijah's being fed by the raven is not really a miracle for the sole benefit of some

Hebrew "prophet." It is the miracle which accomplishes all dense-matter form. This is why we read in the book of Elijah 17:6, "And the ravens brought him bread and fish in the morning, and bread and flesh in the evening; and he drank of the brook."

The symbols should be obvious to anyone who has read this far. The "morning" is a clear reference to the earlier planes of Involution. The "bread" is the bread of life, meaning basic energy-substance out of which life arises. The "fish" is the Life Principle activated, as per the Picean lesson. The "evening" is the last Involutionary plane where substance is brought into the "flesh" of the verse. The "brook" is the River of Life.

Birds of prey, all dark and raven-like, have been used routinely in priestly scare tactics when they thunder about godly judgement and punishment for the "sin" of being alive. Black and sinister they accompany the "old serpent, the Devil" as the Raven accompanies Hydra, in their sermons about how a loving god is going to slaughter the world.

This is a complete inversion of the Watchers' lesson which taught of the natural processes that *must* take place in order for matter to come into form. That honest presentation of how matter forms allows humans to come to grips with what they are, but that is not a profitable commodity for hierarchical religions. It was much more fun and profitable for them to terrorize with tales such as in Revelations 19:17-18. There it is declared that birds are summoned for the purpose of clearing away the carnage in the "final scene." Judgement Day is a horror story written by priest-mythographers. The dark, sinister carrion birds are supposed to accompany religion's (loving?) "king of kings, and lord of (war) lords" when he comes to *judge*.

In medieval times the power structure of Christianity began to associate the dark plumed raven with witches and sorcerers, calling the bird their "familiar spirit." It was through such "familiar spirits", it was declared by the church, that witches and sorcerers cast their "devilish" spells.

The Raven, through influence of such church propaganda, continued to be cast as the bird of augury and ill omen well into the Middle Ages. The bird with its black plumage served as a commanding figure to express the interior monitions or presages of evil. Sometimes the monitions or presages of evil can indeed serve as the heart's peculiar faculty of divination.

*   *   *

Leo and the Promised Land

The ancient lessons presented with Leo in the Zodiac of Constellations provided the material out of which was fashioned the scriptural myth of "the Promised Land."

We first encounter the myth of "the Promised Land" in the book of Genesis. This alone should be enough to convey that it is myth, not history. To whom was the Promised Land promised? To Abram -- who has not yet had the letter H added to his name. This is a clue a enormous consequence. In Eastern myths from which the content and the name was borrowed, the addition of the letter H -- as in Brama-Brahma -- indicates the prephysical elements being personified have reached the Dense Matter plane. This means that Abram, personification of the Life Principle, is still within the prephysical planes.

It is the elementary particles moving through the prephysical planes that are symbolized as the "chosen people." Abram, the Life Principle in action, will carry them as his "seed" into the matter plane, "the Promised Land."

This "land" is not holy, either figuratively or histori- cally. It is *matter* which is first made visible at the Etheric Matter plane. It is here that god tells Abram (Genesis 13:14), "..look from the place thou art northward, and southward, and eastward, and westward: (15) For all the land thou seest, to thee will I give it and to thy seed forever." This is *not* the Middle East region of Canaan-Palestine, it is the plane of dense matter formation.

If this land had been the true Canaan-Palestine region

of Earth spoken of here, then god failed the "chosen people" from the start. Genuine history shows that this region has been predominately under the control of others for as long as can be traced. The Hebrews and the Judaic religious influence within the Hebrew tribes held sway here only sporadically.

What is really meant in this Genesis claim is stated often and with minimum illusion. In verse 16, god is still in his soliloquy, saying, "And I will make thy seed as the dust of the earth..." This is occult cosmology, so it actually means the dust of Earth. To take the speech as meaning some historical person's seed is naive. No human being's "seed" could be "as dust of the earth," either in the implied extraordinary quantity or in its composition.

The verse continues, "...so that if a man can number the dust of the earth, then thy seed also be numbered." Prolific as the Hebrews and Jews might be, they could never add up to all the dust of Earth. What is being spoken to and about is the *world*-seed. This means it is Earth itself which is the "Promised Land" of all hu-man life.

The name Canaan is used symbolically, a region known to the mythmakers and regarded as desirable. It symbolizes prolific Earth just as Egypt symbolizes dense matter in other tales. It is upon this *myth* that organized Zionism lays claim to a geographic region of Earth. Anyone with only a smattering of curiosity can discover for themselves that there is no proof in any history records anywhere that this region was ever the ancestral homeland of the Jews.

If we take the scriptural tales literally we have to ponder, if the "Promised Land" was promised to Abram and his "seed" *forever*, why they apparently couldn't hang on to it. Canaan was to be "..an everlasting possession" (chapter 17:8). Nonetheless, we find in a later book, Exodus, that Moses has to struggle to lead his people toward "the Promised Land." What happened? When and why did they lose their "everlasting possession?" The scriptures never say.

The scriptures never say because it is the same story plot -- not a sequence of happenings but a parallel myth of Creation process. Moses in this version personifies the

Genetic Principle -- being Aries -- Phallus Erectus. He makes his Exodus from primordial-prephysical elements to visible matter fulfillment. Moses leads his "chosen people," the elementary particles, to the borders of the "Promised Land." Moses himself cannot enter. He has generated and delivered the intended matter form, so his role is over. The Dense Matter fulfillment is viewed from the Etheric Matter plane and there he "dies." Literalists add, "and to this day no man knows where he was laid to rest." It makes for romantic mystery but we know that Moses represents the elementary ideation of matter form which is burned off as dense matter forms.

The sign of Leo represents the Etheric Matter period which immediately precedes the formation of dense matter. The ancient Watchers understood and taught that this period was, allegorically speaking, the time when the sweetness of life (spirit) was stored for later redemption. This was part of the life-purpose lessons given with the Zodiac of Signs. The spiritual purpose and the qualified attributes developed on the Dense Matter plane are held for Evolutionary use. These constitute the "milk and honey" which is the reward for achieving passage through "the Promised Land."

In cosmology lessons based upon the Involutionary phases of development, Leo presented the lesson of when the planet-to-be accumulates about its prephysical energies its first visible form. We understand this from science as the gaseous elements coagulating as planetary form. For this to be accomplished the finer prephysical energies are placed in reserve, as it were. Through the first six Involutionary planes it is not necessary for prephysical energy to "shed" any of its gathered essence. That bunglesome experience of shedding spiritual energy-essence occurs only at the dense matter plane.

With the entry of prephysical essence into the plane of Etheric Matter, all spiritual and divine knowledge, at this point, can be said to be affirmed. It is this which is the "sweetness" presented to the world. The development of this sweetness becomes the Is.Ra.El, meaning the overshadowed people -- all of us. This is a far cry from the priestly version that it is at this point when "sin" was presented to the world.

♍ Virgo ♍
The Virgin

the eighth major sign of the Zodiac of Constellations
representing the plane
of Dense Matter

The constellation of Virgo, Latin meaning "virgin," is situated south of the "Big Dipper" handle of Ursa Major on the celestial equator. With the hieroglyph figure of the virgin was presented the eighth lesson of Creation by the ancient Watchers.

Virgo contains about 2500 galaxies, and lies at a distance of around sixty-five million light years (20 parsecs) from Earth. By cosmological standards this is close. Virgo is notable for its numerous nebulae, of which more than five hundred have been identified.

The hieroglyph for this constellation is of a maiden who holds a branch in her right hand, and in her left hand she holds some sheaves of wheat -- some say corn. Emphasis is upon the virginity of the maiden, but she is the virgin who is the holder of the seed.

With this depiction the ancient Watchers sought to present a symbol of the primordial night, the virginal void out of which all creation has its beginning. It was understood to be virginal only in that it is primordial. Life energies converge out of the virginal substance, and here is accomplished the completion of Involutionary formation into its matrix of matter.

For a brief time in some locales Virgo was represented by the figure of a unicorn. The unicorn, a mythical animal, has long been a symbol of virginal purity. It was portrayed as never being overtaken and ever eluding its pursuer. It symbolized, therefore, resistance by avoidance; the evasion of the ignorant who would seek to possess it materially. In association with this constellation the unicorn is mentioned in the book of Job 39:9. There it reads, "Will the unicorn be able to serve thee or abide by thy crib?"

The most prominent star in the Virgo constellation is identified in astronomy as Alpha Virginis. For the rest of the world it is better known as Spica, which is a Latin name meaning "ear of grain." In the branch held by the Virgin is the star which the Chaldeans called *Vindermiatrix*, which meant "branch which cometh." Found in this constellation also is Gamma Virgnis, a double star, each of about equal brilliance.

Virgo dominates the month of September, the bearing month in northern latitudes. It is at this time of year that Nature gives of her ripened grains and fruits, those virgin elements which have formed out of Earth's body. These are to enter into the new life of humanity -- eaten -- as principles of energy and action. The cycles of life could be demonstratably understood from the Zodiac lessons in conjunction with Nature's yield. From the cosmic soul symbolized as the winged virgin, is the soul of Nature refueled -- and from the soul of Nature is sparked the soul of humankind.

In ancient times uncluttered with false theologies, the soul was regarded, because of Zodiac symbolism, to be anchored in the abdominal region. This was held to be so because with the functions in this part of the body all the virgin essences are formulated or compounded. The abdominal area was regarded as the secret part of all beings for it is there that is held the hidden and profound functions of matter-life.

Carried further, the Virgin of the Zodiac was seen more complexly as the subtle chemist presiding over the human crucible, as it were. In this laboratory of the body the elements are renewed for the purpose of a more refined spiritual body, for which the soul is constantly yearning and striving.

This is part of the reason why in ancient Egypt the interior organs of the divine kings were removed and preserved separately from the mummified body. The understanding of the abdominal organs as holding profound meaning to life was also the reason why interior organs of animal sacrifices were studied by diviners and augurs.

It is easy to see how this constellational lesson served as the foundation for various religions' myths. The early Jews, who knew this constellation by the Hebrew name Bethulh, meaning "virgin," liked to think that Virgo represented "the Virgin, the daughter of Zion." To seal Judaism's exclusiveness to god "the Virgin, the daughter of Zion" was declared to be the "wife" of Yahweh.

In the Old Testament book of Isaiah the term *Alma Mater*, "Virgin Mother," is presented. Because of this, Christians like to believe that this verse announced, seven hundred years before the alleged event of Jesus' birth, that their savior would be born of a virgin. All of these religious assertions were drawn directly from the lessons of Creation processes presented with the ancient Zodiac. The stars never prophesized a special individual's birth. They do not prophesize an individual's fate.

Like the priest-mythographers of many other religions before them, the Christian founders presented their savior as the "branch" borne by the Virgin. These authors of "gospel" even had Jesus refer to himself as the seed of wheat which needed to fall and die that it attain its proper fruitfulness (John 12:23-24). This is precisely what previous saviors were presented as saying, the Babylonian Tammuz for example. The cult of Tammuz still flourished and was well known in the time of Rome's decline, the time when Christianity was being molded.

Early Christians regarded the Virgin and Wisdom to be closely associated. It was Peter Chrysologos who allegedly presented the idea of the Virgin as the seven pillared temple which Wisdom built for herself. This is found in the book of Proverbs 9:1, where it says, "Wisdom hath builded her house, she hath hewn out her seven pillars..." The seven "pillars" represent the Involutionary planes into and including the Dense Matter plane, as taught in the lessons given with the Zodiac. The Virgin has "hewn" matter form in which the Life Principle radiates as self-aware consciousness.

Although closely associated with Wisdom, the Virgin was not regarded as Holy Wisdom. That was personified as "Saint Sophia." The wisdom that the Virgin represented was the wisdom of the Zodiac lessons which was couched in self-serving religious terms. The Virgin represents the culmination of energy-consciousness descending through the seven planes of Involution, so bears the "wisdom" of matter generation. In other versions this is known as the "seven sorrows of the Virgin." Out of the primordial night -- or the virginal void -- is issued forth the self-aware consciousness in which qualities are to be achieved. Self-aware consciousness must take on wisdom with its matter experience if it is to proceed into Evolutionary being.

What Peter Chrysologos personified, and the church grabbed onto with a vengeance, was the Virgo lesson of matter-form wisdom. Western religions have never understood the Evolutionary purpose the Virgin represents and so has been locked in empirical materialism ever since.

The lessons presented with Virgo in the Zodiac of Constellations taught some facts that modern science came to understand through the mathematical equation of Einstein, $E=mc^2$. Matter is congealed energy. The creative evolution we see as the universe about us could only result within a field which allows propitiously long reaction time. This is the reason for the Dense Matter plane. It is only because of this slow *reaction* time that *intelligent* reaction can take place.

In proto-galactic -- the formative planes -- the protons and neutrons are under incredible gravitational pressure, and it is there that the creation of pure neutron atoms take place. Later, as creative action evolves into the field of a longer reaction time, that is to say in the plane of dense matter, it is in a lesser stellar gravitational pressure that the creation of conventional atoms take place.

Science, in spite of all the honors heaped upon it, still

finds it impossible to account for the emergence of life. Science is at a loss to explain the appearance of elementary substances, the highly dissimilar molecules, which are obviously necessary for life to be activated. The most profound thing science as an instruction can say with any certainty about life is that "the laws of chance cannot account for the birth of life."

This is a round-about way of saying all life has purpose.

Our dense matter universe takes form within the lowest of the cosmic vibratory rates within the electromagnetic spectrum. It is within this spectrum that the congealing process into dense matter is concluded. Energy is brought down from ideation through the intermediate stages of condensation to manifest as matter. What we know as life is electromagnetic energy acting upon a field of consciousness.

The "seed" held by the Virgin is the coded Divine Wisdom within elementary fields of energy which interact to produce a singular field of self-aware consciousness. Science has not yet found how this process occurs. It may be they cannot explain life because they are looking too far back in the sequence of things.

For example, scientists seek the secret of nuclear fusions by concentrating on bombardment convergence of elementary particles which necessitates ever speedier accelerators. Without the core ingredient of slow gravitational pressure taken into account it is improbable that nuclear fusions will be produced in any laboratory. It may be that science is dedicated to the wrong type of convergence just as religion looks to the wrong end of Creation to find god.

We will leave these problems to the religionists and scientists and get back to the Zodiac lessons. In the plane of dense matter we experience the "hard facts" of our own creative thoughts. We register experience at this plane through use of our five senses. These senses are delicate and receptive. In this way we *embrace and enfold* the world about us, for every sense is, basically, a means of caressing the creation around us. This is the means of bringing the outside creation into our *self* and consequently draw wisdom into our consciousness

With Virgo, in the lessons given with the Zodiac of Constellations, was taught the emergence of matter life. It is with life that the forces which condensed as self-aware spirit-consciousness begin their ascension *from* matter.

In Christian myth this intended ascension of embodied spirit from matter into higher Evolutionary purpose is presented as the Assumption of the Virgin. It is annually enacted when the Sun enters the sign of Virgo on August 15th. The Sun's radiance in the celestial region of Virgo obscures the sign for about three weeks. The "Mother of God" is regarded as taken to heaven at that time to be reunited with her soul and her son. The Roman Catholic Church celebrates the Assumption of the Virgin on August 15th.

*   *   *

––––––––––––––––––––––––– **Coma Berenices** –––––––––––––––––––––––––
or Berenices' Hair
the first decanate of Virgo

This is a small compact cluster of stars of the northern sky situated between Virgo and the "tail" of the Great Bear. This constellation contains a coma cluster of galaxies. Coma in astronomy means the nebulous luminescent cloud surrounding the nucleus of a comet. The nucleus and coma together form the comet's head. This is a contributing factor to this constellation's name Coma Berenices, but there is another reason in a play on the Greek word *koma*, which meant "deep sleep." The name by which we know this constellation was not the name by which the Watchers knew it. Perhaps the Greek meaning holds the clue.

We know this constellation as Coma Berenices thanks to the astronomer of Alexandria named Conon. He was from Samos and flourished in the third century B.C.E. The story he presented for naming this constellation had to do with

Berenikes (Berenice) who was the wife of the Egyptian ruler Ptolemy III Euergetes. Her husband had marched off to a military campaign, so in faith of insuring her husband's safe return she placed her shorn-off hair on the altar in the temple at Zephyrium. The offering supposedly vanished in some unknown manner. The explanation of Conon was that it was placed in the heavens as the constellation. (He did not say what Ptolemy III thought of his stubble-headed wife upon his return.)

To the Egyptian faithful of Isis, the name Coma Berenices served as an anagram to veil celestial wisdom from the uninitiated. To them Berenice's Hair meant "bearing Isis' heir." A royal savior birth, Horus, Creative Principle's offspring. The Latin word Coma comes from the Greek word *kome*, meaning hair, but it was also used as a play upon the Greek word *koma*, meaning "deep sleep." What Coma meant to imply in this use was that the action of bringing forth of the infant was not yet complete and Isis was in "deep sleep" and not yet accomplished.

This served as fertile material in Christian myth of the birth of Jesus that is not yet accomplished, but the radiance of its divine intent announces itself as the "Star of Bethlehem."

In the more ancient picturings of this constellation a divine infant was held in the Virgin's arms. The ancient Egyptians referred to this constellation as Shes Nu, which translates roughly as "the desired son." It was upon this that the priests fashioned their child-god Horus.

In Persian and Hebrew representations the male child was called Ihesu. The Greeks called the child Ieza, who was nourished by the virgin goddess of wisdom and righteousness, Athene.

To the Christians this infant became Jesus, a name similar in pronunciation and meaning. So fanatic are some Christians in their faith that they insist the "Star of Bethlehem" appeared out of the constellation of Coma Berenices. Since this constellation taught the bearing forth of the Life Principle in matter, they are at least figuratively correct.

There is a fact behind the Virgo and Coma constellations that give added dimension to the ancient lessons. The matrix and gravitational center of our galaxy lies in the direction of Virgo. This center is estimated to be around forty million light years away from Earth. This gravitational center is believed by astronomers to be a black hole which they think is located at the center of the radio galaxy they designate as M87. This is the most massive galaxy known. From this region there is being spewed out a jet of gases that extend out for an estimated one hundred thousand light years long. The stars in the M87 galaxy are so densely packed and are propelled so fast into the center that it seems to confirm that a field of densifying matter -- or a black hole -- is generated there.

Discoveries in science repeatedly confirm what the ancient Zodiac lessons had taught.

At other times science may be mislead by what they think they see. A case in point concerns the redshift observations and use of the Doppler effect theory. These are used by astronomers as the so-called "key to cosmology," and is extended as proof that galaxies are receding from us and each other at various rates of speed.

It is believed because of the redshift observations that the more distant the galaxy is from us the faster it is speeding away. The Doppler effect theory is that the wavelength of light seems to change in color value according to the movement of the light source. By extension this is held as proof of the "Big Bang" theory of the "beginning" of the universe.

There may be a flaw in their theory, for there is another possible explanation for the changes of observable wavelengths.

What is being interpreted as the galaxies rushing away from each other may well be but an illusion which is caused by observing *old light oscillation frequency*. Science rates these in terms that apply to the light generated around our terrestrial region of today. Particle masses present billions of years ago were radically different than they are at our matter-stage of development. That is the point of the Creation lessons given with the Zodiac of Constellations.

When we turn our telescopes out into space and look upon the extreme-distant galaxies, what we are seeing is the light from those galaxies that was generated billions of years ago but which are just now reaching us. The particle mass that generated that light was of a completely different particle mass than that in which we now exist. Old light does not have the same oscillation frequencies as light being generated at our present plane of density. To compare them to the light generated at our present oscillation frequencies is like comparing apples to oranges.

It all comes back to the belief that this dense matter plane is what constitutes the total of reality. But matter, the Zodiac lessons said, is only an *illusion* of energy. It is only the "reality" of illusion that we represent mathematically in a four dimensional geometry of space-time. While we are in this illusion, the system works and the order of events can be located by use of space and time coordinates. Material particles can then be charted by one dimensional lines.

The concept that what we perceive as matter-reality is only an illusion of energy may seem to some as unreligious or unscientific. It does, however, echo back some information from the Aquarius lessons which taught of the primordial energies at Creation's fountainhead. The lessons were symbolized with dual jagged lines. This represents perfectly the fundamental fact of specialized science, quantum mechanics, that bits of matter and energy sometimes behave like particles and sometimes like waves.

The bizarre trait of subatomic energy bits is that whichever mundane identity it is seen to assume -- whether wave or particle -- *depends on how it is observed.*

Each bit of subatomic energy contains within itself both particle-wave characteristics. Experimental physics has devised all sort of sophisticated technical apparatus to try to catch both characteristics in action simultaneously. All attempts have failed. Always, when it is under observation, the subatomic energies will display only one of its aspects.

This leads us to wonder, is what we see what we really get? Like Berenike's hair, it is there but it isn't. This was a play of spiritual meaning that delighted Pagan minds. There is always the nagging possibility, which Pagan societies contemplated, that what we perceive to see of the starry heavens is but the reflection of our own material understanding. What we see as the heavens, therefore, would always correspond to our spiritual advancement or retrogression.

Science works hard to calculate with great exactness the movements of planets and stars. In this way the scientists supposedly enable themselves to predict all celestial periods with accuracy. But are the heavens the one-paced field of action that science perceives? The truth is that if all that we observe of the heavens was greatly accelerated or retarded in their movements, there is no way that any of us material-bound beings would be the wiser.

*   *   *

Centaurus
the Centaur
the second decanate of Virgo

We know this constellation by the name Centaurus, which is Latin from the Greek *Kentauros*. This group of stars is visible mainly from places south of the equator, and it is situated between Hydra, first decanate of Leo, and the Southern Cross (Crux, first decanate of Libra).

The brightest star in this constellation is Alpha Centauri, and is the third brightest of all the visible stars to our solar system. Only Sirius and Canopus are brighter. The brightness of Alpha Centauri has attracted the attention of astronomers since the most ancient of times. Alpha Centauri is one of the two stars closest to our solar system, being only 4.35 light years from Earth. The star is actually a double, around which a third star, Proxima Centauri, revolves. If a line is drawn to join Alpha and Beta Centauri it will point nearly to the south pole of the heavens.

Centaurus is the Zodiac's southernmost constellation and it is significant that it is shown above and on each side of the Southern Cross (Crux), the symbol for matter. This constellation has the hieroglyph of a figure that is half man and half horse, which serve to symbolize the two natures -- spiritual and physical -- of the Life Principle in action within the plane of Dense Matter.

The figure is shown bearing a lance, upon the point of which is a slain animal that is being placed upon an altar. With this second decanate of Virgo is shown the matter bound Life Principle that is yet to surmount the demands and limitations of dense-matter life. The figure served to symbolize the intended attainment of mastery over the physical that it may evolve toward Wisdom Consciousness.

The figure is shown as placing his impaled sacrifice upon an altar. This sacrifice is not a recommendation for slaying other living expressions of the Life Principle. It symbolizes the sacrifice of *personal animal nature*. Virgo represents the abdominal area of the Celestial Man, the refining region of the physical being. It is logical that the refining of matter for the betterment of spirit is also one of Virgo's lessons.

There is powerful significance in the depiction of this hieroglyph as shown virtually surrounding three sides of the Southern Cross. It acts as a reinforcing aspect to the lesson on dense matter. It is made still more profound by the fact that its brightest star is the closest star known to our material matter solar system. The double nature of matter life seems to be accented by the fact that Alpha Centauri is actually a double star. Circling this double star system is Proxima Centauri which can be likened to the Life Principle enfolding both the spiritual and substance elements for life evolvement.

Many ancient myths were built upon this Zodiacal representation. Most obvious was the Greek tale of the noble Centaur, Cheiron. The world wise centaur -- representing the courser element -- was willing to die so that Prometheus -- higher mind in man -- might gain immortality.

Centaurus served as the main source of all the world's

mythical saviors, and why they were always presented in a self-sacrificing role. Continuing this tradition, Christianity has always maintained that Jesus grew into manhood possessing two natures, divine and human. The larger truth is that *we all possess these two natures.* Just as Cheiron (and other mythical saviors), Jesus is presented as having chosen to suffer and die that others might be given immortality. The Centaurian sacrifice of animal nature has to be placed upon the altar to approach Divine Wisdom.

Symbolized still further in Christian myth, Centaurus became the soldier on horseback who bound and led away the willing Jesus to be crucified upon Golgotha-Calvary.

The hieroglyph for this decanate of the Virgo lessons represent consciousness which is yet to surmount the demands and limitations of his dense matter experience. His intentions to overcome them is expressed with the offering of his animal nature. Here, surrounded with dense matter, begins the refinement of ego-consciousness for the purpose of evolving toward higher being. *This was the only sacrifice ever stressed in the Zodiac lessons, the sacrifice or putting aside of one's own baser animal nature.*

Compare this to the western world's conception of sacrifice. It is appalling that if we adhere to the letter of the scriptures, we find -- from Genesis to Revelations -- a constant and savage insistence for *blood* offerings.

What is the reasoning that would conclude that the Creative Intelligence would ever demand the slaying of something it had created? Is it sane to hope to flatter an imagined "god" by offering up to it the blood of what it has created? Honors to the Creative Principle should be celebrated with offerings that also honor the higher purpose of humankind, not dishonor everything by a destruction of life forms.

Even the Christian mythical scheme of atonement is the horrid bloody sacrifice of the son by an impassive "father."

Genuine atonement, that is to say personal sacrifice, is the giving of one's heart to a higher purpose. It is not a dying sacrifice but a living one that is the only worthy one. It is in striving to live with higher purpose that one expresses recognition of their at-one-ment to the higher Creative Principle.

All this may seem sacrilegious, blasphemous and heretical -- but who says so? The priest-class -- the preachers, ministers, evangelists, crusaders and that ilk -- who profit exceedingly well from humankind's ignorance. Because they preach at you, and sermonize endlessly, and torture your spirit does not mean they are the voice of reason.

Consider this: each and every person ever born into this world, without exception and without qualification, came into this matter plane as an atheist. The new born infant has had absolutely no exposure to the concept of some supreme being referred to as "god." A new born does not automatically accept this precept. It is an idea that must be implanted and drummed into the trusting acceptance of the growing personality. Since the child has never had nor is it ever given the privilege of comparative or conflicting data, it is unable to defend itself against such indoctrination. Is this the "free will" of religion?

*   *   *

Bootes

the Coming One
the third decanate of Virgo

We are indebted to the Greeks for the name Bootes by which we know this constellation. We are indebted to them also for it being depicted often -- and erroneously -- as a "ploughman." This figure is made senseless for the "plough" faces the wrong direction. The name Bootes comes from *bous*, meaning "ox," which contributed to the idea of ploughman.

The Greeks were not constant in their picturing of this sign, for they also called it Arcturus. This name is also given to the star of first magnitude in this constellation. The constellation under this name is only somewhat closer to the ancient Watchers' intent. *Arktos* means "bear," and *ouros* means "guard." In their picturing this figure is watching what the Greeks named the Greater and Lesser Bear constellations.

Still another name was occasionally given this figure which was Arctophylax, meaning "the Guardian of the Bear." In this regard Bootes with his hounds Asterion and Chara represent the keeper and guardian of what the Greeks regarded as the great cyclic Bear.

The figure representing this constellation is supposed to be looking at the two nearby constellations which properly should be shown as the Lesser and the Greater Sheepfolds. The Watchers presented this constellational hieroglyph we know as Bootes as *the overseer of the sheepfold*. The figure is surveying and supervising the physical yield of the cycle being brought into matter form. He inspects with authority the corporeal or physical bringing forth of Nature through which human harvest is attained. The figure of this third decanate of Virgo is supposed to be *overseeing the bounds of animal principle*. In this regard, as the driver of the sheepfold, he came to be presented in religious myth as the scourger of the Creator.

Bootes, properly understood, is the guardian and keeper of the physical yield of the cycles that is brought in. In a sense, Bootes symbolizes the animal principle to be held in bound during the corporeal bringing forth of physical form.

Showing the confusion of Greek understanding of this Zodiac lesson, the Greeks had still another name for this hieroglyphic figure. The name in this case was Arcas, the son of Zeus by Callisto, the *virgin* attendant of the goddess Artemis. It was in this form that the presentation bore the closest relation to the meanings of the ancient Watchers. Arcas represents the promised "seed of woman" out of the Virgin, and so symbolized the corporeal or physical bringing forth of Nature.

The most ancient picturings for this constellation is of a strong male figure which is striding forward with determination. He carries a spear or a rod in his right hand, and in his left upraised hand he bears a *harvesting sickle*. The sickle represents the cutting off of Creative Ideation, for it has been fulfilled in the Dense Matter plane.

The image is too strong for mythographers to allow to pass without adding some blood to it. This hieroglyphic figure is undoubtedly the source of all the castration myths such as Cronos castrating his sleeping father Uranus, and then flinging the organs into the sea (primordial energies). In some accounts Zeus did the same to his father Cronos. In a Hittie myth Kumarbi, the son and cup-bearer of Anu, bit off his father's genitals.

There is a Jewish midrash version that Noah had been castrated by his son Ham. Another version credits Ham's young son Canaan with the deed. The scriptural account we read which leads up to Noah's putting a curse upon those who saw him naked points to an editing in the text of some sort. The curse is too extreme for the minor offense of seeing Noah drunk and naked.

In the Genesis story of Noah the receding flood (of Creation's energies) leaves Noah and his family upon the planes of matter. Practically the first thing Noah did was plant a vinestock from Eden (others say there was a grape seed in the ark). The vines were mythic vines so they bore fruit the same day. By nightfall Noah made wine of them, the *wine of life*. Like all other mythic characters associated with the vine he became drunk with life.

Noah at this point symbolized the Earth in its earliest dense matter form. There is no vegetation, so he is naked. Ham's actions of covering his naked father represents the garmenting of Earth, a condition not possible until it is completely solidified -- severed -- from its Etheric Matter state. The castration of Noah followed the older myths from various cultures, but they all had to do with the severing of Creative Ideation when Dense Matter is achieved.

From this ancient cosmology lesson given with this figure carrying a sickle, Jewish tradition proscribes that if any priest's testicles are injured in any way he is no longer worthy to be god's priest.

The sickle most certainly was not presented by the Watchers in this hieroglyph as an implement for emasculation. It meant to represent only the cutting off of Creative Ideation once Dense Matter is fulfilled.

In the same sense of physical bringing forth of Nature, this male figure therefore represented the involvement of the Life Principle as "begetter" and overseer of planetary life. Bootes represents what religion interprets as the "promised" seed of woman out of the virgin. In this regard he is one and the same with Christianity's Jesus who personifies the Life Principle and the Etheric Sun, the "virgin born Son" (Sun).

From this decanate of Virgo there was also drawn more elements in the tale regarding Britain's fabled King Arthur. Arthur, who originated and headed the Knights of the Round Table, was said to have been an initiate the ancient astrological wisdom. The "Round Table" and the twelve knights show that it was the Zodiac itself, and Arthur was the pivotal "Sun" of the allegory. Legend says that because of this astronomical knowledge he bore upon his shield the image of the Virgin (Virgo), in emulation of the long promised "seed of woman." Since he was but another personification of this "seed", it is not surprising. It was this emphasis aroused by the Arthur myth that ushered in an age of chivalry and reverence for woman. In spite of this, however, women were never considered man's equal.

The Virgo lessons taught one other understanding of spirit within the matter plane. Virgo represented the beginning of biological life and is, therefore, also representative of the beginning of its *death* in matter. For this reason the sign of Virgo was regarded by the Watchers as the sign of Assumption. With the Virgo lessons was taught not only spirit's entry into matter, but as being also *where would begin the ascension of life forces from matter.* The qualification that is to mark the Evolutionary planes begins with awareness in matter form.

It was noted earlier that this lesson was given symbolic emphasis in the yearly cycle when the Sun enters the sign of Virgo. When this annual cycle repeats itself, the Sun's rays obscure the Virgo constellation so that it seem-

ingly disappears. The yearly disappearance of Virgo is the
basis for the Christian myth of the virgin mother's "Assumption." Although the time or circumstances of Mary's death is
never stated in the New Testament, "revealed wisdom" has
declared that Mary died on an August 13th and rose again
and ascended into Heaven on the third day. That makes it
the 15th -- which apparently by coincidence -- is the time
Virgo begins to be obscured by the passage of the Sun. This
lasts for about three weeks, and when the Sun moves on,
Virgo reappears around September 8th.

In Christian tradition September 8th is regarded as
Mary's "birthday."

*   *   *

The myths regarding divine sons born of a virgin are
many and similar. Common practice among all the myths is
to account for the birth of a divine son or hero in great detail
and then leap forward to the son's entering his manhood. The
intervening years are always neglected or accounted for by
some miraculous action. In Greek myth, for example, as soon
as Apollo, a sun figure, was born he ran down to the nearby
lake, which symbolized the waters of life, leaped into the
waters and swam across the lake and back. When he strode
ashore toward his mother he was a full grown man.

Christian myth does not go quite that far. It simply
brushes the childhood and adolescent years aside and pick
up the story after Jesus has reached manhood. In all
scriptural accounts the birth of the hero -- Noah, Moses,
Samson, and the like all follow that story form.

The point of this is to show that the so-called holy
family, as such, holds no place in the Old Testament or in the
"gospels." The very things that should be presented to show
the shaping and directing of this mythological savior was
completely ignored. This omission of family unity and child
raising does not seem to bother fundamentalists who proclaim that family unity is the ultimate level of this matter-

life achievement. The only reason for such a stand is to create for themselves an aura of superiority. That their claim is equally mythical is disclosed by the high incidents of divorce, child neglect, child abuse, mate bashing, passionless sex, smoldering resentments, feelings of entrapment, and similar *superior* aspects of family life.

Family units are important on a personal level because everyone needs a sense of belonging. In the larger sense, a family unit is important only as a training ground, for family units are microcosmic constellations of the global family. The family should serve as the closed class where one is schooled in the capabilities of tolerance, compassion, non-judgemental understanding, patience, unconditional love, and similar higher qualities.

Global conflicts are conditioned in the "hallowed" family units. It is in the interchange within the family where is experienced the willingness or aversion to hostility and/or violence. It is in the family unit where persons are taught the values they bring into outside interactions.

There is nothing wrong with glorifying family life as long as it is understood that there are higher glories beyond the family.

Libra
The Scales or the Balance

*the ninth major sign of the Zodiac of Constellations
representing the Plant Kingdom*

The southern constellation of Libra is represented by a pair of scales. The name Libra is from the Latin, and its meaning is "balance." This constellation is located between Virgo and Scorpio. The symbol of the balance is given powerful meaning by the fact that the Sun passes into the part of the ecliptic corresponding to Libra at the time of the autumnal equinox. This is when the days and nights are of equal length.

The names of this constellation among ancient peoples convey the meaning of a period of measurement or division. In Coptic this constellation was known as Lambadia, which translates loosely as "station of propitiation," which implies the time to appease or conciliate, to regain good will. In Arabic this constellation is called Al Zubena, meaning "redemption" or "purchase," implying that what one extracts from life must eventually be paid for. In Hebrew this group of stars is known as Mozanaim, meaning "the weighing scales."

The general understanding behind all the various names was *to cause to become favorably inclined.* This understanding issued out of the lessons given with the ancient Zodiac teachings. The Libra lesson in the Zodiac of Signs taught of the conciliating or gaining, of qualities for

Evolutionary unfoldment. It is the reconciliation of matter-experience with creative intelligence (spirit) which instigates qualification for Evolutionary advancement.

In Christian myth Jesus serves in this capacity as the conciliator, the one who reconciles humankind's "sins" with Evolutionary purpose.

The brightest star in the constellation is a double star, which is fitting, and bears the name Kiffa Australis. The binary stars are designated in astronomy as Alpha Librae and Beta Librae. Also included in this group is the globular cluster -- a nebula known as Messier 5.

In all the older depictions of this Zodiac division, Libra was regarded as an independent one. The Greeks, however, represented this constellation as an extension of Scorpio and called it *Chae*, meaning "claws" (of Scorpio). The substitution of the extended claw of Scorpio into this constellation did not radically alter the meaning taught with the ancient Zodiac lessons. The claw, or pincher, allows no escape from penalty; the victim must pay the price of full responsibility for self. In this sense the claw serves also as a "weighing" device, with justice being served by the claw holding the victim for the sting by the Scorpion.

The sign of Libra contained, in the Zodiac of Constellations, the cosmological lessons which taught of the elemental level of matter as the plant kingdom. Vegetation is, figuratively speaking, the innocent life which is martyred by animal life. It is this martyrdom which was experienced by all the world "saviors" -- the giving of lower aspects that the higher might rise into the planes of Evolution.

The hieroglyph of the celestial Scales make up what is basically a cross-form in itself. It serves to reinforce the teaching that matter-form is the penalty the spirit-energy endures in dense matter for advancement toward Divine Wisdom. Libra, as a cross-form, signifies Earth, which is why the lessons given with this Zodiac division was focused on the plant kingdom, the lower life force in matter.

The hieroglyph also served as another reminder of the double nature of all life -- that all life is composed of both spirit and matter, male and female, positive and negative.

Life is most constructively lived by establishing a working balance between extremes. Too much of anything brings with it the sinking of life's ultimate purpose, energy-soul advancement. The lesson presented with the Scales was a reminder that dense-matter life is where one's potential begins to be measured -- qualified -- for Evolutionary development.

The tail of the Hydra, first decanate of Leo symbolizing self love, points to this constellation, Libra. The inference of this placement conveyed the truth that energy-soul qualification (justice) cannot be served by anger, envy, greed or any other of the lower desires.

Numerous scriptural myths hinge upon this sign. Joseph who rose in the land of Egypt (matter) to "judge" his brothers (lower elements) is one. The most obvious is the myth of Daniel who read the "writing on the wall" at King Belshazzar's feast. The stories of Joseph and Daniel are, for all extent and purpose, the same story.

Scripturally, Daniel is Libra. The name Daniel translates in Jewish interpretation as "god is my judge," a variation of Libra's lesson of the judgement of Nature, the relentless and inflexible decrees of matter-life. This is the underlying meaning in the book of Daniel (5:27) where Daniel deciphered the writing on the wall. He translated it to King Belshazzar as "Thou art weighed in the balances, and art found wanting." This simply states an Involutionary fact, not judgement or prophecy. Lower elements and lower nature must be added to -- qualified -- to proceed into the planes of Evolution.

Daniel's refusing to worship idols means that the energy-spirit must refuse to become too engrossed in its matter-form existence. The "idols" alluded to spirit-energy being paralyzed in matter. For refusing to worship these "idols" Daniel was thrown into the lion's den (Leo-matter). Daniel's diet being severely restricted carries the same meaning, that too much devotion to matter weighs down the soul essence.

There is a gram's worth of information to throw upon the scales for consideration. A Babylonian poem from around

1600 B.C.E. tells of a mighty hero who was named Daniel. The scriptural Daniel is but a direct "borrowing" from that poem, complete with all the hero's exploits. What this means is that Daniel was not a Jewish apocalyptist after all.

In the Babylonian poem the hero Daniel lived in a city called Salem, which means "peace." The word Salem later became part of the name of Jerusalem, from *Ur*, meaning "light," and *Salem*, meaning "peace." Perhaps the weight of Libra keeps trying to tell the world something, for Jerusalem, squabbled over for hundreds of years by Jews, Christians and Moslems, has never been a city of light or of peace.

*   *   *

The Old Testament book of Job -- minus the anticlimactic ending tacked on by Jewish priests -- is something of a summation of the ancient Libra lessons. The book is not Hebrew in origin either. The stark reality of the original portion confirms this. The story is not theistically compatible with Hebrew-Judaism, for "god" does not proceed to overrule every law of Nature to prosper Job as he is depicted as doing in the Jewish myths such as Noah, Moses, Joshua, Joseph, Daniel, David and all the rest.

Job personifies the enduring elements within our life-being -- that portion which is tempered with quality and which assures advancement into the planes of Evolution. This is why throughout the first part of the story Job, knowing he is innocent, refuses to accuse or condemn himself. He knows that he is not to blame for the apparent injustice which is so often the paradox of Reality. The pain of life is experienced because raw Nature buffets and hones the Higher Spirit. It is this which polishes the lower matter experience so that consciousness may advance into the planes of Evolution.

The first part of the book of Job is an indictment of "god's" diabolism. It is "god" who is guilty of being the source all the tragedy in this tale, and it is from this same source that is generated all abundance as well. This displayed a true understanding of the action-energies of Involution which the Jewish priest-class personified as "god."

The tale of Job's tribulations was reworked to imply that the diabolic injustices to Job were caused because he was indifferent to the virtues of god. With this rewrite they fashioned a pretzel of supernaturalism to flatter themselves as being the standard bearers of higher moral sense and justice.

*   *   *

With the Zodiac sign of Libra we come to the principle ingredients used in the New Testament as the alleged events leading up to the crucifixion of Jesus. We have the trial (Scales of Libra), the cross (Crux, first decanate of Libra), the sacrifice (Lupus, second decanate), and the crown of thorns (Corona Borealis, third decanate).

If these were presented in their correct fashion, the events of the (spirit's) crucifixion explain the energy and actions within the Involutionary planes which lead into matter-life being, not *out* of matter-life. This reversal of the Zodiac lessons was instigated to disguise the true source of their story material. Properly, the decanates of Libra taught Crux, the taking up of matter form; Lupus, the taking on of animal nature; and Corona Borealis, the taking on of the physical senses.

Libra is also something of a review of Creation, the actions of which first culminates in the lowest of life forms, plant life. In some ways, the lessons of Libra should precede the lessons of Virgo, for plant life preceded higher animal life form. Plant life is the martyred lower life forms used for the advancement of the higher life form. Jesus is the matter-form being martyred for the Evolutionary being symbolized by Christ.

*   *   *

Libra is represented by the hieroglyph of the Balance. This Balance is held to epitomize justice because the Scales show the means of establishing and keeping equilibrium. In the hands of priests the interpretation of equilibrium was reduced to a concept of justice which declared "an eye for an eye, and a tooth for a tooth." This "law" was called *lex talionis*, and was embraced by the tribal Hebrews so enthusiastically that it became practically an article of faith for the Jews. This is not the means of dispensing justice; it is but a primitive code of retaliation.

A sense of justice is a development of Epigenetic Consciousness. That means it is a concept that must be developed within higher awareness. It is not an element in lower plane action. That the modern world's concept of Justice is still warped by religious influence is seen in the laws of every nation.

Justice in most of the world societies is not true justice at all although it is not quite at the level of retaliation either. Justice systems of governments show little moral understanding of what constitutes true justice. Instead, what is instituted as justice is more correctly the practice of regulation. Justice and regulation are not synonymous. They do not balance out.

Governmental justice systems are exacted for one purpose only; not to mete justice, but to control. The exacting of punishments for crimes masquerades as justice but is nothing more than the exerting of force over the perpetrator of a crime.

True justice would be based solely upon bringing back balance into the lives of the victims.

A glaring example of the falseness passing as governmental justice are the confiscatory tax laws. That is more correctly the large scale practice of extortion and blackmail. It is subjective law -- the rules of those in power -- not true justice.

Another case of non-just justice are the laws on so-called "victimless crimes." This is nothing but self-contradicting double-talk. All such laws are on the books only because religious influence has strong-armed their concept of "morality" into an enforced code of what they think is moral. The trouble is that such laws use an immoral means of trying to enforce some personal concepts of what is moral.

True objective justice could never stoop so low as to even consider the enforcement of such examples. In these two examples no one has been harmed, forced, defrauded or coerced, the only things true justice would address. The enforcement of subjective, double laws is the antithesis of justice for *they create problems where none exist.* Such "laws" are the means of exploitation, used to control others by use of force or by the threat of force.

Any society or religion can be defined by whom they feel justified in persecuting. Differing belief systems or life styles are not seen by persons of higher intelligence as being a threat to their own well being. An uncompromising attitude toward others who may differ only reveals cowardliness and ignorance used in place of understanding. The passing of laws aimed to control other people's moral conduct is itself devoid of the moral qualities of tolerance and compassion.

True justice is concerned with individual rights, not an enforcement of arbitrary standards.

*   *   *

Crux
the Cross
first decanate of Libra

One of the most conspicuous star groups in the southern sky is the figure presented by four bright stars in the form of a cross. It is popularly known as the Southern Cross. This distinctive cross form appears in what is about the darkest section of the heavens -- a section apparently devoid of other matter. There is a double star in this group, Alpha Crusis, which is about 230 light years from Earth. The constellation is situated above the Antarctic Circle and is never visible from northern latitudes.

Even so, this obscure constellation served as a lesson symbol presented by the Watchers. The cross represents the taking up of matter-form, so properly it is the entry into physical form, not its exit as presented in Christian myth. But it is from the symbolism and teaching with this Zodiac lesson that has served as model for the worldwide myths of crucified heroes, gods and saviors.

With the starry cross was represented the point in matter formation where spirit voluntarily moved into material elements to "nail" itself upon its innocent matter-form. This is the fulfillment of the first movement of Divine Consciousness toward intention which was introduced with Cygnus, the cross bearing swan, third decanate of Aquarius. At this point, symbolized by Crux, all the Involutionary or primal conditions are removed, and lower life force emerges.

The matter plane is a slower energy field for self-aware consciousness to draw from and rise above. Here, where it enters Dense-Matter expression, Creative Ideation takes up animal-form expression. Energy-spirit activates physical matter and hu-mankind is mutated out of beasthood to begin its limited-action experiences for the purpose of developing Evolutionary potential. It is only through the Life Principle taking on dense-matter experience that the energy-spirit advances itself toward Divine Wisdom.

The lesson stressed with this sign that the energy-spirit is "nailed" only temporarily upon its matter-form where it learns and perceives through virtue of its isolated awareness. This lesson is echoed in the Hebrew name for this constellation which is Adom, and means "cutting off." It is a temporary cutting off of the spirit by its voluntarily taking up matter experience.

The symbol of the cross was revered in all cultures of the prehistory world under this understanding. In broader terms the cross always represented the matter plane itself, and was used in this designation as a mark that the matter is to be found in this place. Treasure maps are a good example where X marks the spot. The Sumerians, Assyrians, Babylonians, Egyptians, Persians, Celts, Gauls, Brahmins, Chinese, Peruvians, Mexicans -- all peoples of the ancient world -- testified to the importance of the cross as a symbol for *matter*.

The link of this constellation to the many crucified savior figures of Pagan myth is obvious. Crucified saviors such as Criti (Chaldean), Tammuz (Babylonian), Attis (Phrygian), Thules (Egyptian), Orontes (Egyptian), Indra (Tibetan), Krishna (India), Iva (Nepalese), Mithra (Persian), Odin (Scandinavian), Hesus (Druidic), Quetzalcoatl (Mexican) -- and others. All such crucified saviors served as priestly personifications of the Life Principle crucifying itself upon matter that Divine Wisdom might be achieved.

This same link, however, is hotly denied by the Christian business machines, and they insist that Jesus was a flesh and blood incarnation as god's son. The fact remains that there is no substantiating proof of their claim of an historical Jesus. Even Origen (185?-254?), probably the most erudite and profound of all biblical scholars, could find no substantiating proof of an actual person from any regions where Jesus allegedly lived and preached.

Origen lived much closer in time to the alleged events of Jesus' crucifixion than we. Even after prodigious and exhaustive searching, he could find no records in Rome, Caesarea or Jerusalem of such a person ever being judged and crucified as maintained. There was only one Jesus to be found in any genuine records, and that was from over a century before the supposed crucifixion. The name was used in that record as a sort of John Doe, and the man was hanged, not crucified. If there were records of that, there would have been some legitimate records somewhere of the crucifixion that "changed the world." None have ever been presented.

This isn't the only case of how far priests have led their followers from any rational understanding of Creation processes at work within the Invo-Evolutionary planes. Misinterpretation of the meaning of crucifixion has stained understanding for over two thousand years. The Judaic priesthood which had lost the meaning of spirit's self inflicted crucifixion saw it only in terms of Mithric-Tammuzian-Christian presentation. So intense were their feelings about the concept of crucifixion that the priests decreed that anyone who might die from being crucified was so defiled they could not be buried in Jewish gravesites.

In Christian myth, the character of Jesus is, in a sense, presented twice as picking up the experience of Dense Matter. Some theologians insist that Jesus took on the mantle of "Christ" at his baptism. According to all mythological standards, they are correct. This is the point in the myth were Jesus, the personification of the Life Principle, enters the Dense Matter plane. This is the same pivotal point of the story where Jacob "wrestled" with the angel, and had his name changed. He was at the end of the Involutionary planes and entering the Evolutionary planes as a matter expression. The baptism of Jesus is also identical in story sequence and meaning as where Abram has his name changed to signify that the action from that point on takes place in the Dense Matter plane.

Baptize means "dipped under the waters of the world." This is the first moment of Jesus' crucifixion, for he has received the *waters of life*. After this point he sets out on his "ministry" which is to say to experience dense matter life. The taking on of matter life is also the meaning of the crucifixion.

The Christian fathers, either through ignorance or cunning, had Jesus then run around the house of matter and come in the door again. They present him as being crucified as the closing drama of their myth. In the myth this is presented as taking place during the Passover observances of the Jews, a highly unlikely event. The Jews would have to run counter to several of their religious laws to murder someone at that holy time.

Passover is observed at the Spring Equinox. This provides added features for the Christian myth. At the Spring Equinox, due to the Earth's movements, the Sun seemingly remains suspended for three days where the ecliptic and equator cross. This is the "cross" upon which the Sun is "crucified" every year. These account for the three days after the crucifixion when Jesus allegedly rose from the dead as Christ.

Upon his resurrection the Son-Sun is said to have shown

himself, now as Christ, to his disciples and followers. He is presented as being radiant as the Etheric Matter sun is radiant in its first visible form. In telling this myth the Christian fathers double crossed billions of gullible believers.

From the "gospel" tales we have to conclude that Jesus has already had his "Second Coming." His baptism and crucifixion means he entered dense matter twice.

There is nothing lost -- except to the Christian business machines -- if there was never an historical Jesus. The underlying spiritual meaning of the crucifixion is what should be important. That meaning was taught by the Watchers in the lessons of Creation processes. Spirit-consciousness willingly takes up the cross of matter, and in doing so thereby gains its own "salvation" -- which is advancement toward Divine Wisdom.

*   *   *

The variation of the cross with the ends of each of the four arms bent at right angles served to symbolize creative motion-matter in the process of formation. This figure is known as swastika, from the Sandskrit which translates, 'It is well."

The swastika stands as an emblem of the cycle or the generative wheel of life. The angled ends of the matter-cross indicate the four lower Involutionary planes; Mental Matter, Astral Matter, and Etheric Matter into Dense Matter. These are the quaternary -- the arena of the spirit-energy's development. The Greeks knew this symbol as Gammadion, from which we get the name gamma-ray, a radioactive ray of shorter wavelength than an X-ray. Among the early Christians the gamma-swastika symbolized Christ as the cornerstone of the Church.

*   *   *

Lupus
the Wolf or the Victim
the second decanate of Libra

Lupus is the Latin word for "wolf." Modern constellational charts show it as a figure of a slain wolf. There is no ancient authority for this particular representation. The Greeks called this constellation Thera, meaning simply "beast." Only occasionally did they call it Lycos, meaning "wolf."

The ancient Watchers taught that this southern constellation represented activated matter form; consequently any animal form could be applied to it. That this sign was not necessarily regarded in a negative context is seen in the Egyptian astrologer-priests presenting it as a small child, the god Horus, who presses his finger to his lips. This served to demonstrate that newly formed matter is to be monitored by the self, to tread softly so that matter does not overwhelm the spirit.

Activated matter-form, symbolized by a beast, is commonly shown as a wolf slain by the spear of the Centaur, second decanate figure of Virgo. The Centaur served to represent the dual aspects of human nature, the spiritual and the material. Lupus, second decanate of Libra, is the animal nature that is to be overcome or "sacrificed" for the soul's advancement. The slain animal on the point of his spear meant to represent that the spirit is to overcome or defeat matter-form sensibilities whereby it may proceed to the Evolutionary planes.

It has been noted that the lessons of Libra regard conditions preceding the emergence of human intellect at the Dense Matter plane. The Libra lessons are concerned about the more primitive life forms, the plant and animal life which developed earlier than the appearance of humankind. This is important in the cosmology lessons, but it is crucial in the life lessons given with the Zodiac of Signs. Here is fashioned the beasthood mutated by the inclusion of higher intellect.

This decanate of Libra is commonly symbolized by the

wolf. Although this is not the likely hieroglyph originally presented, it has subtle meaning behind it. The wolf, like humans, is protective of its young, lives for a time in a family unit, is cunning, carnivorous, fierce, aggressive, predatory, and greedy. It is pure bestial nature, or lower mind, which is to be "victim" or sacrificed by self-aware consciousness.

The second decanate constellation of Virgo, Centaurus, appears above and on each side of Crux, the symbol of matter. This represents self-aware consciousness taking on fully its matter experience. This is the original "death on the cross," self-aware energy-form taking up its self-inflicted experience of matter-form. It has nothing at all to do with someone else dying for our salvation. It has to do with taking up our animal nature and the start of ethical unfoldment or qualification which begins with matter experience.

This ancient understanding that each soul stood responsible for itself was not exactly a hot commercial item. Religious mythographers therefore reworked it to give themselves a product to sell, that product being salvation from "sin" and eternal damnation through the atonement or victimization of a "son of god." The priesthoods have offered the naive multitudes a raft of surrogate agents; Mithra, Tammuz, Attis, Krishna and many others besides Jesus.

Matter-form sensibilities, the subject of Corona Borealis, the third decanate of Libra, are what is to be mastered at this plane of matter. This is achieved only by the self through the development of self-discipline, not through a false surrogate offered by religion. The development of self-discipline is the establishment of equilibrium. Balance.

*   *   *

It is not a spiritual verity that anyone can sidestep the consequences of their choices. The religious shell game of laying one's "sins" at someone else's doorstep to let them pay for us is a repugnant and self-defeating idea. This type of religious teaching has naturally seeped into cultural, social, and governmental ideas of conduct. It colors relationships, international policies and the laws of nations. No wonder the world reels with deceit and victimization of each other.

No exterior being can lift the responsibility from any individual's shoulders. That cross must be borne by each self. The reality in which each person finds themselves is a self-constructed reality. As one alters their thought, so is their reality altered. That is the only salvation anyone can expect. It is far more noble than trying to pass the buck to god's son. In understanding that the reality each of us experiences is an exercise of one's own Creation-power, that power is then set in motion to establish a reality of harmony and competence about yourself.

*   *   *

Corona Borealis
the Crown
third decanate of Libra

Corona Borealis is a constellation of the Northern Hemisphere. It is referred to often as the Northern Crown, but correctly it is the Crown of the North Wind. Within this constellation there is a cluster of galaxies known as the Corona Borealis cluster, and the star Alpheta. In some myths this is presented as the guardian of the silver circled castle at the back of the North Wind. For many ancient cultures the north was linked with the Land of the Dead. Boreas is the name of the personification of the North wind in Greek myth.

The third decanate of Libra, Corona Borealis, is a semicircle of stars which rise between Hercules, third decanate of Scorpio, and Bootes, third decanate of Virgo. Hercules is the Mighty Man of the Zodiac, or rising Evolutionary consciousness; Bootes is the Keeper of the Sheepfold who watches over the incoming physical yield. The placement of the "Crown" is symbolic of the role it plays in human expression.

Because of the arrangement of six of its principle stars, this small bright constellation is easily seen as a diadem or a crown. The lesson given with the constellation Corona Borealis was of the taking on of physical senses. The crown of physical awareness.

The ability to receive and react to stimuli is the purpose of the physical senses. We know these as sight, touch, taste, smell and hearing. These are received and registered on brain impulses. In addition, there is a sixth sense, a power of perception that is often not in any affiliation with the physical senses. For lack of better words, this is regarded as intuitive power. It is of the submerged spirit-consciousness.

These constitute the six principle points in the celestial crown. It is, therefore, not a jeweled crown of glory, but a deceptively glittery estate of matter form which is capped by mockery and pain. Figuratively speaking, it is a *thorny* crown which spirit must wear during its trial in dense matter life, a crown that pierces with sensual and emotional pains.

Further religious interpretation should be unnecessary.

Scorpio ♏
The Scorpion ♏

the tenth major sign of the Zodiac of Constellations representing the Animal Kingdom

This constellation has borne an aura of the cursed from the many religious interpretations drawn upon it. What the ancient Watchers taught of the tenth Creative Principle with this Zodiac division had little in common with religion's twisted version.

The earlier Sumerians referred to this constellation as "the Perverse One" or "the Lawless One." It was not due to the teachings given with this sign, but was probably due to nebulization activities in that vicinity.

The constellation form does not resemble the shape of the scorpion insect. Where, then, did the worldwide depiction as the Scorpion of the Zodiac come from? An astronomical tablet from Babylonian times recording a scene in this constellational sector reads, "a star flared up which radiated bright as day, and as it flared it lashed its tail like an angry scorpion."

The brightest star in Scorpio is Antares, a rare supergiant and one of the brightest and largest stars known. It is possible that due to unstable conditions around Antares in the distant past there may have been comet-like happenings coming out of this constellational region over a long period of time. This is a bit "perverse" and "lawless" -- at least out of the normal to repeatedly have these things happen in one region of space.

Looking into the Scorpio constellation today we find evidence which suggests that activity in this region of space could have affected our own solar system. There are powerful radiations issuing from the Scorpio constellation. Some astronomers have suggested the possibility that Antares, now a red supergiant star, once flared forth as a super nova in a brilliant display that was billions of times larger than our sun.

The Babylonians, one of the descendant civilizations of Sumer, interpreted Scorpio as having been one of the monsters created by Tiamat when she rebelled against the "gods." For this reason they regarded Scorpio to be the opponent of the Sun. Scorpio became almost globally accepted as the symbol of war-like and death-bringing actions. The activity in Scorpio was associated in some way with the catastrophes endured by Earth or it would not have gained that reputation.

The name Antares is Greek, and its meaning is "similar to Aries" (Mars). This is commonly passed over as being in reference to its color which is similar to that of the planet Mars, red. The color hints of blood, but there is more to it than that. Antares and the constellation it dominates was linked as a violent influence to Earth for some reason. Likewise, the planet Mars was suddenly sent upon a rampage which plunged it into a reputation as the planet of destruction. Even in astromancy practice Mars is regarded the "ruler" of Scorpio. Why have the two been linked in character and color from at least early Babylonian times?

There have been no clay tablets found or decoded as yet to give much of any clue. We could take a few things that have been found along with a few mythological references and piece together a possible scenario. With this we will temporarily brush with science fiction.

Let us say that Antares, prior to its flaring forth as a supernova, threw off gaseous particles of itself which flashed forth as comets. When the giant star did flare forth as a supernova it sent shock waves through the universe so violent that they traveled the 220 light years to reach the outer planets of our solar system around 3000 B.C.E.

The turbulence disrupted and possibly even displaced chunks of matter at the outer limits of our system to set Pluto, Uranus and Neptune in their present positions. The axial tilts to the outer planets are extreme. Saturn was perhaps far enough away in its orbit so was not as severely affected.

It was, we shall imagine, another story for Jupiter. The most massive planet of our solar family has an atmosphere thought to be composed of liquefied or frozen methane and ammonia gases. Jupiter took the shock waves almost straight on. The impact was so forceful that the planet's rotation was disturbed which churned the atmosphere. Some astronomers have estimated the atmosphere to be as much as 10,000 miles deep. The temporary disruption of planetary rotation caused an unstable area of super-hot gases to be ejected. This huge glob erupted with such force that it blasted away from the planet to become a rampaging comet.

This was Athena leaping fully armed from out of the head of Zeus in Greek myth.

This was Aphrodite-Venus rising from the foam of the broiling sea where Uranus' severed genitals had been flung.

A strong clue that the planet Jupiter suffered extreme turmoil sometime in the distant past lies in the fact that its magnetic poles are extraordinarily far removed from its axis of rotation.

Eventually the comet interacted with Earth and Mars. This brought calamity to Earth for many generations. It was worse for Mars. To the inhabitants of Earth it must well have appeared there was a "war in heaven" as Mars and the comet interacted with electromagnetic discharges. It may have been at the second and closest approach between the two that the atmosphere of Mars was drained away. Venus then took up its present orbit, but Mars was thrown out of its orbital path to rampage around the heavens for more generations.

From these events, not surprisingly, astronomers of Earth made the correlation between the supernova blast in Scorpio which sent Mars into a rampage bringing destruction on Earth. This is the probable reason that Mars came to be regarded as "ruler' of Scorpio in astromancy practice.

Worldwide astrological records prior to this proposed scenario indicates that Venus *did not exist* in our solar system. Worldwide astrological records prior to this proposed scenario indicates that Mars was a peaceful, benign, and an almost uninteresting planet.

This is, admittedly, only speculative. Whether or not celestial events occurred in this manner is not as important as the lessons which had been presented with the Zodiac prior to the time in question.

*   *   *

In the original lessons presented with the Zodiac of Constellations, Scorpio was regarded as something of an alembic -- something that transforms and refines. It is at this point that the spirit consciousness takes up desire-nature and mental-emotional function.

Here the characteristics of the Animal Kingdom are confronted by the awakened matter-life elements to begin the hardest, most challenging struggle. That is to find and recognize its higher purpose so that it may elevate out of its matter commitment. In this ancient lesson, Scorpio taught of the soul struggling and approaching the threshold of its success.

Zodiacal picturing of this constellation is today shown as the Scorpion, its tail curled as if ready to strike at the left foot of the male figure which represents the constellation of Ophiuchus who is holding Serpens -- the combined first and second decanates of Scorpio. The Scorpion, in turn, is commonly pictured as about to be crushed by the right foot of this male figure. The "heart" of Scorpio is the fiery red, first magnitude star Antares. In Arabic, this star's name means "the wounding."

The lesson taught by the ancient Watchers with this celestial presentation was of the struggle for existence when the spirit consciousness fully awakens within the animal-form. From this lesson of Scorpio the constellation came to be looked upon as representing the seat of greed, desire and passion aroused in the Animal Kingdom. In this regard Scorpio could be seen as being "at war" with matter. After the world events which have been speculated upon, there would be additional reason for seeing Scorpio as a killer, "lawless and perverse." Global events caused some change in the hieroglyph presented with this sign. It was then regarded as being undeniably sinister and touched with evil.

From this ancient Zodiacal presentation of Scorpio, together with its three decanates, was built the scriptural references to "Woman's Seed," meaning animal matter-form, in conflict with the Serpent, or Higher Wisdom. In this struggle, man (humankind) is depicted as being mortally wounded in the foot as he struggled. The sting of a scorpion rarely causes death in adults. The sting is painful but the usual result is that the sting induces a stupor upon the limbs of humans.

Much of the material used in the myth of the "Fall of Man" was drawn from this Zodiacal lesson. The awakening of matter-life is also the beginning of death as a matter-form. Matter is the door being passed through to reach the Evolutionary planes of higher being. This is not a "fall" from grace, not some affront to the Creative Principle which cunning priests have presented as "original sin." The taking on of animal form is the temporary but necessary step for the purpose of refining self awareness and thus acquire higher qualities.

In Genesis, Eve is instructed (myth says she was "tempted") to take up animal-life form by Higher Wisdom symbolized by the Serpent. There was no deception played in this -- except by the priest-mythographers who told the tale as a means of setting up a scam for control of others. In order to advance into Evolutionary beings the matter-life experience has to be passed through. So forget the false guilt trip laid on the world about "original sin." It is a con game designed to profit the priest-class, and there is not a word of truth in it.

Also in the book of Genesis (myths of beginning),

Scorpio is presented as the dying "blessing" given by Jacob which was supposedly prophetic of the "tribes" of Israel. The "blessing" reads like some lines put into a fictional character's mouth, which it is. Jacob says, "Dan shall be a serpent by the way, an adder in the path, that biteth the horse heels, so that his rider shall fall backward..." (Genesis 49:17). This is but the personification of Scorpio wrongly jumbled with the half-man half-horse hieroglyph of Sagittarius. Man does not "fall" from this horse either, it is his animal nature which he is to rise above. The Genesis "blessing" is therefore in no way historical and definitely not prophetic.

In association with the Lesser Zodiac of Signs, Scorpio was represented as the genital region of the Celestial Man, the seat of biological passion. Scorpio is assigned the general month of November. This is the season often marked by golden meteoric showers. In northern latitudes this marks the season where Nature drops or casts off her glory and pride to enter "the winter of her discontent."

*   *   *

Sex is the biggest stumbling block for western religions. It is the seat of generative power, and the source of physical ecstasy. Except for the very lowest of life forms -- the elementary monocellular organisms and even the more complex Coelenterata, Platyhelminthes and Annelida (worms) -- reproduction is achieved through sexual union of opposites. Sex is equivalent to death, religions say. This is true as far as it goes. The beginning of life is also the beginning of its death in matter. As usual half-truths are the means of religious control.

Asexual reproduction -- the division of cells into two individual cells which also will divide in their turn -- would insure immortality on the matter plane. Cell organisms, by the process of dividing, reproduce the same characteristics indefinitely. In other words, they never die-except accidentally. They are in this way physically immortal and never suffer the confusion of hereditary modifications. It seems the ideal way of reproduction.

Sexual reproduction of a species seems, if looked at critically, a bunglesome and unlikely mode of reproduction. Why the evolution of sex for reproduction when asexual -- cloning -- assures that the progeny inherits *all* the genes of an organism instead of only half as is allowed for in sexual genetics? Asexual means of reproduction is, by far, much more efficient and time saving since it does away with the need -- a somewhat dangerous pursuit at times -- of seeking and gaining the interest of a mate.

Immortality at the matter plane could hardly be said to be an elevated or blessed estate. It would be like a child never advancing beyond a certain grade in school. That would not and could not bring qualities of wisdom.

What this means is that the reason for sexual reproduction with fecundation is precisely *to suppress the matter immortality of the individual.* The energy-soul is meant to go on to acquire qualities of wisdom so it may eventually elevate into the higher planes as Evolutionary being.

Knowing this it should be obvious that there is more to sex than simply a means of reproduction. Sexual reproduction is more accurately the means of establishing a system of checks and balances so the soul does not get stuck in this slowest plane of energy. Because sensual ecstasy is more often the driving force behind sexual union than a desire to reproduce, it indicates that reproduction by sexual means is of only secondary importance. There is something more profound about sexual conjoining than physical reproduction.

The answer is in the puzzle itself. The experience of conjoining is the experience of blending with another. Sexual ecstasy has in it the attribute of surrender to a force more elevating than the ego. It is a means of self-abandonment by being united with and combining energies with another. Sexual passion permits the organism to experience its spontaneous reactions as no other means on the physical plane can achieve.

That is why religions denounce sex so vehemently; it proves the spirit does not need their rites and dogmas and hypocrisies to achieve elevated awareness.

Religion smears our natural sexual spontaneity with unproven claims that such shared spontaneity in some inexplicable way demeans the spirit and threatens the soul. But nothing in the universe backs that assertion. Nowhere in Nature is anything inclined to be ashamed of sexual interest. Nor is Nature, which could be said to be the Life Principle in action (or god), ever inclined to be economical or restrained in its expressions of sexual love.

The issue of sexual spontaneity, more than any other, shows how far the pointing, grubby fingers of religious hypocrites have missed the pulse of spiritual and physical reality.

*   *   *

Western religions have a long history of deception where sexual meaning is concerned. Honesty about sexual things has never been a policy of the Judeo-Christian ethics. The result it that most people who read the "revealed word of god," scriptural myth, do not even know what they are reading. Not even the priests, preachers, ministers and the like.

In biblical myth, for example, the word "thigh" is commonly employed as an *euphemism* -- a word used as substitute for one that might offend the delicate sensibilities of the reader. It should go without saying that to indulge in such practice is going to lead to misunderstandings. It is still another way scriptures are used to teach people to be dishonest. In this example the word "thigh" is used when it really means "sex organs."

An example of this use is seen (Genesis 24:9) where we read that Abraham ordered his slave-servant, Eliezer, to put his hand "under the thigh of Abraham" and swear. This is instruction to cup Abraham's sex organs, principally the testes. This was a common practice of swearing the most solemn oaths throughout the Near East, especially among the Hebrews, of early times. It is from this means of swearing solemnly upon the "sac of life" that we received our words testify, testimony, and testament -- as in Old Testament and New Testament.

In the story of Jacob, also in Genesis, the book of beginnings, when he wrestles with the angel stranger the "hollow of Jacob's thigh was out of Joint..." Genesis 32:24). Then in verse 31 "And as he passed over Penuel the sun rose upon him, and he halted upon his thigh." The sun represents the unencumbered spirit, in Etheric Matter, at the point where it is "crippled" by matter.

The wresting match allegorizes the entry of prephysical energy-substance into the matter plane, and "spirit" is symbolically crippled. More to the point, upon entering the dense-matter plane, life-form is there generated through use of the sex organs. It is because of prephysical substance's entry into the matter plane that the means of generation is localized in the sex organs. In standard myth-telling technique, once the personification reaches the matter plane the name of the character is changed, in this case from Jacob to Israel because the principle has changed.

Later in the Jacob-turned-Israel tale (verse 32), the reader comes upon what appears to be the instigation of dietary prohibitions. It says, "Therefore the children of Israel eat not of the sinew which shrank, which is upon the hallow of the thigh, unto this day; because he touched the hollow of Jacob's thigh in the sinew that shrank."

The "children of Israel" are in reference to matter elements. The "sinew that shrank" refers to the prephysical Generative Principle which "shrank" or withdrew as a directive principle when matter-form was taken on. In the matter plane the Generative Principle is represented by the erect phallus. What the priests instigated with this myth was the dietary prohibition of eating the sex organs of animal meats. With this allegorical tale Judaism entered into what could be termed a dietary religion.

The final "thigh" illustration is another reference to oath taking. When Jacob-Israel approaches death we read in Genesis 47:29 "And the time drew nigh that Israel must die; and he called his son Joseph, and said unto him, If now I have found grace in thy sight, put, I pray thee, thy hand under my thigh, and deal kindly and truly with me; bury me not I pray, in Egypt;.." Joseph is instructed to carry Jacob "out of Egypt" in verse 30.

Jacob-Israel, of course, cannot remain in matter which is symbolized by Egypt. Joseph, personification of the Creative Principle at this point, vows by the Generative Principle that Israel will be taken out of Egypt (matter).

*   *   *

Serpens and Opiuchus
the Serpent and the Serpent Holder
the first and second decanates of Scorpio

(because they are intermingled they will be studied as a unit)

In the lessons of Creation from the Zodiac of Constellations, the Serpent symbol always represented some aspect of wisdom of the Creative Principle. The Serpent in this lesson is a discerning symbol of the Creative Principle in the role of the Life Principle in generative action. The meaning of the Serpent is given additional emphasis when we remember that all biological life is propelled by the microscopic serpentine cells of the spermazoon, the male sexual cell whose function is to fertilize the egg.

It is apropos that in the Zodiac of Signs this lesson falls in the anatomical portion of the Celestial Man which is the genital region.

In the hieroglyphic figures of Serpens and Ophiuchus, the male figure is shown holding the Serpent. The male figure is not in any mortal struggle with the Serpent, nor is this a symbol of carnal desire as often erroneously presented. Ophiuchus stands for the Life Principle -- as the generative force -- and the Serpent he holds, Creative Wisdom, is held so it faces the Corona Borealis the crown of sensual and emotional pains through which is achieved transformation and regeneration of spirit. This Zodiac lesson was quite the opposite of carnal desire, for it taught of the wisdom that permits one to overcome desire and matter illusion.

Applied at the level of personal guidance, Serpens represents the spirit or higher intelligence assessing and accepting full responsibility of its matter-self. Ophiuchus, the Life Principle, lifts personal intelligence toward the symbol of the sensual crown, suggesting the aim of matter-life is to aspire to and become an ideal *being* -- develop into the Evolutionary being or Omniself -- through overcoming its sensual matter-life experience.

This is what is meant in the book of Luke where in chapter ten, verse nineteen, it reads, "Behold I have given you authority to tread upon serpents and scorpions, and over all the power of the enemy: and nothing shall in any wise hurt you." Jesus is the Life Principle speaking as the Ophiuchus-Serpens lesson which taught that the disciplined qualities of the soul are to exercise dominion over the lower desires and emotions. The illusions with which lower desires charm animal nature cannot affect one once they are armed with truth and wisdom.

The next verse winds up by saying, "...rejoice, because your names are written in heaven." In other words, the purpose of passing through matter life is to develop qualities for elevating into the Evolutionary planes and into *Omniself* status.

The triune nature of Scorpio was meant to be presented in this part of the Scorpio lesson. With Scorpio was taught the lessons of sex, death and transformation, which on the surface seem a strange combination. The Creative Principle in action at this point first appears to be a deadly image. Matter life is generated through sexual union only to be canceled by the sting of death. But sexual generation on the matter plane is itself only symbolic of the multiplying functions of spirit on the higher Evolutionary planes. This indicates existence beyond what we call death. The Serpent represents higher wisdom to be attained and used to, figuratively, procreate ourselves through the higher Evolutionary planes. Ophiuchus, the Life Principle within us, is the highest manifestation of our matter-life existence.

Death is problematic only for the ego. In nonviolent natural conditions the organism releases or disentangles itself in a kind of ecstasy. The ego, that part of us most enraptured by matter, is taught by our religio-cultural training to regard death as being somehow a loss of status. What we term death is the withdrawal of energy consciousness from matter. It is a mandatory experience only of the matter plane. It is part of the natural and biological order which the Libra lessons taught.

Life is not opposed to death, nor is death the result of "inherited sin" that cannot be washed out of our matter-life form. When we discard our physical expression, the inner identity -- or inner energy which projected us into the matter plane -- draws back into the Etheric-Astral energies. It was through these energies that was radiated the extension of "self" that was projected as electromagnetic fields of light (matter). What we regard as "life" is then registered as experience by means of a focusing technique we call "ego."

In all ancient mythologies the Serpent was always depicted in the role of initiator, and almost as often pictured as the guardian of some great treasure. Used as symbolic of Wisdom in an initiating action, the Serpent was said to "speak." This is why in scriptural myth the Serpent, standing guard at the "Tree of Life," is portrayed as speaking with Eve and advising her. Eve, as prephysical element-substance, is initiated toward wisdom by Creative Principle by being counselled to take up the intended purpose which is achieved only through matter-form tribulations.

The tale of Eve and the Serpent was taken from extremely ancient understandings that it was the luminous or celestial Serpent who initiated and taught the concepts of morality. Serpent-like figures, indicating Creative Wisdom at work, have a role in several of the Zodiac lessons. The first movement toward what could be termed "moral" conduct occurred out of the mutual regard of elementary substances for each other that were gathered through the prephysical planes. Out of this is initiated the higher concept of morality which raises the soul-being through considerate regard of others.

The ancient meaning of this Serpent is hardly the "evil" or diabolical initiator as it is presented in the garbled version of the "holy book."

All peoples of antiquity regarded the celestial Serpent and Dragon as symbolic of the initiative forces which brought wisdom and civilization to humankind. The ancient historian, Sanchoniathon, wrote that the venerated serpent was not a crawling snake, but was a luminous creature that moved through the skies with astonishing speed. In a deliberate move to turn this ancient understanding upside down, the priests of organized religions maligned it as Pagan absurdity to be mocked and condemned. The free access to, or perpetuation of genuine wisdom has never been the ideal of the priest-class.

Under a program of ceaseless propaganda from religion's power machines, humankind had figures such as "Saint George" and "Saint Michael" thrust upon them as replacements for wisdom. These and like characters were presented as being righteous for the murdering of the celestial initiators, the Serpent and the Dragon of Wisdom. What these tales represent is actually the allegorical re-counting of the deliberate extinguishing of ancient knowledge.

The Bible, as worked and reworked and edited as it is, still hints that the Serpent was earlier understood as the progenitor of higher knowledge.

*   *   *

In the original words of the scriptural tales there were often little plays upon words. Many of these do not translate. Most of such word-plays were completely lost on those who translated the words into different languages. To them everything was taken literally, and the great loss to original understanding was the result.

"Serpent" is one such word which wound up presented in purely literal terms meaning "snake." However, there was always much more meaning behind the original telling. In biblical verses the term used for serpent is taken from the word *nahash* which, indeed, is the word for snake. This word for snake evolved from the Hebrew root NHSH, which meant to decipher or to make out the meaning of. This adheres closely to the more ancient associations of the serpent as a symbol for truth and wisdom.

*   *   *

The serpent figure shown forming a circle by holding its tail in its mouth was an extended understanding of Creative Wisdom. Both the serpent and the spiral served to represent the coiled energy of the universe. Within the encirclement life was created from inert material. The grasp of this universal understanding of serpent spiral symbology reached full exemplification in some old Chinese writings. In the **Huai Nan Tzu** book (about 120 B.C.E.) as well as in **Lun Heng** of Wang Chung (about the year 82 C.E.) there is expressed the concepts of centripetal cosmogony. In these works is presented the cosmogony where spiral action -- or "whirlpools" -- materialize worlds out of primary matter. Cosmologists of today have come to the same conclusion that this is the manner in which galaxies form.

*   *   *

Hercules
the Mighty Man
the third decanate of Scorpio

We know this constellation by the name Hercules which is Latin for the Greek Herakles, meaning "with Hera's glory." This headed Scorpio's third decanate lesson which taught of the awakening consciousness within its animal matter form. A form of consciousness exists in all living things and these are interrelated in action as well as in purpose.

Hu-man consciousness differs in one vital regard to other conscious life forms. That difference rests in an awareness of a more immediate and direct comprehension of higher purpose than linear intelligence of matter-mind -- or ego -- can perceive.

The celestial figure for this constellation was known as the Mighty Man to prehistory peoples. The legend of the Mighty Man can be traced back at least as far as Chaldea. Because this legend was fully developed even then, it is certain that the understanding of the celestial Mighty Man goes back even further. Similar legends, with nearly identical aspects, were prevalent not only in Greece and Rome, but in Egypt, Phoenicia, and even India.

The Mighty Man personified the Evolutionary life that is taken up at the Dense Matter plane. A more comprehensive definition for some of what the Mighty Man represented might be Divine Will -- that aspect within human consciousness which has the power to subdue and master the Lower desires and passions of the animal nature it experiences.

In the course of many generations, numerous aspects of the legend became somewhat altered. We are probably most familiar with the Mighty Man legend through the Herakles-Hercules myths. Even Aristotle admitted that there were changes and additions to the Greek version "after the mythical style."

Herakles was in every way the "savior" figure of Greek mythology. He was born of a virgin (Alcmene); the highest god (Zeus) was his father; he was called the "only begotten son" of the father; he was called the "good shepherd;" he was called the "Prince of Peace;" he died in agony; he descended into the lower world; and then ascended to heaven (placed as a constellation).

The Greek story of Herakles is recognized for what it is: myth. The story of Jesus which follows the identical format is, on the other hand, vehemently declared to be *history*. There are none so bind as those who refuse to see.

Besides the identical instances mentioned above,

there are other clues that the Christian story is but the same myth. Herakles died an agonizing death from putting on the *purple* robe of the Centaur (Sagittarius) named Nessus. Purple is the color of the Centaur, the next Zodiac sign, and the vibratory color of royalty. The color represents the ascending spirit into the Evolutionary planes. These are the reasons we read in the "gospels" of Jesus (Herakles renamed) being declared "king of the Jews," and wearing a crown of thorns (the Corona Borealis, last decanate of Virgo, the virgin). The final touch to this is given in John 19:5 where it says, "Then came Jesus forth, wearing the crown of thorns and the purple robe."

The story details regarding both Herakles' torment and the mockery of Jesus can be traced to an ancient Babylonian (priest invented) ceremonial called the *Sacaea*, a New Year's festival. The Sacaea was highlighted by the slaying of a victim who masqueraded as the king. Wearing a crown and a purple robe, the victim was either hanged or crucified in the expectation that his sacrifice would insure another favorable year for the people. The festival was based on the misunderstanding of ancient Zodiac lessons -- or more likely due to deliberate priestly perversion of the lessons.

The Jews in their historically verifiable captivity in Babylon would certainly have been familiar with this annual affair. It is the probable source of the *Purim*, one of the later Jewish festivals invented in honor of the deliverance of the "nation" as presented in the book of Esther. The fasting which precedes Purim (celebrated on 14 to 15 Adar) was most likely inspired by the fasting and ceremonial mourning rites for the Babylonian god Tammuz-Adonis. The Babylonians portrayed this son of god dying annually for the "betterment" of humankind.

As representative of the Evolutionary Life Principle, this is a natural pattern. Other "Mighty Man" versions of this character arose as central figures of various priest-inspired religions. Mithra, Krishna, Attis, Tammuz, Jesus and others served as priesthood's personifications of the Life Principle which is destined to rise from its Dense-Matter experience.

The Zodiac lessons taught that we are all conceived out of primordial elements and so we are all, in essence, "virgin born." As such we are each "fathered" by the Divine Principle. We each wear the crown of physical senses, and matter-life is the trial and mockery of the destined Evolutionary being -- the Omniself.

*   *   *

From the Mighty Man, representative of the Evolutionary Life Principle, we will soon progress into the Hu-man Kingdom which was taught with Sagittarius. All matter-life shares more principles in common than they do differences, a fact that surface features may seem to belie.

All matter is energy. All matter-life is energy. There has to be an elementary point from which all living matter diverged. There is a relationship between all forms of living matter even though their final matter-forms appear to be profoundly different.

From looking at things like trees, plants, snails, whales, four legged animals and hu-mans, they seem to have little in common. In truth everything is related. All these have, for example, a circulatory system that operates on the same principle.

The "blood" of a plant is called sap. The circulatory pigments of algae and plants is chlorophyll. This is the simpler "blood" which is built around an atom of magnesium. The molecular weight of the chlorophyll pigments is 904.

The "blood" of various arthropods (insects, arachnids and crustaceans) and mollusks (slugs, snails, mussels, clams, limpets, etc.) contain a pigment built around an atom of copper. The molecular weight of the pigment varies from species to species so weight ranges between 400,000 to 6,700,000.

The blood of higher animals contain red pigmentation known as hemoglobin which is characterized by the presence of one atom of iron in its molecule. The molecular weight of the iron pigment varies from one species to another, but the mean molecular weight is 69,000. The molecule of hemoglobin is quite large and considerably more complicated, but it still holds relationship to the circulatory substances of all other living things.

This similarity of life's flow is not surprising to us when we have had access to the Creation and life lessons given with the Zodiac teachings. We then understand that all life forms are first built up out of and through the elemental forces. Then at the Mental Matter plane these elemental forces take on their purpose as intended matter forms. These are the archetypal forms which are to take on their atomic structure and thus define themselves.

The mineral kingdom, although not commonly perceived as such, is composed of living matter. It is not, however, endowed with consciousness to know it exists. Minerals are the Astral-Etheric energies held in collective and continuous form to be drawn upon and used by active matter.

The plant kingdom draws directly from these living Astral-Etheric energy forms to transform that energy as substance-material for higher life forms. The plants, in turn, produce food, utensil material, fiber material, shelter, and even produces oxygen for animal life.

The animal kingdom is the level of lower intelligence which is awakened through sense-desire. It is here that mental activity is excited and quickened through want, curiosity and instinct. The Animal Kingdom reflects all the many and various properties that reside within each human being. The Animal Kingdom is important to human existence not only because the human physical form has been mutated out of animal nature but because all creatures mirror the nature which activates human experience. How humans treat and regard animal life -- with compassion or with contempt -- serves to index how far the individual has advanced above their own animal nature.

The Watchers taught, with justification, that to dishonor other forms of life was equal to dishonoring the self. Humans were *not* elevated out of animal nature to take dominion over it -- which is an idea precious to western religious thought.   In our human life experience we stand only at the threshold of our Evolutionary advancement. If we have not yet gained dominion over our selves, how can we claim dominion over the natural world? The hu-man species was not elevated out of beasthood to take dominion of it, but to serve as custodians for those less advanced life-form expressions. Through religious and cultural direction the human species has failed miserably in its responsibility to Nature.

Sagittarius
The Archer

the eleventh major sign of the Zodiac of Constellations representing Genetic Force — Human Kingdom

Sagittarius is from Latin and its meaning is "archer." This southern constellation lies partly in the Milky Way. The hieroglyph figure is of a centaur, a mythological figure whose lower body is of a horse and whose upper body is the torso of a man. The Centaur is usually shown as in the act of drawing his bow to release an arrow. In western cultures the Centaur is usually considered to represent the wise Centaur from Greek mythology named Cheiron.

This constellation contains many star clusters, variable stars, and nebulae. The brightest star, Rukbat, is but of fourth magnitude. Other stars in Sagittarius include Kans Australis and Nunki. The Sun is in Sagittarius at the time of the winter solstice in northern latitudes. It is at this point when the Sun apparently stands still for three days in its southward movement. This occurs about December 22nd, and is the first point of Capricornus. The Sun's movement northward begins around December 25th, and is therefore regarded the "birthday" of world savior figures.

In ancient Akkadian, the name for this constellation was Nun-ki, which meant "Prince of the Earth." In the Egyptian temple at Dendera, this constellation carried the hieroglyphic word identification of Knem, which means "the conquerors." In Hebrew, this constellation was known as

Kesith, meaning "the Archer." The Greeks knew it as Cheiron.

The Centaur was first presented as the second decanate figure of Virgo which taught of spirit's entry into dense matter form. At that point the figure, spirit bound with animal power, confronted the dilemma of having to sacrifice personal animal nature if it wished to proceed with its higher purpose. Here, as the symbol of Sagittarius, the dynamic and unrestrained state seen in the Virgo lesson is brought under control. The Centaur is a symbol of cosmic success.

In this Zodiac lesson the Centaur figure carries an archer's bow. If the figure is shown as shooting an arrow, it is either aimed upwards or directed at the heart of Scorpio -- to end the struggle of spirit and matter.

The Centaur hieroglyph represents the double nature of matter-life which possesses both higher and lower -- spirit in matter. Sagittarius represents that phase in spirit's "conflict" with matter where spirit begins full mastery over matter. The loosening of the arrow upward symbolizes the achievement of Evolutionary wisdom overcoming savage nature and thereby bringing peace to the soul. The Archer symbolizes the at-one-ment with higher Evolutionary purpose.

Sagittarius represents the victory of spirit in the struggle which originated out of the first four creative planes. It is from this ancient teaching that "Saint John the Divine" borrowed all the images which included the Four Horsemen of the Apocalypse. The priest-mythographers who fashioned that tale depicted them as four different colored horses which, properly understood, are symbolic of the four lower Involutionary planes.

The lessons which had been presented by the Watchers with the sign of Sagittarius provided the material upon which the latter part of the "prophetic" New Testament book of Revelations is built. It must be remembered that all of the book of Revelations is but a recounting or summary of all the ancient Zodiac lessons. The priestly mythographers fashioned these into fearsome imagery to strike terror into the hearts of the gullible and thereby establish power advantages for themselves.

Some of these connections have already been touched upon elsewhere in these pages. From here on will be shown the intimate ties of the ancient Zodiac lessons to the book of Revelations -- which is Christendom's supposed "prophecy" of heaven and Earth's doom.

Zodiacal hieroglyphic images pop up everywhere in Revelations -- so abundantly in fact that it seems ludicrous that anyone would miss their Zodiac references. In chapter 13, verse 11, for example, John supposedly sees "...another beast coming up out of the Earth; and he had two horns like a lamb, and he spake as a dragon."

Let us hope so. The mass-soul of humankind could use a little genuine wisdom about now.

This is more priest-class bastardization of the ancient Zodiac lessons for their own ends. The verse quoted here uses Zodiac lesson emblems for the Creative Principle and for Wisdom Consciousness and turns them upside down and inside out to present them as some deceptive "antichrist." They paint these in the precise role that organized religion is itself playing. It is a cunning move, and one practiced in the shuffle of religious power machines from time out of mind.

In the ancient Zodiac lessons, from the last of Scorpio through Sagittarius and Capricornus, was presented instructions of spirit approaching the higher planes of Evolution. This became reworked in a field-day exercise of priestly horror stories.

The horrific imagery where the "loving" angels pour out the seven "vials" of god's wrath upon the Earth to bring forth the seven last plagues is too fiendish to be considered "holy." Chapter sixteen goes into great detail of the horror brought about with each "vial." The first brings "...a noisome and grievous sore upon the men which had the mark of the beast, and upon them which worshipped his image." The second vial kills every living soul in the sea, the third turns Earth's rivers and fountains into blood, and the fourth causes the Sun to flare forth scorching men with fire. The fifth vial brings excruciating pains and sores to men. The sixth dries up the waters of Euphrates and those who kept their "garments" on are gathered "into a place called in the Hebrew tongue Armageddon."

The seventh vial is poured into the air, which brings a voice from the temple of heaven saying "It is done." Thunder, lightning, hail-and earthquake "...such as was not since men were upon the earth..." make sure that the "..cities of the nations fell..." Babylon, always the symbol of Earth itself, "...came in remembrance before god, to give unto her the cup of wine of the fierceness of his wrath."

If this doesn't convince one of god's great wisdom and unconditional love, it is reinforced by a follow-up of seven dooms.

All of this is the deliberate disfigurement of the ancient Zodiac lessons which concerned the actions within the seven Involutionary planes *leading into matter formation.* For all matter-life this represents the process of *past* actions. This would not do for priests hungry for material power, so it was palmed off as being "prophetic" of future horrors. After the seven dooms we are treated to the rantings and ravings of Babylon and fornication and harlots replete with all the threats of the "bottomless pit." From here we arrive at last to still *more* horror.

We thunder and roar right up to Armageddon, priesthood's gory excuse for the Zodiacal lesson of spirit's victory over its matter-life experience. This is priesthood's blaring announcement of the "second coming" of the "prince of peace" who is to judge and *make war.* Everyone seems to be too afraid to question all the contradictions and the setting aside of divine character in these images.

This hasty summarization of Revelations' nasty imagery brings us to that point in the Zodiac lessons presented with Sagittarius. We will skip over religion's boogie-man, Satan, presented at this point of the myth, and look at the next batch of "revelatory" images.

The "white horse" of Revelations (19:11) stands for Sagittarius itself. It is the White Horse of the Avatar whose wisdom brings peace to the spirit that *was* locked in the violent nature of its matter-form. It is at this point where the supposed author of Revelations, "John," reports seeing a new heaven and new Earth. Accordingly, "...the first heaven and first earth were passed away."

Of course they were. The lessons with Sagittarius taught that the Involutionary planes and their dense-matter expressions must be left behind by the liberated spirit. This is not terrifying, it is glorious. At this point the spirit is conscious that its aim is upward -- as signified by the arrow being loosened from the Archer's bow.

This is the meaning behind chapter six, verse two of Revelations: "And I saw, and behold, a white horse, and he that sat thereon had a bow; and there was given unto him a crown; and he came forth conquering and to conquer." He conquers his *own animal nature* to proceed into the Evolutionary planes. His "crown" is higher wisdom. To render this beautiful truth into blood and guts terror is a disgrace to Divine Wisdom.

Later in chapter twenty-one, verse two, "John" sees "...the holy city, new Jerusalem, coming dawn..." The priest mythographers gushed on that this holy city came "from god out of heaven (out of the Zodiac lessons), prepared as a *bride* adorned for her husband." In verse four, in reference to the Evolutionary planes, it goes on "...and there shall be no more death, neither sorrow, nor crying, neither shall there be any more pain; for the former things are passed away."

The Dense Matter plane is the only plane where spirit must disentangle itself from a cocoon it builds around itself. Its grub-life is surmounted. Its cumbersome, impedient involvement with sluggish matter is abandoned.

After twenty chapters of horror and disgusting images, we finally arrive at the brief offering of seven heavenly goodies awarded to the victors and survivors of this imaginary priestly *carnage*. These seven new things of Revelations (chapters 21 and 22) are but the seven Evolutionary planes which follow through the dense-matter plane. Priest-mythographers have always been notoriously ignorant of spiritual things, and that is apparent in the list of prizes suggested in Revelations. The seven rewards listed show no familiarity with the fact that the Evolutionary planes refine the soul consciousness with wisdom which transforms the soul as Omniself to become one with Divine Wisdom.

The best John could see coming out of the Evolutionary planes was: 1) a new heaven, 2) new Earth, 3) new "people", 4) new Jerusalem <as the "Lamb's" wife>, 5) new temple, 6) new light, and finally 7) new paradise. From this new paradise there is seen *a river of the water of life*, described as issuing from "the throne of god and of the lamb." Like the Zodiac lessons, we have moved full circle back to the Aquarian waters.

*   *   *

The central core of our Milky Way galaxy lies beyond the constellation of Sagittarius some 30,000 light years away. A misty glow of light there marks our galaxy's center. Looking into this area we can see only about ten percent of the distance toward the center before the line of sight becomes obscured by celestial dust and a profusion of stars.

With radio and X-ray emissions, however, it has been confirmed that the dark center of our galaxy is located there. During December the Sun is in Sagittarius and marks the direction of that dark core about which over a trillion suns revolve.

The lesson given with the constellation Sagittarius concerned that which is beyond our mortal sight -- the evolution of soul-qualities.   Similar to peering into the direction pointed by Sagittarius, we can see only about ten percent of the Evolutionary path lying beyond us. The lesson of Sagittarius sought to clarify the direction, aim and destiny that is the core of Evolutionary purpose. That core of purpose about which we revolve is to gather qualities which are to be refined into the state of Divine Wisdom.

The canonical hoax of Revelations does nothing to enlighten the soul. Remembering that we will proceed to the first decanate lesson of Sagittarius.

*   *   *

Lyra

the Lyre or Harp
first decanate of Sagittarius

The name Lyra is Latin, taken from the Greek, which means "lyre" or "harp." This northern constellation is situated between Cygnus (the Swan, third decanate of Aquarius) and Hercules (third decanate of Scorpio). Lyra is most easily identified by the triangle it describes, with the first magnitude star Vega (Alpha Lyra) as one of its apexes.

The presentation of the Lyre or harp as the hieroglyph for this constellation is another recent addition from Greek influence. In older representations the hieroglyphic figure for this constellation was of an Eagle. Because this caused some confusion with the second decanate of Capricornus, Aquila, the eagle which soars *upward*, this decanate of Sagittarius was sometimes presented as a hawk, or in rare instances as a vulture.

Borrowing from the more ancient hieroglyph for this constellation, modern atlases generally show it as a figure of an eagle but which is holding a harp in its talons. In some picturings the harp is shown superimposed over the body of the eagle. Even in Sumerian times the harp was used in conjunction with this lesson, but the philosophical Greeks favored the lyre for this lesson because it represented harmony.

The eagle hieroglyph, when used by the ancient Watchers as symbolic of this lesson, meant to symbolize the suddenness and power of a vanquisher swooping down upon its prey (matter) from on high. This meant to indicate the power of spirit which, reclaiming its purpose swiftly and with great energy, can subdue and conquer the hold of the matter-senses.

The changed hieroglyph does not alter the signifi-cance of the lesson presented with this constellation. Both the Eagle and the Harp indicate the awakening of Cosmic Consciousness. The Eagle, when shown holding the harp, is representative of the soul-spirit; the harp beautifully symbolizes the harmony to be attained upon the shedding of dense-matter experience, when it is destined -- as symbolized in Aquila -- to soar (as with eagle's wings) into fulfillment through the planes of Evolution.

The Eagle hieroglyph for this decanate of Sagittarius was of the Eagle swooping *downward*. Its "prey" was the animal matter-senses. The substitution of a hawk or of a vulture meant to clarify the action symbolized was of the *lower nature being removed by higher purpose*.

The Eagle holding the Lyre indicated the purpose of removing lower nature was to establish harmony. The *harmonized* conditions of soul are what opens the way into higher planes of being. The strings of the Lyre represent the animal desires which have been brought into harmony and transmutes self-aware consciousness into higher Evolutionary planes. The higher emotions are then activated in complete harmony to receive from the Evolutionary summit the outpouring of love and truth.

The first magnitude star Vega of this constellation is the brightest star in the heavens of the Northern Hemisphere. It is calculated to be the fourth brightest star in the sky, and glows with a distinct bluish tinge. It is the dominant celestial body in the vicinity of the solar apex, and is approximately twenty-six light-years away from Earth.

The name for this star is from Medieval Latin taken from the Arabic (*al nasr*) *al wagi*, which means "the falling (vulture)." The brightest star's name therefore reaffirms the teaching given with this constellation. The meaning is of the transmuting power whereby the lower nature is, in a sense, consumed, releasing the higher nature to its purpose. The higher self is emerging and it is first conceived as being an obnoxious image because it threatens the lower self with extinction. This emerging self has often been referred to in religious myth as the "wrath of God."

To modern cultures the spiritual significance of the vulture has been lost and it is understood only in its matter-form role -- a raptorial bird that subsists mainly on carrion. The Vulture was used to symbolize the emerging higher self which is to do away with the lower. It was in this understanding that the image of the vulture was placed on the neck of Egyptian mummies as an amulet of protection. This is why, also, the Egyptians often showed the vulture hovering in the air with outstretched wings and holding in each claw the symbol for *life*. Matter life was perceived as being only the basis for achieving higher life.

Understanding the spiritual symbolism explains the reason behind the Parsees -- members of a Zoroastrian religious sect -- delivering over to the vultures the bodies of their dead. Once again it is a case of mistaking a symbol used for spiritual instruction with a literal interpretation. Because their "divinely inspired scriptures" implies that the personality is to be consumed and transmuted by the vulture in order to liberate the ego from lower nature they feel bound to the letter of "the Word."

In this lesson given with Lyra was taught the transmuting power of higher self. The lower self is "consumed," and the soul emerges into activity amid higher qualities. All that the lower ego-self regarded as "reality" is overturned.

*   *   *

──────────────── Ara ────────────────
the Altar
second decanate of Sagittarius

The constellation of Ara, Latin meaning "altar," located south of Scorpio, continued the lesson of the spirit's triumph over its dense-matter experience. The hieroglyph used for this constellation in the temple at Dendera was of a throned human figure which was wielding a flail over a jackal. This symbolized that the lower darker animal-nature is to be brought under domination of the spirit, its four "skins" of "accursed matter" slashed away. (Here is where "circumcision" of spirit from matter takes place. Hence, Abraham was 99 when he was circumcised.)

Ara appears as one of the more peculiar hieroglyphs of the Zodiac lessons in as much as the altar is upside down and the fire upon it burns downward -- toward the matter plane. This served to indicate the "sacrifice" of spirit's matter-form is to be fulfilled by the removal or the burning off (through radiation) of its "skins" of matter.

Among ancient cultures these four matter-energies were presented as four "elements": earth, air, fire, and water. That these were meant as being symbolic only is shown by the fact that fire is not a *material* element. Not even the most primitive cultures would consider fire to be a material element. These four "elements" were meant to symbolize the four primal energies that propelled ideation into the Involutional construction; that is to say, into its dense-matter form. Once qualities of self-aware consciousness is achieved these "elements" are burnt off.

With the lesson of Ara it was taught that these dynamic energies of matter-form expression are to be cut off (circumcised) to achieve the qualifying actions necessary to rise into higher Evolutionary planes. It is out of this that the Judaic priesthood fashioned the mark of god's alleged covenant with them -- the removal of the foreskin of the penis. The phallus has, from time out of mind, always served as symbolic of the Life Principle — hence the "mark" placed upon the genitals of all male followers of Judaism.

In the more ancient Zodiac lessons it was taught that it is through radiation and disintegration that spirit-consciousness is purified to create its higher form. The lesson of Ara explained that it is upon spiritual idealism that the lower qualities are burned away (radiation) for the sake of the higher. The fire upon the altar symbolizes spirit which purifies and transmutes the base, which is why the fire burns downward.

Priesthoods have never been inclined nor dedicated to genuine spiritual enlightenment, so this was altered as the "reproach of accursed matter." The Chaldean priesthood were the first to present this interpretation. This understanding was later picked up by the captive Jews who, at the same time, acquired observance of the Chaldean Sabbath. It was in this same period that the priest mythographers of Judaism became acquainted with East Indian Brahmanic legends upon which their "seed bearer" Abram-Abraham was fashioned.

All this led to one of the most incredible interpretations of the Zodiac lessons regarding the shedding of matter to ever be foisted upon a people by a priesthood. The practice of physical mutilation called circumcision.

The Jews, coming away from their Babylonian captivity, accepted meekly their priest-politicians' demands of observing the Sabbath. It was a familiar practice and it honored higher spiritual purpose if not the understanding of it.

The Judaic priest-politicians had been introduced to and had become enamored with the East Indian Brahmanic legends while in Babylon. They found these to be a stimulating means for recording occult cosmology. If it could be worked also into a hypnotizing doctrine of religious *exclusivity*, so much the better. Thus from the Brama-Brahma legends the Judaic priests anagramatically transposed their "seed bearer" Abram-Abraham. This purely mythological character was so well presented that it has been taken up by Christians and Moslems (who know him as Ibrahim) as having been an historical person!

With the Abram-Abraham myth the Jewish priesthood then introduced a *literal* interpretation of the "reproach of accursed matter." It was the practice of circumcision as a bloody religious rite. Properly, this skin-shedding marks the leaving of matter-life experience, but religio-political domination and control was the purpose of this scam.

In scriptural myth the character of Abram personifies the prephysical stages up to the Virgo lesson where spirit's movements into the Dense Matter plane is signified by the addition of the letter H to the name. The letter H signifies life and so is added to names like AbraHam, SaraH, ElisHa, and others just as it had been used in the Brahmanic legends.

At this point the Judaic priests who were fashioning the articles of faith and ceremonial rites jumped ahead in the proper evolutionary unfolding of things. The Zodiac lessons had taught (with Sagittarius lessons) of the removal or cutting off of matter which enables spirit to advance into the Evolutionary planes.   These   were taken out of proper sequence, inserted into the story where Abram becomes Abraham -- or clothes himself as matter form -- where they have "god" insist that Abram remove his fore-(four)skin as a sign of devotion.

According to scriptural myth Abram "was ninety years old and nine" when "the Lord" appeared to him (Genesis 17:1) and demanded the mutilation of Abram's genitals. Abram was not startled by the demand, and up to the bloody challenge. At verse five Abram therefore becomes AbraHam, and by verse nine circumcision is established (by the priests) as the sign of the "Abrahamaic Covenant." By verse fourteen "the Lord" is fired up: "And the uncircumcised man child whose flesh of his foreskin is not circumcised, that soul shall be cut off from his people; he hath broken my covenant."

Can anyone seriously believe the Creative Principle would disown the men who have not been circumcised physically? It is ludicrous. We know that what is being spoken of is *the removal of the four elements of matter*, or four "skins," that must take place at the beginning of the soul's *Evolutionary ascent.* If matter is not removed at that point the soul would indeed be "cut off from his people:" the *soul could not advance.* The butchery practiced on infants "in the name of the Lord" then becomes, although hygienically acceptable, an appalling practice.

The reworking of the Brahmanic legend accomplished a great deal of control over the followers of Judaism. With enforced circumcision of infant boys there is impressed upon the subconscious the idea that their mutilation is a mark of "chosen" status. Never in their lives will any Jewish male not be subconsciously reminded of his alleged "covenantal" specialness. The scars do not really mark a covenant with the Lord, but simply symbolize the priest's authority over the people. As such, the practice of circumcision upon defense-less infants is not a worthy interpretation from the noble Zodiac lesson of Ara.

*   *   *

The hieroglyph of the overturned altar and the fire burning downward symbolizes the spirit's burning off of the lower-plane senses. The altar itself symbolizes the lower nature to be overturned. It is upon this "altar" that the individual ego has built its higher nature.

In a real sense the Earth is the altar of life from which arises the qualified higher self. Lower qualities are cast off (sacrificed) for the sake of the higher. The Involutionary being which manifested in the Dense Matter plane must qualify itself for Evolutionary development. Here, in Dense Matter experience, the spirit-fire transmutes itself -- the alchemy of spirit which will bring union of the individual consciousness with the Absolute.

This is the meaning behind the story of Noah where, once he reaches the Dense Matter plane upon the flood of Creation's energies, he is presented as building an altar. Upon this altar he "...took of every clean beast and every clean fowl, and offered burnt offerings on the altar" (Genesis 8:20). Did the Lord have Noah carry two of these things into safety just so they could be burned up as a sacrifice? *Of course not.*

The "clean" fowl and beasts represent the desires, emotions and passions that are the means of offering the latent soul to the Higher Self.

If only the biblical verses were clean enough to offer up to Truth.

*   *   *

------------------------------ **Draco** ------------------------------
the Dragon
third decanate of Sagittarius

Draco is Latin from the Greek *Drakon*, which means "dragon" or "serpent." This northern circumpolar constellation is located partially between Ursa Minor and Ursa Major -- first and second decanate of Cancer -- with Cepheus, second decanate of Pisces, located westerly above its arched spine. This hieroglyphic figure twists across at least one half of the northern sky. The second magnitude star Etamin, also know as Draconis, is the brightest star in this constellation.

Around forty-five to forty-eight centuries ago, the star Thubin in this group was the North Pole Star. Today this star is below the third magnitude, but in those days it was extremely bright.

With the constellational lesson presented with Draco, we once again come upon a serpent-like figure, but now *it is grown huge.* The hieroglyphic figure of a Dragon has no zoological basis, and it served to symbolize the cosmic wisdom of all Creation with all the coiled energy of the universe at its command. It is this Creation wisdom and power which is at the command of the evolved soul, but is fully accessible only after the life altar has been overturned.

It is significant that when the Watchers taught the world through use of the Zodiac lessons, the Pole Star was taking up position in this sign of great cosmic wisdom. Since that time the world has turned away from that wisdom, and the world no longer points its axis to this sign. Humankind has, however, reached a high stage of basic cosmic technology, not through wisdom but through sheer brute nature. The consequence is that our Cosmic Consciousness is lagging some twenty-five centuries behind our technological accomplishments.

If Cosmic Consciousness is not attained by humankind within the foreseeable future, our cosmic technology will most likely recoil and hurl us back to the world conditions equal to our primitive spiritual consciousness. We cannot be allowed to become citizens of the universe until our Cosmic Consciousness is developed to balance technical ability.

In this point of the Zodiac lessons, Ara, the altar of spirit's sacrifice of its matter experience, lies behind the rising spirit, indicating that higher consciousness has come into the realm of the Evolutionary planes which opens access to cosmic wisdom. Here, in Revelation's imagery, is seen the "new heaven, new Earth, and new people."

Pagan antiquity did not regard the mythological dragon to be representative of evil or malevolence as Judeo-Christian propaganda has chosen to regard it. The Dragon, with its serpentine body, clawed feet, fiery breath and membrane wings, although fearsome in appearance, was credited with beneficent powers. The Dragon hieroglyph with all these attributes served to symbolize the embodiment of all the secrets of the Creative Cosmic Consciousness. These secrets the Dragon willingly conveyed and taught to humankind that they might progress into the Evolutionary planes. The fearsome qualities, far from representing evil, were understood as Wisdom's protective influence -- for wisdom *can* be a frightening thing.

The Dragon, in its fearsome appearance, represented the protector and guardian to the struggling spirit-soul in its "conflict" to pierce the illusion of matter.

In that age it was standard practice to present the Creative Wisdom Consciousness in the form of a Dragon to indicate its directive use of the raw, indisciplined primal energies. The Serpent represented wisdom, the Dragon represented the Wisdom Consciousness through which Creation's energies could be directed. For this reason the Serpent and the Dragon, symbols of wisdom, and the shorthand figure of a spiral could all be used to represent the coiled cosmic energy.

With the loss of the ancient Zodiac lessons a number of the Zodiac hieroglyphic figures became jumbled and misrepresented. Aspects of Cetus (the Whale, second decanate of Aries), and Hydra (water serpent, first decanate of Leo), and Serpens (first decanate of Scorpio) became muddled with Draco the Dragon. The errors and misinterpretations this brought has blighted the understanding of the natural cyclic process of Causation and Creation ever since.

In the Creation Epic of the Babylonians, one of the central figures of the legend was the goddess Tiamat, presented as a dragon-like being who personified the primordial energies (creation's waters). This imagery brought in its wake a confused understanding that continues into this day.

The dragon-like personification could then be presented as being "slain" so the hero (the Life Principle) could create from its "body" the heavens and Earth.

Within the ancient cultures there were those who kept some untainted memory of the Zodiac lessons and correctly credited the Dragon with beneficent powers. Even into classical Greek and Roman times the dragon was believed to possess the ability to understand and covey to humans the secrets of Earth and higher being.

The folklore of northern Europe presented dragons as a beneficent and protective influence although terror inspiring in appearance. Ancient Norsemen adorned the prows of their ships with carved likenesses of dragons. The Celtic conquerors of Britain used the dragon as symbol of sovereignty. In later British history the Teutonic tribes invaded Britain, and upon their shields was depicted the dragon. It is probably because of all this that the patron "saint" of Britain is credited with slaying the dragon -- which is to say *destroyed wisdom.*

Various Oriental countries, notably China and Japan, have honored mythological dragon from antiquity. The Taoist religion deified the dragon. It was the national emblem of the Chinese empire, and it is still traditionally regarded as symbolic of good fortune.

In scriptural imagery, however, written after the Jew's authentic Babylonian Captivity, serpent-like figures such as the dragon came to be used by the priest-class as representative of evil and death. Being peoples who inhabited areas infested by venomous reptiles, and having lost the key to the ancient Zodiac meanings, the mythological dragon was used by the Judaic priest-class in their folklore as symbolic of destruction and evil. It is also likely that the Jewish priest-class knew something of the ancient Zodiac teachings, and it would be to their advantage to cast such symbols in a negative light.

Christian mythology inherited the Judaic conception of the dragon, and it came to play the heavy role in all of the important apocalyptic literature of the Bible. By the time it had passed through the Dark Ages of understanding the traditions arose such as "Saint" George killing the dragon. The true meaning of the Dragon was still known among some seekers of truth -- who are usually spoken of contemptuously as practitioners of *alchemy.* The symbol of wisdom often used by them was of the Dragon holding its own tail in its mouth. They knew the false interpretation given the Dragon by the church, and knew it would be self-defeating to slay the Dragon of wisdom as was presented by Christian mythographers.

Christian interpretation won out, not through wisdom but by arms, intimidation, inquisition, and subterfuge. Christian art made the Dragon their favored symbol for "sin." In that role it was commonly represented as crushed beneath the feet of "saints" and martyrs. This was supposed to show the triumph of Christianity over Paganism.

The Dragon is mentioned seven times in the book of Revelations. In 12:3 we are treated with this: "And another sign was seen in heaven, and look' a great fiery-colored dragon with seven heads and ten horns and upon its seven heads seven diadems...."

Yes, John's dragon is the constellation Draco. Its "seven heads" are in reference to the seven planes of Evolution ushered in with the lesson of Draco. The seven diadems crown the heads because the wisdom within the Creation processes is the elevating principle. The ten horns are the lessons of Creative Wisdom presented in the ten Zodiac signs from Aquarius through Scorpio.

Verse four continues where verse three had been chopped off with a semicolon. "....and its tail draws a third of the stars of heaven, and it hurled them down to the Earth. And the dragon kept standing before the woman who was about to give birth, that, when she did give birth, it might devour the child."

Hmmm. Perhaps "John" had imbibed too much of the "prophet's herb." The dragon he "saw", who with "its tail, draws a third of the (northern circumpolar) stars," goes so undisguised that it is incredible anyone could ever regard the description as being "prophetic." It must have been John's bloodshot eyes that made him think it was fiery.

Draco, located partially between Ursa Minor and Ursa Major (second and third decanates of Cancer) is nowhere near Virgo, the virgin whose child is claimed to be in danger of being devoured. The Dragon does, however, look at Cygnus the cross-bearing Swan (third decanate of Aquarius). Priest mythographers of this "revelation" were not at all interested in astronomical accuracy, only in using established image-symbols for their own ends.

Draco faces the cross-bearing Swan, symbolically confronting the Swan with the purpose of its matter-life experience -- which is the acquisition of wisdom. The Dragon was never presented as carnivorous. On the other hand a pack of spiritually starved priests have always proven to be some of the most carnivorous creatures in our matter-plane.

To this end the priest-mythographers treated the world with such as this: verse seven, chapter twelve of Revelations, "And there was war in heaven: Mi'cha-el and his angels fought against the dragon...."

Mi'cha-el, presented in Judeo-Christian-Islamic myths as an *archangel*, is, if properly understood, symbolic of the higher self which delivers the soul from its captivity to the lower planes. This is accomplished only through attaining wisdom. *Attainment of wisdom is not taken as spoils of some war*, but is achieved only through evolving into it. Blood thirsty priests have never understood this.

Poor Draco. Typically, it is again vilified as the priest-class excuse for any apparent chaotic but purely natural cyclic events of the Invo-Evolutionary processes. Without their "sin" and their mythical "Satan," the parasitic priest-class would have no business. Though not genuinely wise, they are cunning. They point to the Zodiac hieroglyph of the Dragon of wisdom and universal energy, and credit it with doing *their* dirty work of (Revelations 12:9) "..misleading the entire inhabited Earth....."

*   *   *

The stars Etamin (also known as Draconis) and Rastaben are regarded as the gleaming eyes of the Dragon. These stars seem to bid seekers to open their eyes to see where they have placed themselves in their life experience. In the newly found enlightened perception they will no longer walk in self-imposed darkness.

As we have noted, the ancient Watchers always presented serpentine figures especially the Dragon -- to be symbolic of wisdom and truth. The greater percentage of the world's cultures still hold the dragonlike figures as symbolic of *benefits* for humankind. It is, therefore, disturbing to note that there are over thirty allusions to the dragon in scriptural myths, and in all of them it is constantly used as symbolic of evil or "sin" or of false gods or false beliefs. The Judeo-Christian faith systems *have never honored wisdom.* Their sole intent is power in this limited plane of action.

Even so, the scriptural allusions have inadvertently let a few things slip by that show the old symbolism for wisdom was the Dragon. For example, there is a verse which reads, "The owl and dragon shall honor me." Both of these figures have been used as symbols for intelligence and wisdom from time out of mind. If they represented false gods or false beliefs, as priestly propaganda would have us believe, the priestly dream of receiving honor from these symbols is a bit peculiar.

*   *   *

The "Four Horsemen of the Apocalypse" given in the book of Revelations were purposely mixed up in an attempt to disguise that their symbolism was taken from the ancient lessons given with the Zodiac. What the Four Horsemen really represent are the planes from Devolution into Evolution which, in the Zodiac of Constellations, were taught with the lessons of Virgo, Libra, Scorpio and Sagittarius.

In Revelations the first horse symbol is presented as being a *black* horse. By the most ancient Zodiac lessons this would be Libra. Black symbolizes the darkness of densest matter, which is to say the mineral kingdom. In other words, the Earth.

The second horse presented in the Revelations horror tale is said to be a *pale* horse. In the ancient Zodiac presentations this would be Virgo. It is "pale" because it symbolized the etheric energy -- the most simple of life forms -- the plant kingdom.

The third horse ridden upon is given as being a *red* horse. This horse is Scorpio, and it is red because it symbolizes the awakening astral element in the animal kingdom.

The fourth horse of the Apocalyptical "vision" is reported to be a *white* horse. This is Sagittarius, the archer with his bow, the symbol of genetic force -- the human kingdom. The purpose of human experience is to acquire wisdom and through it rise out of baser Nature.

The rider of the white horse is consciousness which is to take mastery over energy -- the energy which dominated the experience of matter-life from Gemini onward. The four planes represented by Virgo, Libra, Scorpio and Sagittarius are what constitutes the Revelations battle scene of Armageddon. It is *not* a future doomsday battle, but an ongoing struggle everyone passes through. We are each in our Armageddon battle right now.

The word Armageddon comes from the Hebrew word *har*, meaning mountain, and *mergiddon*, meaning the plain of Mergiddo. The plain of Mergiddo was where several battles allegedly occurred between Israelites and their enemies (Judges 5:19). From this Old Testament claim some later Christian mythographer borrowed the site name to present the "prophetic" tale of the final struggle between good and evil, which priests envision as heaven-approved orgy of hideous butchery.

There is an open acknowledgment to the symbolic use of the Hebrew name in Revelations 16:16 where it says, "And he gathered them together into a place called in the Hebrew tongue Armageddon." This is the only place in the entire Bible where that particular name is ever used. Doesn't it

ever strike anyone as strange that god should plan to crowd
not only the entire human race but angels and devils as well
into the plain of Mergiddo so he can watch them butcher
each other?

The book of Revelations can be called a book of
"prophecy" only in that it borrowed its outline from the
ancient Zodiac lessons which taught of the Evolutionary
processes. The higher Evolutionary planes are opened to the
spirit-ego only after it has experienced the plane of resistance known as Dense Matter. What the "visions" of
Revelations really pertain to is the struggle of spirit over
matter, not a demented scene of future god-approved carnage.

The authors of the book of Revelations, with twisted
mentalities, contrived a sick "mystery" and horror scenario
for use in a scam operation offering spiritual insurance. It
was a despicable deceit foisted upon human gullibility in the
name of their mythological savior.

The Evolutionary planes are our destiny. We struggle
here -- perhaps more than one lifetime -- but we all will
become the master over our baser experiences. This
beautiful promise of soul-success was made into the ugly
tale of Revelations.

Capricornus
The Sea Goat

the twelfth and final sign
of the ancient Zodiac of Constellations
representing Wisdom Consciousness

Capricornus, commonly known as Capricorn, is the Latin name for this constellation, from *caper,* meaning "a goat," and *cornu,* meaning "a horn." The literal translation is "goat-horn."

This constellation has been depicted from earliest times either as a goat or as a mythological figure with the forepart of a goat and its hind part as the tail of a fish. The emphasis is upon the goat, which properly is a horned white he-goat. The hieroglyph of the mythological "sea-goat" indicates the higher self surmounting the lower planes, having risen out of its primordial origin to gain mastery over the "waters" of Creation.

Since the half-goat half-fish hieroglyph figure appeared as early as the Sumerians, it must cling closely to the original figure used with the Zodiac lessons presented by the Watchers. Among ancient peoples this sign was regarded as containing the knowledge of "the gateway into life of those who know not death." That understanding was drawn from the Watchers' lessons taught with this Zodiac division. Capricornus represents the fully recombined energy and consciousness that had to be temporarily divided at the plane of Mental Matter, Gemini.

This inconspicuous constellation in the equatorial region of the Southern Hemisphere is situated between Aquarius and Sagittarius. The Sun enters this sign at the winter solstice about December twenty-second, traversing the sign until January twentieth. At the winter solstice the Sun reaches its point farthest south of the celestial equator where it seemingly hangs suspended for three days. For this reason Capricornus was referred to as "the Southern Gate of the Sun."

In Hebrew this constellation was called Gedi, which translates as "the kid." It can also mean "cut off." In this case, the Sun's descent is *cut off* and light will again increase.

The lessons given by the Watchers with Capricornus taught the completion of the Involutionary-Evolutionary process. Creation energies have moved, in effect, full circle, from Divine Consciousness (Aquarius) to fulfillment as Wisdom Consciousness (Capricornus). The spirit has qualified itself to take on its mastery as Higher Self -- or Omniself.

To the ancient Watchers this was considered to be the most important of all the lessons from the Zodiac of Constellations. The matter-weary soul-consciousness is at the point of attaining its Evolutionary fulfillment. The indomitable spirit-soul now moves masterfully upon the waters (energies) flowing to-from-around Divine Wisdom Consciousness. The spirit-soul has come of age and is about to enter into true cosmic order where it is to take up its obligations as Omniself.

The lessons of Capricornus taught the purpose of creative action in their cyclic rhythm on the Evolutionary planes. Poetic imagery has spoken of this as the "heavens being rolled up as they are rolled down." The intellect-spirit has, at this point, shed completely its "skins" of matter, and takes on the elemental form of higher wisdom. This was refashioned by the priests for religious marketing as "the gateway into life of those who know not death."

The Babylonians referred to this constellation as the "Father of Light." It was occasionally identified as well with Ea, their personification of the universal Creative Wisdom. It was Ea, in their version of the "Flood" which preceded the scriptural account, who warned Utnapishtim, the Babylonian Noah, of the impending Flood. Ea personifies the evolved spirit-intellect as creative wisdom, which is Capricornus. The "Flood", we have seen, is really in reference to the initiatory movement or rush of Creation's energies -- the "beginning" of Involutionary action.

Capricornus became, due to priestly mix-up of Zodiac lessons, associated as well with Oannes, the Babylonian's half-fish god. In Babylonian and Assyrian myths, Oannes came to be presented as the founder of civilization. This was the mythographer's way of saying the establishment of higher order and understanding of conduct and behavior-which is the lesson of Capricornus.

The Philistines and Phoenicians, too, associated Capricornus with their half-fish god Dagon, which is known in the **Talmud** as Dag. Properly, Dagon represents the Aquarius-Pisces Patriarchal Principles. Because of the Philistine-Phoenician mix-up the Talmudic Dag, taken from Dagon, is presented as the Judaic Messiah. It is from this that the Christian's mythical messiah or "savior" was devised. Like other world "saviors," such as Mithra, Zoroaster, Osiris an others, the Christian "savior" was "born" at the Winter Solstice which begins December 22nd After "hanging" at that point in the heavens for three days, the Sun begins its northerly passage on December 25th—which accounts for the "birthday" of Jesus. This brings "the light of the world" back to the northern hemisphere.

The earlier Greeks associated this sign with Phoebos, "the Bright One" or "the Pure One." This was the Sun as symbolic of increase and higher development. Later on, somewhere between 1200 and 850 B.C.E., epic poetry attributed to the Greek poet Homer made Phoebos an epithet of Apollo. Homer was to the ancient Greeks the equivalent to the Bible and Shakespeare wrapped up as one. As Phoebus-Apollo, the increasing blessings of the Sun, he was regarded as the god of such seemingly unrelated things as prophecy, music, poetry, archery, medicine, the bucolic arts, law, philosophy, and the purifier "from all stains of sin."

The sign of Capricornus was given by the Watchers as

governing over the time following the winter solstice. In Pagan antiquity the crossing of the solstice signaled mounting *luminary blessings*, and this reinforced the teachings of the spirit-intellect attainment of Higher Self. For these reasons the period of time at the winter solstice was set aside as a time of celebration in honor of the spirit-soul's eventual Evolutionary transition.

The Sun's entry into the constellation Capricornus was therefore observed by the Pagans of antiquity with a midnight rite called the "Vigil of Light." This night was called "Mother Night," for at midnight of the winter solstice the constellation of the virgin, Virgo, begins to rise above the eastern horizon with the great star Spica in the seed. The star Spica is the so-called "seed of woman" in "Gospel" myth. This appears approximately December 25th. This is how the virgin is tied to the birth of the "son"- Sun.

Because of the appearance upon the eastern horizon of Virgo, hieroglyph for the Dense Matter plane, this cyclic period became a time of joy in expectation of the soul's evolution. This was too vital to be ignored by the priestly con artists who where intent upon building their business machine called religion. For example, the priests of the Persian religion Zoroastrianism celebrated the birth of their savior, Zoroaster, on December 25th, long before the Christians adopted the observance.

The Pagan's "Vigil of Light" rite was in recognition that here occurs the longest night of the year. Therefore, the Pagans customarily observed the Sun's midwinter descent below the equator by the ceremony of burning the "Yule Wheel." This is scorned by present religious machines as ignorant "heathen" practice.

The word *yule* means "that which turns or revolves." It has nothing to do with some mythological character's "nativity." Yuletide, properly understood, means the time of when the Sun appears to stand at it lowest ebb just before it turns back from its southerly course. In other words, yuletide refers to the three days of the Sun's apparent motionless position at the winter solstice. The Pagan's rite of burning the Yule Wheel and rolling it blazing down a hillside into a lake or other water represented symbolically the Sun's descent into its period of rest. This "ignorant" rite displayed a closer understanding of cosmic processes than any "birthday" feast celebration carried out for a fictional character.

The burning of the Yule Wheel, which is derided as a heathen practice, is nonetheless preserved among Christians with the burning of the Yule Log in the fireplace at Christmas Eve. This custom is preserved because of still another tangled connection to the ancient "heathens."

The word *yule* in Chaldae is said to mean "infant" or "little child." Since the star Spica in Virgo was known to make its appearance at the time of the winter solstice, the celebration of Yule Day was observed by the Chaldeans on December 25th. The night preceding Yule Day was known as "Mother Night." The yule -- or infant -- was identified with the "divine infant Jesus" as the "light of the world." Burning of a Yule log, therefore, was not seen as being Paganistic and was overlaid and transformed by the Christian institution.

In the nation of ancient Egypt, the birth of the son of Isis, Horus, god of *day*, was also celebrated on this date. The Persians, as we have seen, celebrated the "birth" of their savior, Zoroaster, on December 25th. In Pagan Rome the twenty-fifth of December was the time of the celebration called *Natalis Solis Invicti*, meaning "the birthday of the Sun" -- not son.

These widespread "Pagan" celebrations at the winter solstice marked the commencement of a new yearly cycle that echoed the coming action which is expected to follow the soul's entry into the Evolutionary planes. The darkest nights were over, and the festivals were joyous in hopeful expectation of the Evolutionary cycle as a "Deliverer." From this we get the "saviors" of various religions. This Pagan understanding was a happy reason for gift giving, a practice carried over in the myth of the Magi bearing gifts to the infant "saviors" such as Zoroaster, Mithra, Tammuz, Jesus, and the rest.

Mythical significance was placed upon the fact that at the winter solstice the great star Spica of the virgin, Virgo, is on the meridian at midnight. This was seen as the virgin giving "birth" to the Life Principle. The Sun begins the seasons of lengthening light, so in Christian myth Jesus is the personification of the Life Principle and *light*. It should be remembered that the name Jesus is a derivation of the name Joshua, which was an ancient Hebrew solar deity. Knowing this explains why Jesus is quoted as saying, "I am the light."

The reason for the Christian myth of Jesus being born in a manger (Astral Matter, Cancer) among "lower" animals is a direct Zodiac influence. The "birth" represents the Sun beginning a new yearly cycle at the winter solstice. It is just leaving Sagittarius, symbolized by the horse, and entering Capricornus, symbolized by the horned white he-goat. The suggestion of "lower" animals in attendance at the "birth" of the Life Principle is also a veiled reference to the Involutionary side of the Zodiac, particularly those signs following Pisces. The animal signs of the Involutionary lessons are Aries-Ram, *Taurus*-Bull, Gemini-Goat Kids -- all gathered at the "manger" which is itself a section of the Cancer (Astral Matter) lessons. Nearby are also found the Asses of Ascelli, the same asses that Jesus is later portrayed as riding upon as he enters Jerusalem to meet his sacrificial fate.

The Jewish festival of Hanukkah (or Chanukah), the Festival of Lights, is celebrated at the time of the winter solstice and lasts for eight days. Hanukkah means "dedication," and is properly the Feast of Dedication -- *to light* -- which is celebrated from the 25th of Kislev to the first of Tebet of the Jewish calendar. It, too, is an outbranching from the ancient Pagan recognition of *seasonal increase of light* which was honored with the Vigil of Light.

Jewish myth, typically, does not acknowledge the celestial procession of increasing sunlight but reduces their celebration to an alleged "miracle" performed *just for them* at the Temple at Jerusalem.   The Jewish Festival of Lights ignores the benevolent blessings upon all the Earth by the Sun. There is nothing exclusive in that -- everyone gets blessed. Instead they celebrate a myth of pretended exclusivity. The feast of Hanukkah supposedly commemorates the rededication to Yahweh of the Temple at Jerusalem by Judas Maccabaeus in 165 B.C.E. According to Talmudic tradition there could be found only one cruse of pure olive oil blessed by the high priest and necessary for the ritual which was to last eight days. Yahweh could not let his "chosen" celebrate in the dark, so that small quantity of oil burned miraculously for eight consecutive days.

*   *   *

Sagitta
the Arrow
first decanate of Capricornus

Sagitta is the Latin name for this star group near Aquila, second decanate of Capricornus, and Cygnus, third decanate of Aquarius. All ancient peoples knew this small northern constellation as the "Arrow" even though the stars in the group do not form a straight line. In some earlier charts the hieroglyph of the Arrow was pictured as clutched in the talons of Aquila (the Eagle), second decanate of Capricornus.

The arrow, usually thought of as a symbol of destruction or destroying powers, is in this case the upward soaring arrow of spirit loosened by the Centaur, Sagittarius. The arrow, therefore, symbolizes the higher purpose of the Life Principle, but which individual will has bent to its own use in its passage through the dense-matter plane. Even though this arrow has been distorted by dense-matter experience, its aim toward Evolutionary wisdom remains true.

Sagitta represents Higher Will -- or spirit-intellect ego. The arrow released by the Centaur penetrates the higher planes, its target the summit of being, Wisdom Consciousness. The Arrow is spiritual force aimed above personality.

An arrow seems to suggest a weapon, but it symbolizes victory and triumph. It does not destroy life, although it does represent the end to matter illusion.

The understanding of the Arrow constellation became lost through the turbulent ages after the Watchers had withdrawn.   There was left only a vague memory of its meaning -- that it somehow indicated future conditions. Out of this arose the practice of "divining" with arrows or rods in hopes of discerning the future. This practice is referred to in the Bible. In the book of Numbers, for example, there is given instruction for making twelve rods to be placed upon the altar so god could show which of the twelve tribes of Israel he favored for priesthood honors.

This practice is a variation of casting of lots to determine a question by chance.   In gospel accounts the soldiers present at Jesus' crucifixion cast lots for his garments. It is from the Greek word *kleros*, meaning "lots" or literally that which is assigned by lot, *gambling*, that we receive our word for those who are ordained for "religious service," the clergy. The word *clergymen* is supposed to mean those who are authorized to preach the gospel and administer its ordinances. What is admitted here is that these persons are ordained as gambling men. In the word clergy, from *kleros*, to gamble by lots, we can see why religion has always missed its spiritual mark.

*   *   *

In archery terms the stele or shaft of an arrow, when it is made of a single piece of wood and is not reinforced, is said to be *self*. This term seems peculiarly appropriate when we understand this lesson taught of the spiritual force aimed above personality.

When this term is coupled with a philosophical puzzle presented by the Greek philosopher Zeno of Elea (flourished in the 5th century B.C.E.), in conjunction with the Zodiac lessons of planes of development, we face a great question of Creation. Zeno's question was this: If the arrow is at every instant of its flight at rest in a space equal to its length, when then does it move?

*   *   *

Aquila

the Eagle
second decanate of Capricornus

Aquila, Latin meaning "Eagle," is a small northern constellation in the Milky Way, and contains about eighty stars that range from the first to the sixth magnitude. A few references have also called it the Vulture. The principle star in this constellation is of the first magnitude and known as Al-tair, which is Arabic meaning "the star" or "the flying." It is a double, variable star approximately eight times as bright as the Sun, and is the eleventh brightest in the heavens. It is approximately 15.7 light years from Earth.

To the Persians and the Greeks the Eagle was held to be sacred to the Sun, *to higher light.* The eagle has been almost universally regarded as a royal bird. Thus Aquila symbolizes the "royal" or divine powers which are to be inherited by the ascending consciousness.

Eagles are solitary and predatory birds. With keenness of vision, remarkable strength, and indomitable courage, they hold dominion of the skies. These traits made the Eagle the ideal symbol for the spirit-soul that has been freed of its matter-form.

The Eagle as the hieroglyph for this Capricornus lesson served to symbolize the freed spirit. Ancient legends relate that only the eagle can look into the dazzling brilliance of the Sun. This legend was taken from the Aquila lesson of the soul's ascension and looking into the brilliance of its mastery.

In the original Zodiac lessons, Aquila taught of the soul's intended purpose. That purpose, once the higher Evolutionary planes are penetrated, is the rapid "coming" into its divinity where it will carry all the divine powers of higher wisdom. The Greek myth of Zeus taking the form of an eagle to carry away to Olympus the beautiful boy Ganymede is from this Zodiac lesson. In that myth Zeus personifies the Creative Principle, Olympus symbolizes the Evolutionary summit, and Ganymede personifies the spirit-soul raised swiftly into higher purpose. Modern cultures, tutored by spiritually blind religious interpretations, see only same homoerotic lust behind the story.

It is natural that Ganymede would be much loved by Zeus -- Creative Principle. The beautiful Ganymede is the soul that is made ready for its Evolutionary purpose -- the bearer of divine powers. This is why, in the Greek myth, Ganymede is presented as being made the personal cupbearer to Zeus.

The Zodiac lesson taught with this decanate of Capricornus was of the spirit as soul or Higher Self rising to its higher domain, into the planes of Wisdom Consciousness. All its dense-matter experiences have fallen away behind it, and with them are abandoned all the self-serving (predatory) habits and actions indulged in on the matter plane. This lesson announced the rapid manner in which the soul may ascend to its divinity once it has shed its dense-matter experience.

In New Testament terms this was ineffectually rewritten as "prophetic vision." The book of Revelations, fashioned upon the Zodiac lessons, offers this substitute: "Look! I am coming quickly, and the reward I give is with me, to render to each one as his work is" (Rev. 22:12). A few verses on is added: "He that bears witness of these things (Creative Principle) says, 'Yes, I am coming quickly' " (Rev. 22:20).

The Eagle hieroglyph for this constellation is identical in meaning as the legendary Phoenix for, dauntless, it rises from its matter-experience (ashes) and soars into full Evolutionary life. The Eagle as Phoenix has often been erroneously attributed to Scorpio as its highest manifestation. The soaring Eagle and the Phoenix symbolize the purified spirit-intellect, therefore both are emblems of the qualified spirit at the highest planes.

The eagle as the royal bird had its wings borrowed and assigned symbolically to the higher aspects of soul capabilities. In this manner the "angels" so dear the religious myths came to be depicted as having wings.

*   *   *

Delphinus
the Dolphin
third decanate of Capricornus

Delphinus, a small constellation in the Northern Hemisphere, is located between Aquila and Pegasus (second decanate of Aquarius, horse of the gushing fountain). The name is Latin from Greek *delphis, delphin,* meaning a "dolphin." The hieroglyph for this constellation is popularly portrayed as a dolphin leaping up out of the sea (of creative energies).

The Chaldeans referred to this group of stars as Rotaneu, which translates loosely as "swiftly running," as a stream. The Persian representation of this constellation was of a fish and a stream of water, reminiscent of Piscis Austrinus, the first decanate of Aquarius. Since this is the last sign before touching again upon Aquarius, it indicates the "waters" of Creation flow down, up and around the fountainhead. With this final sign, the Zodiac shows us that Creation -- that which we see as the universe -- turns ever back upon itself.

The Dolphin hieroglyph may not be the original figure used for this constellation lesson. It may be another Greek adaptation. On the other hand it is known that by at least 3500 B.C.E., dolphin figures were common subjects for funereal art throughout the Mediterranean area. It was widely believed that dolphins accompanied into the hereafter the souls of the dead. Accordingly, the dolphin was used as a symbol of the soul's liberation from earthly life.

The Dolphin is commonly, but incorrectly, called a "fish." It is a much higher evolved creature. It is a gregarious aquatic mammal, and probably the most intelligent creature living in the seas. The dolphin has the largest brain relative to its size of any animal after human. The dolphin has a long tradition as symbolizing truth-wisdom. Their graceful movements, joy and ease in the waters suggested achieving freedom from the tralldom of physical illusion.

For these reasons the Dolphin serves as an appropriate symbol of the spirit-soul's full entry into the "waters" of Creative Consciousness which flows through the Evolutionary planes to reunite with its source.

Dolphins are extremely intelligent mammals, and so serve as an excellent symbols for wisdom attained, and the joy that wisdom brings. The third decanate of Capricornus symbolizes the soul's full entry into the finer spectrum of Wisdom Consciousness as a graceful swimmer -- as a master. The hieroglyph of a leaping dolphin symbolizes not only the joy of the soul being fully at ease in the finer streams of wisdom, but indicates that our purpose is always the qualifying of self in wisdom.

The Dolphin frolicking at the Source conveys the final truth of Creation. This truth was still understood and taught in ancient Greece. In the words of the Greek philosopher Heraclitus (c.535-c.475 B.C.E.), "The way up and the way down are one and the same." The process of Creation is by degrees which the Zodiac lessons taught as planes of Involution (the way "down" to matter) and Evolution (the way "up" to refined quality).

Heraclitus also taught that what we think of as *being* and *not being* is a part of everything. By this he meant the only possible real state one can experience is *the transitional state of becoming*. Matter-life experience is only a small part of the transitional state of becoming.

The greater understanding of Creation, cosmology, nature, and purpose was offered in the ancient Zodiac lessons. Organized hierarchical religions have long tried to destroy the Zodiac teachings calling the Zodiac itself a "devilish deception." Even so, the ancient lessons have always served as the off-limits treasure house which these same condemners freely pillaged for their own doctrinal purposes.

This final lesson from the ancient Zodiac of Constellations is summarized in the book of Revelations, 22:17 with the verse ending as "And let anyone thirsting come: let anyone that wishes take life's waters free."

For sharing this stolen truth the priests still expect to be paid.

*   *   *

Delphinus represents Evolutionary fulfillment -- that is to say the point where individual consciousness merges with Higher Wisdom Consciousness. In the book of Revelations 1:8 this is what is referred to when it says, "I am the Alpha and the Omega saith the Lord God, which is and which was and which is to come, the Almighty."

Similar in meaning -- without the endless barrage of words -- was the Roman god Janus who gave his name to the month of January. Janus was pictured as having two faces which looked forward and backward, and was regarded the guardian of thresholds, doors and gates -- the entryways into another region. He was generally shown with the facial features of one being alert and watchful, and the opposite face looking away in a dreamy or reflective mood. Janus, observing both directions at once, personified the junction of Capricornus with Aquarius -- the beginning and end of the Zodiac lessons, and the end and beginning of a new yearly cycle.

In the oldest Roman times one particular archway was always used by the army in the time of war. This gate was used only by the army marching off on their way to war and it was the gate by which the army also made its return. The gates opened either way, and were always kept closed except in times of war. The Latin name for gate or an opening is *janua*.

In Praise of Starlight

The twelve Zodiac signs and the associated decanates were presented by the ancient Watchers as the sacred arcana of the patriarchal mysteries. The Zodiac with all its remarkable hieroglyphic figures set forth the principles of Creation and humankind's place within it. The heavens still keep the ancient order, and the primeval wisdom that set forth that order may still be found in the lessons given with the stars if theological blinders are cast off.

Some may ask why, if the stars proclaim a divine teaching, is not the message made more plain for human mind to understand? The answer to this has been suggested already -- with the Cancer lesson and the analogy of the mind with the Moon.

Understanding the celestial hieroglyphs is not simply a matter of visual comprehension. The mind, like the Moon, must be illuminated that it may reflect in life experience the real significance of higher being. Mental illumination depends upon each person's stage of development.

For example, a child learning to read will linger upon every letter -- or the alphabet -- of a word. At that learning stage the child is not aware that the letters can be combined and associated to spell out an endless variety of messages. It is the same with the celestial figures. To read the Zodiac lessons one must first learn the principles and the nuances which each figure represents. Those principles apply to everything that exists, and so are far more important and all-encompassing than is suspected through the childish application of the celestial figures in astromancy practice.

Why would the Zodiac with all its intricate divisions, colorful imagery, star names, and development of complicated symbolism be fashioned simply to entertain as a fortune telling device? The technical skill needed and the familiarity with deep space phenomena necessary to fashion the Zodiac indicate that the Zodiac was intended for more serious purposes than fortune telling.

The Zodiac is an imaginary band in the heavens extending for about eight degrees on either side of the apparent path of the Sun. This band of the celestial sphere is divided into twelve equal parts, each of which is further divided into equal zones of thirty degrees. This band is commonly considered to have been defined by Chaldean astronomers sometime around 3000 B.C.E. The problem with that assessment is that clay texts from the most ancient Sumerian times regarded the Zodiac divisions and figures assigned to them to be *ancient even then.*

If the Zodiac was devised simply to serve as a kind of gameboard by Chaldeans for people to play with their personal fate, why and how did the intricate, arbitrary assignment of the stars become worldwide in ancient times? The Egyptians had the same twelve divisions. They acknowledged receiving this understanding from Sumerian sources. But what of the Chinese? Did they also have access to the Sumerian understanding of dividing the celestial realms into twelve equal divisions? Was it all for personal amusement? Did the ancient empires of the Americas, by coincidence, adopt the same twelve-fold division of the heavens as seen from Earth? There is more than coincidence involved when the majority of the constellations -- arbitrary groupings of stars -- also have the same hieroglyphic figures assigned to represent them.

The fashioning of the arbitrary groups of stars into sequential patterns required a knowledge of the heavens that was far beyond what we consider to be the "primitive" ages of humankind. The sequential patterns of the Zodiac are fashioned as a circle containing 360 degrees. This required instruments and technical skills beyond "primitive" comprehension.

Accurate star charts can be fashioned only by beings who have an intimate, working association with the stars. Star charts are necessary for space navigation, for example. With the Zodiac "star charts" the Watchers taught how and why we are to navigate through our life experience. We can only wonder if those "charts" also indicated other connections -- other routes to be followed. It is interesting that even in our "space age" the ancient Zodiac still provides the basis of nomenclature for the stars.

Whoever the Watchers were who conceived the Zodiac, they understood the universe to be a living thing -- a vast unified *consciousness*. When they looked out into the universe they perceived something at work that was much grander than religion's personification of a pouty, petulant "god." The Watchers adored the universe with an intimacy that the practice of ecclesiasticism can never experience. The Watchers knew with divine certainty that each being is a necessary part of the universal consciousness. That is a far more noble understanding of the universe and Creation than the religious contention that god stands apart and aloof from everything "he" created.

Humankind's invented religions always leave their followers with vague feelings of unfulfillment -- of spiritual malnutrition. They are belief systems in which one must *will* themselves to believe. Religions such as Judaism, Christianity and Islam are not faiths which one can feel as natural expressions of the inner consciousness. They are systems which deny feeling. The reason behind this is that to open oneself to feel something is regarded a feminine aspect of being and so is regarded as not worthy of being cultivated.

Judaism, Christianity and Islam are religions that are infected with notions of the heroic, the vigorous, the manly. They are faith systems designed for strutting, combat, competition, and carefully tended hypocrisy. The result is that these religions have always been at war with *something*. For spiritual understanding the priests of these religions force-feed the seekers with images and glorifications of angel-warriors, wars in heaven, "holy wars," the glorification of blood sacrifice, and combats with "sin." Heaven is a fortress to be stormed. In church one is to sit in strict militaristic rows, obey orders to rise, to sit, to sing -- to *pay*. We are expected to find spiritual comfort in such verses as Psalm 18:34, "He teacheth my hands to war..." Even the hymns, more often than not, are couched in militaristic terms. For example the Christian hymn, "Onward Christian soldiers, marching as to war...."

What a horrid idea to present as spiritual enlightenment.

In Christian "houses of worship" one often finds the cordoned-off sanctuary where the celestial light of the open sky is allowed entry only through the filtering system of leaded, etched and stained glass windows. God's pure, natural light is unacceptable. Nature is forsaken for a theater of artificiality. From pulpits of gold, during the magic-show called religious service, the priest-class has the gall to preach that we are to forsake materialism.

True, unvarnished history has proven that the definition of "religion" should be understood as the practice of deception for gain and control. More acts of violence, disregard for others, wars, destruction and the like have been carried out "in the name of god" than for all other reasons combined.

Organized religions are routinely intent upon suppressing the specialness of each individual. What religions want to do is crush each person's specialness until it disappears into the sterile personality of the religion itself. In this regard religion's spiritual ambition becomes no higher than that of social insects where the individual life is lost in the impersonal "personality" of the hive or nest. Organized religions, in trying to prove their bogus claim of some godly exclusiveness, are really seeking to destroy the very qualities that lead the soul into godhood.

An individual's higher purpose is not to simply act as some separate organ to some religious social structure. The individual does not and can not evolve if they blindly and mindlessly pursue the task of perpetuating that religion. Adherents of such religious thought are reduced to being little more than the hive workers and breeders who, through mental conditioning, would find emotional survival virtually impossible if separated from the body of their religion. This is not the path to spiritual evolution.

Nothing in what is recognized as religion really offers to explain, enlighten or guide one to an understanding of who or what the "I" is when we speak of our individual sense of awareness. Religions imply only that human life is played out for the sole amusement or frustration of a "god." We are also to understand that this "god" is so detached from his creations that only a specialist can get through to his distant abode.

Nothing in the major religions of the world offers any cognizant explanation -- or even awareness -- of the incredible vastness and seemingly unnecessary multitude of galaxies in what we know is the curving space-time continuum. It is as though the rest of the universe has no meaning.

Religious systems seem to prefer to treat any wonderment of the universe as some kind of spiritual disease. Questions regarding the rest of Creation are avoided as if they were instruments of contamination. Such religious aloofness gives no means of making common sense of Creation and the universe in which we live. Such an attitude is not the path into enlightenment.

What religions -- especially western religions -- have always offered as enlightenment has been nothing more than the cultivation of a hostile attitude. For enlightenment they tell us to conquer "sin", gain dominion over Nature, deny our natural self, resist evil, spurn the un-"saved," or the un-"chosen." In short, they have always advocated what is a kind of resentful hostility to all that is around us. That is hardly the ideal path into spiritual understanding of life and its purpose let alone open any insight as to the meaning or purpose of the rest of the universe.

An underlying trait of the human condition is to fear what is not understood. In not understanding something the common result is to learn to hate it. The hatred that underscores Jewish, Christian and Islamic chauvinism is rooted in extremely limited understanding of the cosmic purpose for our being here. Ritual, rite, rote, ceremony and "tradition" are presented by priests, ministers, preachers, evangelists, crusaders and the like as substitutes for *seeking to understand*. The more these things are clung to, the less one is likely to reach out for understanding: in not seeking to understand, the unknown is allowed to fester into hatred.

Religions have always prospered because there is a beautiful transcendent unity within all people which is the yearning of the human spirit for illumination. When the spirit becomes mired down in the concrete of ritual, rite, rote and tradition, the light they seek has been shrouded in mesmeristic practice that permits little light to shine through.

It is vital that humankind turn its attention away from these things and learn once again to pause to gaze in hushed awe into the wondrous universe. The great picture book in the heavens known as the Zodiac has fascinated the peoples of the world for millenniums. Upon it have been woven fairy tales and legends, myths and epics. Its hieroglyphs have fired the imaginations of poets and bards, and served as the treasure trove for marauding priests who fashioned for themselves a "history" that allowed them to assume authority.

The lessons presented by the ancient Watchers with the Zodiac of Constellations and the Zodiac of Signs were, and still remain, greatly superior to the theologies of organized religions. Even Pagan myths were superior, for Pagan intelligence never made self-serving philosophical or religious presumptions, as theology freely does. Myths could assume sacred importance for anyone inclined to see behind them, but nothing about Pagan myths ever demanded a priestly endorsement of belief. The glaring difference between mythology and theology lies in the fact that theology always masquerades as a pseudo-science -- the "science" of divine things -- which implies certainty and truth.

The theologies of organized religions have done little else than suggest that all Creation is divided into feuding camps. That is not how Creation holds together.

The heavens still bear witness to the flow of Creation. We need only to remove the blinders placed over our eyes by those who would take advantage of our blindness. What is more stirring to the soul than looking up into the light of countless stars? Lured away from the stars, humankind has been "guided" to seek spiritual upliftment by huddling together in echoing "sanctified" enclosures. There, the devout are given role models of heroes and "saints," saviors and kings who would never have dreamed of huddling together in an imprisoning box with uniform seating.

The Watchers knew the soul better. They fashioned their lessons across all the observable heavens because they knew the soul forever craves freedom to roam unencumbered wherever it wishes. With the glittering, beckoning stars, the wise Watchers long ago inscribed this benediction for all who gazed heavenward:

May the light of Wisdom Consciousness forever watch over you.

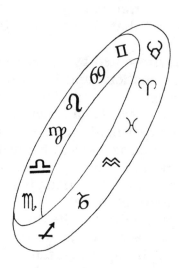

Selected Bibliography

A Guide to the Babylonian & Assyrian Antiquities
British Museum Edition, 1900

Abhedanada, Swami. Great Saviors of the World, Volume 1
The Vedanta Society, NY 1911

Allen, E. L. Christianity Among the Religions
Beacon Press, Boston 1960

Appleton, E. R. An Outline of Religion
H. C. Kinsey & Co., Inc. 1934

Bentwich, Norman. Josephus
The Jewish Publication Society of America, Philadelphia 1914-1945

Berry, Gerald L. Religions of the World
Barnes & Noble, Inc. (Everyday Handbook Series) 1947-1954

Boorstin, Daniel J. The Discoverers
Random House, NY 1983

Bouquet, A. C. Sacred Books of the World
Penguin Books, Baltimore, MD. 1954

de Vore, Nicholas. Encyclopedia of Astrology
Philosophical Library, NY 1947

Doblhofer, Ernst. Voices in Stone
Collier Books, NY 1957-1961

Durant, Will and Ariel. The Lessons of History
New York 1968

Eliade, Mircea. The Forge and the Crucible
Harper & Brothers, NY 1956-1962

Fairservis, Walter A. Jr. The Ancient Kingdoms of the Nile
New American Library Mentor Book, NY 1962

Frank, Adolphe. The Kabbalah (translated from the French)
Bell Publishing Co., NY 1960

Frazer, Sir James George. The Golden Bough
Macmillan Co. 1922-1950

Godwin, Joscelyn. Mystery Religions in the Ancient World
Harper & Row, Publishers, San Francisco 1981

Graham, Lloyd M. Deceptions and Myths of the Bible
Bell Publishing Co. NY 1975

Graves, Robert. and Raphael Patai. Hebrew Myths
Doubleday & Co. NY 1983-1984

Graves, Robert. The White Goddess
Creative Age Press, NY 1948

Hawkins, Gerald S. Stonehenge Decoded
Delta Books, NY 1965

Heninger, S. K. Jr. A Handbook of Renaissance Meteorology
Greenwood Press Publishers, NY 1968

Hislop, Rev. Alexander. The Two Babylons
Loizeaux Brothers, New Jersey 1916-1959

Hoyle, Fred. Astronomy and Cosmology, A Modern Course
W. H. Freeman & Co., San Francisco 1975

Hoyle, Fred. Frontiers of Astronomy
New American Library-Mentor Books, NY

Hyma, Alber. Ancient History (College Course Outline Series)
Barnes & Noble, Inc. NY 1940-1955

Jones, Miss M. Nineveh and its Story
T. Nelson & Sons, Edinburgh, NY 1883

Larue, Gerald. Sex and the Bible
Prometheus Books, NY 1983

Macchioro, V. D. From Orpheus to Paul
Henry Holt & Co. 1930

Menzel, Donald H. A Field Guide to the Stars and Planets: Including
the Moon, Satellites, Comets and Other Features of the Universe
2nd ed. Houghton Mifflin, 1983

Ohiera, Edward. They Wrote on Clay
University of Chicago Press 1933

Pagels, Elaine. The Gnostic Gospels
Random House 1979

Paine, Thomas. The Age of Reason
Citadel Press, New Jersey 1974

Robertons, J. M. Pagan Christs
Dorset Press, NY 1903

Russell, Bertrand. Religion and Science
Henry Holt and Co., Inc. NY 1935

Sachar, Aabram Leon. A History of the Jews
Alfred A. Knoph, NY 1935

Sacs, A. Babylonian Horoscopes
Journal of Cuniform Studies, VI, No. 2, 49; 1952

Sagan, Carl. Cosmos
Random House, NY 1980

Sayce, A. H. Assyria, Its Princes, Priests, and People
Fleming H. Revell Co., NY-Chicago 1893

Scott, Ralph W. Biblical Crime
Nelson-Hall, Chicago, 1979

Seligmann, Kurt. The History of Magic
Pantheon Books, NY 1948

Shipman, Harry L. Blackholes, Quasars and the Universe
Houghton Mifflin Co., Boston 1976
Spence, Lewis. Myths and Legends of Babylonia and Assyria
George G. Harrap & Co., London 1916

Velikovsky, Immanuel. Earth in Upheaval
Dell Publishing Co., Inc. NY 1955

Velikovsky, Immanuel. Worlds in Collision
Macmillan Co., NY 1950

White, Andrew D. A History of the Warfare of Science with Theology
in Christendom. George Braziller, NY 1955

Wilson, Edmund. Scrolls from the Dead Sea
Oxford University Press, NY 1955

Index